A Jubilee in the Hardwood Trade 1945-1995

TO COMMEMORATE
50 YEARS IN THE
TIMBER TRADE

by
Dan Kemp

THE KEMP HOUSE PRESS
Oxford
2007

A Jubilee in the Hardwood Trade

Published by THE KEMP HOUSE PRESS
Kemp House, Cumnor Hill, Oxford OX2 9PH

ISBN 978-0-9555848-0-0

Designed and produced by Hunts Limited, Oxford.
www.hunts.co.uk

The text pages are printed on paper made from sustainable forest wood pulp and is TCF (Totally Chlorine Free). This book is recyclable.

Contents

Contents continued

Foreword

This book is dedicated to my father, Ludwig Kemp, who founded Timbmet.

My aim in writing these memoirs is to record the family's early days in Czechoslovakia and the changes that have taken place during the first fifty years of Timbmet. I trust that the reader will be able to appreciate my father's dedication and vision, and how together we have built on his foundation and followed his principles.

Dan Kemp
May 2007

Acknowledgment

I would like to thank Elizabeth Carter for the help given to me in editing the text and proof reading my book.

I am also grateful to Timon Colegrove and his staff at Hunts who gave me guidance and assistance on many aspects of production and advice on the choice of images and book jacket.

CHAPTER 1

My Origins

The background

When Emperor Joseph II, who was also King of Austria, Hungary and Bohemia promulgated the Edict of Tolerance in January 1782, life improved for the Jews living in the countries he ruled. Jews were permitted to follow most trades and occupations, to own land and property, as well as study in a *gymnasium* and gain admittance to universities. All of this lasted until 1914 when the First World War broke out. In 1918 when the fighting ended, the Austro-Hungarian Empire was broken up.

At negotiations between all parties in Versailles, and later at Trianon, various new countries were created. These included Czechoslovakia, which became a democratic republic headed by the humanitarian Dr Masaryk. Jews lived in more freedom than ever until the early 1930s when the fascist parties in neighbouring countries started to influence right wing elements, particularly the Hlinka party in Slovakia.

The Kampfner Family

The Kampfner family lived in Surany, near Nove Zamky, in south-west Slovakia, for at least 150 years. Surany was a large village and the only industry was a substantial sugar beet processing plant.

Daniel Kampfner, my grandfather, and his family must have been reasonably well off, judging by their life style. Their farmhouse was in the middle of the village in the market place with barns, cow sheds, the usual outbuildings, stables and coach-house. They had an adjoining market garden where they grew vegetables, and an orchard with fruit trees: produce from the farm was sold primarily to private consumers and there was also a butcher's shop. They grew wheat and sugar beet on the arable land outside the village.

Daniel and Berta Kampfner (née Schrotter)

Daniel died in the influenza epidemic of 1922. My grandparents had five children, two sons and three daughters

Ludwig (my late father) 1890-1959; and a male who perished in the 1914-18 War

Three daughters

I can no longer remember the first names of the two younger daughters. The eldest, Etelka, married Adolf Klein who continued to manage the farm and also had a butcher's shop on the premises. They had one son, Gyula (Julius) who joined the partisans about 1940 and was never heard of again.

The second daughter married Leopold (Poldi) Weiss. He was a gentlemens' and ladies' outfitter with a sizeable local store; they had one daughter and two sons, Juraj and Janko, who emigrated on youth transports in rusty old river steamers in 1940 or 1941 down the Danube, and eventually reached Palestine. Neither is still alive. The parents and daughter perished in Auschwitz.

The third daughter married Emil Fiala; he was a wholesale grain merchant in Surany. They had two sons, whose names I am unable to remember. Tragically all four died in Auschwitz.

*****

My brother Fred and I enjoyed being with our grandmother, Omama, and our cousins in the school holidays. Life was less strict and we learnt about country life from our eldest cousin and drank the non-pasteurised milk from the cows.

The population in Surany was principally Slovak. Most people also spoke Hungarian and some German; south of Surany the population was Hungarian but lived in Slovakia. As we all know, political boundaries cannot always be drawn according to the ethnic minorities.

Ludwig Kemp (Kampfner) 1890 – 1959

The Mayer family in Bratislava (Pressburg)

My mother's ancestors had lived in Pressburg, the German name for the city, from about 1770 until 1939. One who was a jeweller, Elkan Mayer, was murdered in January 1785 at the 'Green Tree' Inn. All the gruelling details appeared in a local daily paper a few years ago with a picture of the grave. The article mentioned the names of direct descendants still living overseas.

My maternal grandfather, Simon Mayer (1861-1943), was a draper and haberdasher. He married Johanna Eva Mayer (née Schrotter) who was born in 1871 and died in the 'flu epidemic in the winter of 1922. They had five children, three sons and two daughters.

Ludwig (1892-1971), who married Edith Kornfeld, was a wine producer and merchant, a member of the Slovak National Parliament and very active in local Jewish affairs. They had two daughters named Eva (b.1925) and Trude (b.1928). Eva was with us in England. Trude, Ludwig and his wife Edith were hidden by decent Slovak farmers: one day Auntie Edith ventured back to their home town and was caught in the street. She was never seen again.

Ludwig Mayer and his daughters went to live in Australia about 1948, and Eva died in 1995. The second daughter, Trude, is alive and living with her husband Richard Aldor, who was from Bratislava. They have a grown-up married son Leslie who has two children: they are all living in Melbourne.

Josef Mayer, the second son, died in the army in the 1914 - 18 War.

The third son, Eduard (1904-44) married Esther Rosenzweig (1902-44). They lived in Vrable, mid-Slovakia. Eduard joined his father-in-law's business which produced fine fruit based liqueurs. They had two daughters, Judit (1926-44) and Martha (b.1928). Martha survived, but her parents and sister died in the concentration camps in 1944.

Martha emigrated to the USA in 1945 and married Albert Nadler, a physiotherapist. Both are still alive and have two sons. Edward, a mathematical genius, is married and has two children. The second son, Peter, born in 1958, is an international lawyer living in Japan and is also married with two children.

Margit (Margaret), the first daughter (1898-1990) married Ludwig Kampfner (1890-1959) from Surany on 7 March, 1920. They had two sons Dezider Daniel born in 1922 and Frederich Evzen born in 1926.

Etelka, the second daughter (1902-1944) married Andor Deutch (1898-1944). They lived in Subotica, Yugoslavia. The Deutch were a prominent family in the town and very active in Jewish communal affairs. They had four daughters; Eva (1922-2003), Terri (1923-44), Lilly (b.1928) and Ditta (1936-44). Etel, Andor and his parents, Terry and Ditta all died in the Holocaust in 1944.

Eva survived in a local labour camp in Hungary and married Jeno Gutmann after the war. They emigrated to the USA, after the Hungarian uprising against Russia in 1956. They had no children.

Lilly was in a labour concentration camp in Germany and met Berek Bornstein (1915-92). In 1945 they got permission to live in Palestine and married. They were unable to have children. They lived in Israel for some years then went to America and made a 'mini pile'. They returned to Tel Aviv where they retired and lived very happily. Berek died in 1992; Lilly is still alive and enjoys reasonable old age in a very elegant retirement home in Ramat Gan.

Bratislava (Pressburg)

Bratislava is a medieval walled city, and has been a trading centre and a river port since the early Middle Ages. There is a fortified castle on top of the hill above the city. It was the traditional seat of the Hapsburg dynasty Crown Prince and had an old established university with the classical four faculties of theology, medicine, philosophy and humanities. The city also had a military garrison. The Turks never invaded although they were close by in southern Hungary. The population in the 1920s and 30s was approximately 120,000 of whom about 10% were Jews. Some 7,000 or 8,000 belonged to the orthodox congregation, and the rest to the progressive community (Neologen Gemeinde).

There was also a small but influential ultra orthodox congregation, very loyal followers of the rabbinical family, and descendants of the Chatam Sofer. The Pressburger Yeshiva had a very high reputation for scholarship. The majority of this community have perished but there is a small commune living in Jerusalem.

The Bratislava ghetto was demolished post war during the communist regime. The site has become a motorway leading to a new bridge built over the Danube, and the great synagogue nearby still lies in ruins.

CHAPTER 2

The life and early achievements of Ludwig Kemp (Kampfner)

Ludwig attended elementary school in Surany. At the age of 14 he left and was apprenticed in his uncles' businesses, Ludwig Schrotter, the saw miller and timber merchant in Nitra, and Heinrich Schrotter, who had an ironmongers' and builders' merchant business in Topolcany.

In 1914 he was conscripted into the Austro-Hungarian army where he served until 1919, achieving the rank of lieutenant in the supply corps. Soon after demobilisation he started his own ironmongers' and builders' merchants business in Bratislava, mainly retail, trading as Kampfner & Mayer. Whether he started from scratch or bought a partnership into an existing business we shall never know. I left it too late to gather the information from our relatives and friends. I am convinced that Eduard Mayer, his brother-in-law, was his partner until he married and went to work with his father-in-law.

My father must have had an exceptional natural flair for business. The postwar development of a new state no doubt helped, but without researching I would not know who provided the development capital. Foreign currency was very carefully husbanded, particularly British sterling, as many essential raw materials were mainly available from the British Empire. His retail business prospered and grew quite rapidly. He started to import scythes for harvesting the field crops and canisters for spraying vines and fruit trees.

Around 1927 he made a licensing arrangement with a Hungarian engineer to manufacture slow combustion stoves using wood fuel, which were far superior to the many heating stoves used at the time. Different size stoves were available according to the size of the room, and finished in pastel shades; the bright colours proved very attractive in older dwellings which were not suitable for conversion to central heating. The heat was emitted from 100mm pipes, and the stoves only needed attention once a day. They were sold under the trade name 'Zephir' and patented.

From about 1928 onwards my father exported softwood pine, spruce and some beech from Slovakia. I do not remember so much about the export of timber; this must have been handled by staff that I did not know personally. The transactions were carefully monitored by the Ministry for Trade to ensure that the proceeds were returned to the country from which the goods originated.

It was a much harder task to persuade the ministry granting import licences that additional volumes of reinforced steel bars were required to satisfy the needs of the building industry in the CSR [Czecholslovak Republic.]

The demand for tin plate and steel bars to reinforce concrete columns in newly-built high rise buildings must have been larger than the production capacity of the steel works in Plzen and Moravska Ostrava. It was in my father's favour that he exported timber of which there was an abundance in the country and he gradually got his way. He spent two days of most weeks in Prague: he left by the late evening sleeper train and had early breakfast on the train and by 8.00 am he was in the government offices situated close to the station. When he finished his business he returned by the early afternoon train to Bratislava.

It is most important to note that this could hardly be considered barter (counter) trade. The proceeds of the export business had to be remitted back and returned in full to the satisfaction of the ministry.

Before goods could be imported, full permission had to be obtained and the National Bank's consent procured. On the import side, most of the goods came from steel mills in Charleroi, Belgium and also Lyons in France. Urgent orders were freighted by rail to Passau on the German Austrian border and from there transferred by river barges on the Danube to Bratislava, and mostly distributed ex-port on arrival. The majority was taken by the slower but cheaper route, using rail to Antwerp, ship from there by sea to Danzig (Gdynia) and then by rail again, often straight to larger building sites and inland distributors, or to the company yards in Bratislava.

Ludwig travelled to visit customers and suppliers regularly in Holland, Belgium and France and more occasionally to England. He must have led a very full and very busy life. He acquired a working knowledge of spoken French and English.

We did not see as much of our father as other families, but in the winter we went on short holidays with him to the Tatra Mountains. Obviously he did not have a lot of time to do communal work, but always gave generously to good causes.

In 1928 the National Socialist Party (the Nazi Party) did not do well in the federal elections to the Reichstag, but they succeeded in obtaining a majority in the Bavarian State Parliament in 1929. There was a lot of discontent in neighbouring Austria, with regular violent clashes between the National Socialist and left wing parties.

With great care and foresight, my father started surreptitiously to accumulate a fraction of 1% from his export transactions in the west, as an emergency reserve, and by the time it was needed he had enough golden sovereigns in the Broad Street safe deposit in London to make a new start in another part of the world.

About this time, the Kampfner family sold some of their land in Surany and divided the proceeds. Ludwig put some additional capital to his share and purchased an agricultural holding of 347 acres of mainly good arable land, growing wheat and potatoes at Tura, a village near Levice.

The main house was a mini mansion, Central European style, and was divided into a large dwelling unit of 7,800 square feet (not large by English standards), occupied by the tenant farmer and his family. The smaller unit was comfortably furnished for the owners. The holding included a garden, fruit orchard and amenity woodland but 325 acres of the land was under the plough. The tenant had a long lease on a profit sharing basis. The farm had the usual outbuildings, barns, stables and several cottages.

The information about the farm above, and description of the block of flats below, was copied from a sworn statement by a surveyor from Czechoslovakia who attended the hearing with my parents at the Foreign Compensation Commission. The hearing was held at HM Foreign Office in London on 31 October, 1952. This property was in part of southern Slovakia, ceded to Hungary at the time of the Munich Agreement in September 1938. We did not often go to Tura for recreation, as the main attraction for my brother and me was to visit Omama and see our boy cousins, and for my parents to see the adult family. My father was very attached to his sisters: they were all living in Surany.

Surprisingly, in spite of uncertain times, my father built a substantial modern block of flats, warehouse and office at Dunajska Ulica 21 in Bratislava; construction commenced in 1935 and the building was ready for occupation in spring 1936. The government gave grants and encouraged building.

The property had ten flats. We occupied a double unit on the first floor; there were three shops on the ground floor in addition to an arched drive into the rear to the warehouse and office. The structure had reinforced concrete frames and brick walls, all in the best materials, and the interior throughout had first-class fittings.

My father's enterprises continued to trade successfully from 1936 to 1939. Ludwig, as ever, travelled a great deal, sometimes by passenger plane (which he denied as it worried my mother) and often by Orient Express. The train made a small diversion twice a week and stopped in Bratislava. You can imagine two excited schoolboys at the station waiting for their father to step off the train. My mother also had the opportunity occasionally to accompany him to Belgium, and might once have had a treat and visited Paris.

The Central European temperament blended quite well with the Western European nations, so it was easier for my father to befriend some of the executives and owners with whom he did business in Western Europe. Due to international cartels after 1945 my father found it impossible to trade with his old connections in Belgium and France.

In London he got to know a young able accountant by the name of Bernard Summers who had a small office in the city. Postwar this became Summers & Greenbury, in the West End, until the partnership merged with Hacker Young: Bernard Summers became a friend for life.

Ludwig formed a very good friendship with two partners at Phillips & Lyons, metal brokers, with substantial offices in Finsbury Square, Moorgate. Possibly he speculated on tin futures on the London International Metal Exchange. This firm merged with an even larger company a few years ago, but there is no trace of the old name in any current directory.

My father's exports to England were comparatively small. His agent was Mr E T Jones, who had a city office and was, I presume, a general agent and broker; he was helpful to my father and his commission rates were very reasonable. Until a few years ago, every limited company in England with foreign owners had to have an English director on the board. When Timbmet was formed in 1942, Mr Jones became a director and received an annual fee. He was handsomely rewarded as he lived to a ripe old age. Once we lived in England, he just signed the annual accounts and never wanted any business or social contact.

CHAPTER 3

Storm clouds gather 1933-39

In 1933 Hitler and his party won the general elections in Germany and soon afterwards began to carry out his policies and threats. He held many national rallies where huge crowds of all ages and backgrounds proclaimed their loyalty and support. Some of these meetings were quite frightening. He arranged very conveniently to have the parliament building burned down. He started to re-arm, and reoccupied the industrial Saarland. All this was against the agreements made with the allies in 1919, principally the treaty of Versailles.

Although I was only eleven years old, my grandfather, Simon Mayer, had made me listen to the radio broadcast of one of the first mass Nazi rallies. I was regularly updated by his commentary of events and made aware of the seriousness of the situation.

By 1934 the persecution of the Jews in Germany was well under way. At first all university and research institutes' very learned professors were replaced, and Government officers, teachers and municipal employees were sacked. Aryan administrators were appointed to large Jewish companies. Jews had to wear yellow badges and were therefore barred from public places of entertainment etc. Occasionally, when trying to put up resistance, Jews were badly beaten up. Much worse was to follow as time progressed. A baptised Jew or anyone with one Jewish grandparent was considered Jewish by the Nazis to be Jewish.

Hitler found a lot of support amongst the discontented Austrian population. The country was in a poor economic state as a result of the break up of the Austro-Hungarian Empire. When he decided to send his troops to occupy Austria on 13 March 1938, Hitler and his army, the SS and SA storm troopers, received a triumphant welcome in Vienna.

Bratislava, where we lived, was only ten kilometres from the Austrian border with Czechoslovakia, and barely forty kilometres from the centre of Vienna.

In 1937, my father put into action the first part of his plan to move our family to safety, if only for a temporary period.

In May 1937, two months after the Anschluss, he gave me the opportunity to go to a summer school for the holidays in a boarding institute at Bain les Bains in Switzerland. He secretly hoped that I would like it and ask to continue my education there, but I pleaded to come back. When, almost a year later, in March 1938 my father explained things to me, I readily agreed to travel to England with him and live with a Jewish family where I would continue my education in London. He feared that otherwise he would never get my mother to emigrate when the situation became really dangerous. I arrived in Dover on 26 May, 1938 with permission to stay as a student, but forbidden to undertake any work, paid or unpaid, due to the high unemployment in England.

I settled in quite well to my new surroundings and made friends of my own age in the local community. My father enrolled me for three months in the London Schools of English and Foreign Languages, at 19 Oxford Street, W1. I learned quickly. I had an underground season ticket; in my spare time I walked the streets of London and visited museums and historical sites.

Meanwhile, the political and racial upheaval continued. The Germans whipped up hatred among the Sudeten Germans living on the fringe of Bohemia in the Czech part of the republic. The enthusiasm was not as apparent as that shown by the Austrians: nevertheless, well over half the population in the border areas expressed a desire to become part of the German Reich. With the full consent of the League of Nations based in Geneva, Great Britain, France and the Soviet Union guaranteed the Czechoslovak borders but as the summer of 1938 progressed the position became untenable.

To political and military observers it became obvious that the allies were not adequately armed or even prepared to undertake the pledges made in Geneva. The foreign ministers of the three nations met constantly. Lord Halifax was comparatively weak, George Bonnet, the French statesman, was stronger and von Ribbentrop was, or pretended to be, a mighty giant who constantly threatened the others.

There were a few full plenary sessions of all the members of the League of Nations in August and September 1938, and it was decided that the British Prime Minister and his advisers would be despatched for a final talk to Hitler's mountain retreat in Berchtesgarden. As feared, Czechoslovakia, an emerging modern and progressive country, was betrayed by the West in order to gain a year's postponement of the major conflict that was bound to follow. Neville Chamberlain flew back to England in September 1938, arriving at Heston airport, stepped off the plane and proclaimed 'peace for our time'.

By mid September I was enrolled on a commercial course at the City of London College, now known as the City University. I usually walked to

Moorgate station at lunch time with two of my English fellow students, and the three of us shared an *Evening Standard*. They held up the paper and read the latest on the test match in South Africa and other cricket news on the back page, while I anxiously read the political news on the developing crisis on the front page. Sadly, most people in England were completely apolitical at the time and not really interested in the events in mid-Europe.

The new borders of Czechoslovakia were drawn up in early October 1938; and the second President of the Republic, Dr Benes, resigned. Large areas of Bohemia on the border with Germany became part of the Reich. Part of northern Moravia, known as Silesia, with good coal and iron ore reserves and a steel producing complex, was ceded to Poland, then still an ally of Germany; and a substantial part of southern Slovakia became Hungary.

Soon it grew obvious that the country's communications were truncated and that economically it would also become very hard to manage. It was likely that the central government authority would be undermined and gradually lose control.

In Slovakia uncertainty was greater than elsewhere in the country. As the sizeable Catholic pro-Nazi Hlinka party became more dominant, anti-Semitic posters appeared on billboards and Jews were bodily attacked in the streets. Ludwig decided to send his wife and son to our relatives in Subotica: they came back, then returned again but also spent a little time in Budapest. I can well imagine how my brother's education suffered.

By February 1939 the patriotic Czech people, and the minority of genuine Slovaks, who did not want to be affiliated to the German Reich, must have been pretty demoralised. International trade suffered. The Nazi propaganda machine relentlessly accused the Czech people of persecuting the German minority who were still supposed to have been in the middle of the country after the border adjustments were made.

On Friday 10 March, 1939, the parties led by Father Hlinka and Father Tiso declared the wish to form an independent republic under the protection of Germany. On Monday 12 March a treaty was ratified between the two parties and the new Slovak republic was established, *de facto*, if not *de jure*.

My father and mother must have packed suitcases a few weeks beforehand with enough to last for a two or three week holiday. On 10 March Ludwig took Margaret and my brother Fred to Prague by train. He felt safer there. They stayed at a hotel in the city centre awaiting further developments.

On Wednesday 15 March, 1939 my father, walking in Wenceslas Square, saw German troops entering the town centre. No resistance had been offered by the CSR army on the way from the border.

CHAPTER 4

Ludwig implements his most daring plan

I think Ludwig had the railway tickets to Brussels in his wallet. Mother told me that he went to the bank in Prague and withdrew cash which he had in a safety box. They boarded an early afternoon international express in Prague. The train left late, but when the train reached Pilser (Plzen) all passengers had to disembark. My parents and brother went to the station restaurant, and may have teamed up with a very eccentric and wealthy Belgian lady and a young man of our acquaintance from Bratislava. Ludwig left them and told them not say much to anyone, and not to be unduly afraid.

He went to the station taxi rank and must have disclosed his plans to a taxi owner with a large powerful car, no doubt offering an exceptional reward. The size of the reward for the favour was never disclosed by my father. They proceeded to the CSR border with Germany, about 60 kilometres from Cheb. I believe the locals were not difficult, but in tears due to events. Ludwig then crossed to the German border post and pretended to be an Aryan due to go on holiday to a German spa who did not wish to have his plans disturbed. Who believed what? After some hours he returned to Plzen station and warned every one not to speak, and the five persons got into the car with the luggage and set off into the unknown.

My brother disclosed that he and the others were very frightened; the journey to the German border was heavy with traffic in the opposite direction, German army tanks, lorries, supplies and equipment. The Czech taxi driver managed to locate two swastika flags which he prominently displayed on his vehicle: they were not stopped or molested on the way. When they arrived at the Czech border crossing, there was only one customs officer left who was in tears, and intoxicated. According to my brother, Father stamped the passports for himself and provided a bottle of brandy. These are my brother's recollections.

The car proceeded to the German border post and stopped. In their passport is an entry dated 16th March, and it must have been past midnight. How my father negotiated this we have never found out. There is evidence for this information based on passports that were stamped and saved and are available.

The car took them about 80 kilometres further to the town of Nurnberg in middle Franconia, a major railway junction. The international train from Prague to Brussels normally stopped in Plzen and Nurnberg. In the morning of 16th March, a train left Nurnberg going to Brussels and the family boarded using the tickets originally booked for the journey. They alighted in Köln (Cologne).

According to Fred, my father went to a bank to change CSR krowns for deutschmarks. The teller laughed as the money was temporarily valueless, but he had pity on him and gave him the minimum required to buy railway tickets to Aachen. They travelled by train from Köln to Aachen and then purposely changed on to a workmen's train which daily carried Belgian factory workers from Aachen to Aix la Chapelle and back. The same faces were there day in, day out, and by the time the German customs officers had spotted the strangers, the train had left the station. The Belgian customs had no objections as my parents had current visas in his passport granting entry to Belgium. The family was safe! I do not think they phoned me until 17 March as no doubt they were exhausted. I could not believe it at first, and feel sure I burst into tears of joy.

None of this could have happened, of course, if my father had not had a current visa allowing him entry into Belgium at all times.

The family stayed in Brussels for a few days. No doubt it did not take my father long to think ahead: he was convinced that Hitler would overrun the whole of Europe, but would be unable to cross the English Channel and occupy England. He was also certain that eventually the Nazis would be defeated and that we would return to the homeland in four or five years' time.

My mother would have preferred the comfort and luxuries of her home and domestic staff. She knew the difference between a reserved England, with the very quiet home life, and the café society of Central Europe. Around 22nd or 23rd March, a week after the German occupation of the CSR, the British Foreign Office introduced compulsory entry visas for Czechoslovak passport holders from 1st April, so as to avoid having to turn a large number of asylum seekers back at the UK entry points. I am sure this enabled my father to persuade my mother to carry out the last part of his exodus plan.

Ludwig was undoubtedly aware that he had a fair chance of gaining entry to England because of his entry visa to Belgium while Belgium was a free country: this was six months before the start of the Second World War. I firmly recollect that he also had a letter from a high official of the Belgian Ministry of Trade, authorising entry for himself and his family to the country at all times.

My father, mother and brother took the boat train from Brussels to Harwich on 28th March, 1939. According to Fred, my father had difficulty in obtaining permission to enter the country. On the evidence of Ludwig's passport, the initial permission was for a month: the month is lightly crossed out and substituted by "three months." I am willing to believe that he persuaded the officer to make this change. He understood circumstances in the country well enough to know that to offer an inducement would have had a disastrous effect. Anyone in Britain in a government position would have been upright and reliable and very proud of King and country. In addition, he obtained a visa from the foreign office dated 30th March 1939, allowing three months' stay, which enabled him to travel outside the UK and guaranteed him a return entry. They landed on condition that they did not engage in any employment, paid or unpaid; fortunately they had not been bodily searched on the journey. so the family jewellery that my mother had hidden in her bra was not found.

They came to live in England just before Passover 5699, and a few days before my brother's thirteenth birthday, in time to celebrate, very modestly, his Bar-Mitzvah.

CHAPTER 5

The family in England 1939-42

After arriving at Harwich, my parents and brother stayed for a few days in a private hotel at West Hampstead, London. They quickly found a furnished flat in Compayne Gardens NW6.

It was at this time that as a family we were really starting upon a new phase in our lives. My mother was still convinced that we would have been all right if we had gone into hiding somewhere in the Slovakian countryside; she never really came to see that Father's foresight managed to get all of us to freedom just in time.

A great number of those fortunate enough to reach England had suffered both bodily and mentally and were grateful to be here living in whatever conditions they could find. They accepted work of any kind, legal or otherwise. My father was just over fifty years old on arrival, and had great difficulty in finding an occupation. He had to help my mother for the first few months until she learnt to speak some English and became accustomed to life in England.

The summer school term had started. I was lucky enough to find a place for my brother at a GLC middle school in Kentish Town, and for a few weeks my father had to take Fred to and from school. Fred learned English very quickly, but it included a lot of bad language and swear words. Meanwhile I continued to live with my host family in north London and carried on with my course at the City of London College until the end of term, when I went to live with my parents.

I had an opportunity to go with a Jewish youth group to a summer camp at Buxton where there was a Bernard Shaw festival at the theatre. I bought a ticket and felt that I would understand enough to enjoy the play. I put on my best plus-four suit and was amazed to find the whole audience was in evening dress. I sat next to a young couple who turned out to be related to the Earl of Derby; the young man gave me his card and implored me to keep in touch.

The political situation in Europe deteriorated day by day. The allies warned Hitler that if he invaded Poland, they would declare war. He took no notice and on 1 September 1939 sent his troops to invade Poland. The British premier, Neville Chamberlain, gave Hitler a few hours to stop hostilities. He did not obey and the allies declared all out war.

Ludwig Kemp's passport entries leaving Czechoslovakia at night 15/03/1939, entering Germany early morning 16/03/1939, entering Belgium late 16/03/1939. After a short sojourn arriving Harwich on 13/04/1939.

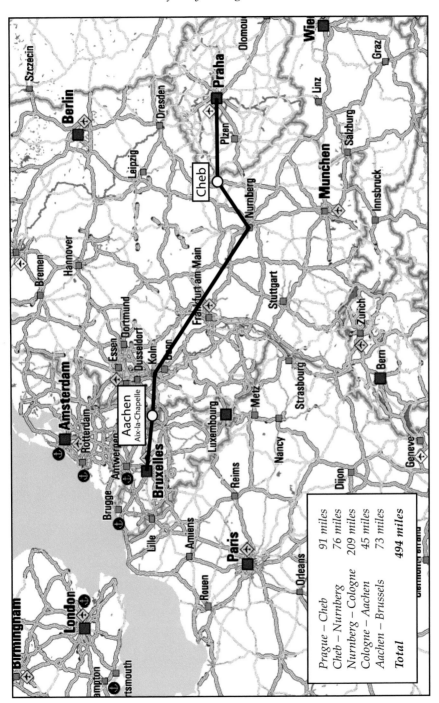

Prague – Cheb	91 miles	
Cheb – Nurnberg	76 miles	
Nurnberg – Cologne	209 miles	
Cologne – Aachen	45 miles	
Aachen – Brussels	73 miles	
Total	**494 miles**	

Map of route

Meanwhile, on the personal side, my father was in touch with several German Jewish refugee families who had settled in Cardiff. These groups came with the encouragement of the British government as they had manufacturing skills in light engineering, paint production and similar trades. They were given limited help to establish themselves on the Treforest Industrial Estate, near Cardiff, to help reduce local unemployment. Ludwig tried to establish partnerships, but nothing ever materialised. He also had a few business acquaintances in the Bristol area, among them a medium-sized shoe manufacturer who made 'Britton' brand men's shoes and boots. My parents' newly acquired friends persuaded them to come to Cardiff for safety from impending air attacks. They must have found them a partly furnished flat, in the Cathedral Road area, and we all voluntarily evacuated ourselves by the middle of September.

During the months before war broke out, it was possible to communicate with Germany and the Nazi occupied countries. A few people from Slovakia came legally to England if only on domestic work permits; we began to understand about the new conditions in Slovakia, and became more appreciative of our life in the UK.

After the outbreak of the war the Germans created a great fear of an impending invasion of these islands. All foreigners in Britain came under great suspicion. The position got worse once the regular heavy bombing raids, started by the Luftwaffe, concentrated on all major ports. All enemy aliens had to move twenty five miles inland from coastal areas; and all other foreign nationals had to apply for a special residence permit to remain on the coast. My parents decided to move inland to Aberdare where they found an old fashioned house on the outskirts of the town. My brother easily found a place at the local grammar school, and he has happy memories of the headmaster there who loved his music and Latin.

I applied to remain in Cardiff. Permission was readily granted especially as I enlisted part time in the ARP. All foreigners who were permitted to remain on the coast had to observe a night curfew although I was exempt when "on duty." The country needed more manpower, but any foreigners without special qualifications were still unwanted, even in 1940; I managed to find two low paid, unskilled jobs in Cardiff which gave me enough to make a meagre living. It was easy to find clean lodgings in the port area.

In May 1940 when allied morale was at its lowest and I was eighteen years of age, I applied to join the RAF flying branch. I passed the tests easily as I had not long left high school, and I was encouraged by the recruiting officer to help others with the tests. I was desperately disappointed to receive a letter from the Air Ministry to say that as I was not British they could not enlist me, but thanking me for applying, and for my loyalty.

In June 1941 it was suggested to me by the local labour exchange that I should attend a crash course in engineering at a government training centre in Treforest. I readily accepted, and after six months it was put to me that I should work in London where labour was short, no doubt due to many more young Brits being called up to the forces and some older people disappearing because of the blitz. I started work in north London on 19 January, 1942, and I was allowed to become a dilutee member of the Amalgamated Engineering Union. I soon found digs at nearby Finsbury Park and joined the local ARP group. (Note. The ARP was a voluntary body responsible for air raid precautions: warning people of fire risk and helping in a practical way during and after air attacks wherever they could.)

My father may have earned some money by a few speculative deals in metals and furs. This was still possible in the first two years of the war. He also went regularly to the Board of Trade Timber Control offices in London and Bristol as well as to the Forestry Commission offices in Surrey. No doubt the family lived for a time from the reserves my father had deposited in gold sovereigns in England before the war.

Soon after the war began, the British government decreed that everyone must surrender any gold coins, gold bars and other precious metals to help the war effort. You were only allowed to keep jewellery and odd coins of sentimental value. My father collected his coins from the safe deposit and took them to Rothschilds where he duly sold them and received the equivalent in English money. He believed he was one of the first foreign Jews in England to do so. The bank wanted to call the press, but my father managed to persuade them not to, as he feared any possible consequences postwar when he returned home. I cannot recollect the date when this order was made.

In December 1942 my parents decided to move to Oxford.

CHAPTER 6

Early beginnings

The Board of Trade and home timber production

In the United Kingdom, all commodity trading before the war was unrestricted. In 1936, central government instructed the Board of Trade to prepare a strategic plan for the import of raw materials to control the consumption and introduce licensing schemes. A small number of staff was recruited from the Forestry Commission and the timber trade to have everything ready for any emergency.

In the First World War, raw material procurement was not organised and some of the shortages led to prolongation of the conflict and great hardship for the armed forces as well as the civilian population. When the war broke out in 1939 a skeleton staff, to be known as the Board of Trade Timber Control, was in place to take over the purchase, import and distribution to priority users. It is easy to appreciate that it would take time for such a large conglomerate to work as a team. Disagreements arose between government officials, the Forestry Commission and those from the private sector until they all began to function properly together.

In the summer of 1941, a separate home timber production department was formed and the organised output of both native hardwoods and softwoods began to increase. By the following year the consumption of home-grown softwoods was about 45% of the total. Landowners were encouraged to allow extra quantities to be felled on their estates; and the Treasury granted excess profit tax relief where appropriate.

My father was only a very minor cog in a vast organisation. He became an official timber contractor attached to the Forestry Commission in Bristol and was allocated tracts of softwood forests to fell. The ground was cleared for replanting or most likely to grow food. He was advised to obtain his labour from the MOD, mainly German, with some Italian POWs. The Germans were preferred, but the Italians were the better cooks, who could distinguish edible plants and weeds and make some very tasty stews with the rabbits shot by the guards. Every one was happy except the neighbouring farmers.

The British army treated its prisoners very fairly, well above the minimum standards laid down by the Swiss Red Cross Geneva Convention. The employers of labour paid the MOD full trade union rates, and were encouraged to provide extra goodies such as cigarettes and chocolates. My father did not agree with this as he knew how badly British prisoners were treated by the Germans and their allies.

Ludwig engaged a very strong and powerful Irish man, Paddy Ferris, who remained with us to the end of his working life. Together they trained the men. Paddy eventually retired to a local village and we kept in touch. On some roadside sites, the round softwood crosscut logs awaiting collection proved a great temptation to thieves, so my father employed a sprightly elderly man as his watchman who sometimes lived on site. We found out later that he was not very trustworthy, to say the least.

By restarting in business, however humble, father regained his self confidence and his health improved greatly. He sought the advice of home-grown timber merchants about business and working methods in England, and the late Fred Scarsbrook, a much respected burgher of Woodstock, and the Linnell family in Silverstone, were always most helpful. We remained friends with both families in the following generation. To this day John Scarsbrook, grandson of Fred, is a highly regarded member of the Oxford Timbmet staff.

As well as being allocated sites to clear and fell, it was possible to buy stands of trees by private negotiation, subject to a felling licence. When this was granted, my father would be given instructions on where to dispose of the felled softwood. On a valuation trip around the Oxford country villages in 1942, Father was on his bicycle assessing standing timber. He was unknown in the area and, being an alien, the local policeman arrested him and kept him in custody for some hours until his identity was established by the Oxford police. Then he was let free, and everyone apologised with handshakes all round.

Early in his timber trade career Ludwig was very fortunate to meet Mr Hart-Synnot, the estate bursar of St John's College, Oxford, who gave him a lot of advice and assistance. Later in life my father would often refer to him.

Registration of Timbmet Ltd.

In April 1942 my father registered the company of Timbmet Ltd. His first choice of Woodmet Ltd was already trading as manufacturers of wooden trays and trolleys. I have on record that Ludwig opened a personal bank account with Barclays Bank, Aberdare on 1 April, 1941, which was transferred to Barclays Old Bank, High Street, Oxford. Timbmet Ltd has banked with Barclays right from its inception.

How do you make a modest profit when everything is strictly controlled? Home grown timber companies were offered parcels of round timber by the forestry department: one was not compelled to make a purchase but it was possible to make a counter offer. Likewise, if you found a parcel of standing softwood privately and purchased it, you could fell the logs, subject to licence, and offer the produce to a consumer who had a permit to use it.

Father was instructed to crosscut the round timber after felling to the required lengths and to de-bark, for which he got the controlled price in round measure (hoppus measure) delivered. He was encouraged to select out any straight logs for telegraph poles. These were individually inspected and, if up to standard, would fetch above the normal price for roundwood. The manufacturers of the wood wool [shredded narrow strips of fibre] were not keen to receive larger logs so my father was able to sell these at slightly higher prices to the nearest home grown sawmills.

Timber Control produced price schedules for round timber, based on quality and size. The larger the logs, the higher the price. All of this had to be strictly recorded, but with waste in conversion of any round timber, there was always a margin of error. It was partly dependent on judgement and luck as to what class of timber the woodland contained and what profit was achieved.

A better legal average price could be obtained by sorting the logs for various end uses rather than selling a bulk deal. Sometimes when my father finished felling a parcel of logs, a neighbouring saw miller would try and force him to sell it all at stump. The government officials were very fair minded, and this allowed my father to complete his harvesting.

CHAPTER 7

1945
The war in Europe ends

Timbmet continued trading in round softwood as described. Turnover increased a little annually: Ludwig had very few overheads and the business was profitable even with the strict margins permitted.

As the war in Europe came to an end in early 1945, details became known of the horrific atrocities committed by the Nazis. We realised that we had lost most of our relatives, the majority of whom had been put to death in the gas chambers. My father particularly grieved for the loss of his sisters. We and all other survivors were in deep mourning. The strong willed Ludwig was more affected than the rest of us, however: he suffered from shingles, and found it difficult to run his little business. At the time I was not fully aware of his condition.

In April 1945, without telling me, he applied to the Oxford Divisional Ministry of Labour for my release from Dormer & Wadsworth at Tooting in south west London where I was employed as a toolmaker. The rate was 1/7d (about 7.5p) per hour, and with a bonus the total was 2/2d per hour (equivalent to about 11p in old currency.) Flying bombs permitting, I went to night school to learn engineering drawing. So I was rather surprised when on 15 May I was called to the office at Messrs Dormer & Wadsworth and it was politely explained to me that although my work was entirely satisfactory, the Divisional Office of Labour had applied for my release; and I was ordered to work at Timbmet for my father, who was also assisting the war effort. My letter of engagement states that Timbmet had permission to expand and therefore was able to give me a job. This was a month after the European war had ended and Germany and its allies had surrendered, but Japan was still fighting the allied forces.

I packed my toolbags, bade farewell to fellow workers, thanked my landlord and his wife, and came to live with my parents at Oxford. As was mandatory for aliens, I registered my change of address and occupation at the Oxford police station on 18 May, 1945, the day after my twenty third birthday.

Looking back after all this time, I am surprised by how much skill I had acquired. I had thought my chosen career was going to be in engineering. I was grateful for what my father had done for his family and had great respect for him, and never resented the manner in which he had insisted that I join him in the business.

Dan joins Timbmet May 1945

As my father was not well when I joined him, I did not receive any training and had to learn as I went along. At the time Timbmet was felling a large parcel of softwood near the most picturesque village of Great Tew. The extraction was uphill to a roadside, with few machines and little fuel available, and it was a back breaking job.

I joined the team, and lived during the week in the village in a lovely cottage which had no electricity or running water. Paddy taught me how to calculate the volume handled, and to complete all the usual associated paperwork and statutory government forms. To get to the site, I travelled by bus from Oxford to Enstone and from there cycled to Great Tew. Within a few weeks I had gained weight, and felt healthier and refreshed. I enjoyed country life after the grim wartime experiences in the metropolis.

My father's health improved and so did his will to work and to build a business. The future of Timbmet became his main objective. He called on the Board of Trade Timber Control, no doubt with a recommendation from the Forestry Commission home timber production department, requesting that Timbmet be recognised as an established timber merchants.

Private imports of some species of hardwoods, mainly from Europe, were allowed by timber control in 1946, after the war had ended. Timber control knew that my father had worked well for the Forestry Commission and granted his request. It was also possible for priority users in government work to apply for a permit to purchase a new car and my father was allocated a grey Austin 10 with the licence plate number 'JJO 411'. He was also allowed additional petrol coupons, which made everyday life much easier.

Some timber controls eased

Timbmet was now permitted to trade in native hardwoods as well as import timber like the well-established firms. However, we had no access to the national hardwood stock as Timbmet was not yet a member of the Timber Trades Federation.

The national stock of timber which included a large volume of hardwoods from all over the world was started by Timber Control in the autumn of 1939 and maintained until about the middle of 1952 when it was fully wound up, The government then allowed the trade to resume its activities freely, except for currency restrictions, particularly for timber which had to be paid in US$.

Until the trade became fully independent of government controls, there were tables for maximum prices. Maximum prices for standing round English softwoods and hardwoods were determined by the quality and size of the logs, e.g.:

- Prices for felled timber at stump
- Additional prices for fresh sawn logs
- Extra for square edging
- An additional premium for sticking timber and part drying for a few months

The trade itself was classified as:

- Country mill
- Town mill
- Port city mill

For both English and imported woods this system allowed an extra small profit for those operating in the cities and less for the small country sawmill. Timbmet was given permission to operate as a port city mill.

Timbmet deals in native sawn hardwoods

We started to purchase fresh sawn English hardwoods from country mills. Some home grown mills had accumulated hidden reserves during the war and were able to offer dry hardwoods. We were allowed to buy these goods providing we gave the sawmills our trading licence number and kept clear records of our purchases.

To enable Timbmet to make a sale, a consumer had to provide us with his licence from the furniture manufacturers' Board of Control. We would endorse his quota and thereby diminish any further purchase he could make in the three monthly period for which it was valid. It must have been enormously complicated, but it worked and quality control ensured that the 'utility' furniture available in 1948 and onwards was of a good standard of manufacture. This procedure was similar in other industries using raw materials for post-war reconstruction.

CHAPTER 8

Growth in the postwar years
1946-1950

Timbmet was geographically close to High Wycombe and we had good beech and oak to offer to a few cabinet manufacturers and chair makers. As we were only a very small company, we endeavoured to concentrate on a limited number only. Most of these firms are no longer in existence. The three largest were Castle Bros of Cressex, High Wycombe, Gomme who became 'G' Plan, and Furniture Industries, owned by the Ercolani family. Ercol had a sawmill and converted most of their requirements from round English elm, beech and oak logs.

We got on exceptionally well with Castle Bros. Mr Tucker the managing director appeared to have a lot of respect for my father; Mr Castle, the chairman, would pay when requested and I had the honour to collect the cheques personally. I also worked in their timber yard for a few weeks under their yard foreman, Reg Hall, who was one of my teachers.

Even fresh sawn good quality hardwoods were in short supply in the immediate postwar period so it is not surprising that the large firms were only too willing to trade with a small merchant. As time went by we opened new accounts in High Wycombe; gradually many smaller firms resumed normal production. High Wycombe was the principal centre for chair manufacturing in the UK, employing over 10,000 manual operatives in about 120 production units. Once adequate supplies of beech and oak were available, it became harder to sell and almost impossible to achieve a reasonable profit margin.

By travelling around southern England, we got to know a number of English saw millers, nearly all old established family businesses; sometimes part of the family also engaged in farming. In the counties around Oxfordshire, an abundance of English elm grew in hedgerows and also in the middle of meadows. This was the traditional wood for coffin boards. We were not always well received as mill owners remembered the period between the two world wars when timber from Central Europe was exceptionally cheap and this had depressed prices for hardwoods in England.

By the end of 1946, or early 1947, elm production for coffin boards was permitted again. During the war, coffins had been made only of reinforced cardboard, and there was an immediate market for fresh sawn and dry elm. The majority of coffins were manufactured in Lancashire and Yorkshire. The population here, being friendlier by nature, was more welcoming to a foreigner speaking with an accent, and Ludwig's regular visits brought good results. These warm hearted people were tough business men, but appreciated a hard bargain provided they got a fair deal at the end of it, and some of these customers became good personal friends.

In a few sawmills it was possible to purchase fresh sawn timber and have it put into stick for seasoning and to remain drying for limited periods, at an extra cost. In the government pricing structure, there was a provision for rental charges. The national hardwood stock was stored as much as possible in country districts where the risk from bomb damage was much lower away from the ports. The wharfing charges at the ports were applied in country sawmills and other sites where the timber was stored by Timber Control.

I persuaded Ludwig to rent a suitable site for timber seasoning and storage. I was convinced we could develop our business better if potential customers came to inspect timber on our own premises. He relented, and decided to rent part of the Chawley Timber, Brick and Tile Works at the top of Cumnor Hill, on the outskirts of the city, rather than on low-lying land which was liable to flooding, near the town centre and canal at Osney Mead where St John's College had a lot of land going cheap.

Expansion: the Chawley Works site

In 1946 Timbmet agreed to a five year lease for part of Chawley Works through the Earl of Abingdon's estate agents, Tipping & Co, whose senior partner was Cecil Jones.

At first we hired two men and began to clear and level the land to enable us to put timber into stick for air drying. By making prompt payment for the stock, in spite of general shortages, we managed to obtain supplies of good sawn English elm and oak as well as beech. Ludwig was not the most patient teacher, but I tried to be a good pupil. He taught me and his other employees the simplest principles of timber drying and storage:

- Use clear and flat land
- Allow good air circulation around the piles
- Pile well above ground on good bearers at least 15cm off the ground

- Leave gaps between the piles
- Use accurately sawn dry clean softwood stickers
- Cover tops of piles with low grade boards
- Put all stickers straight one above another on top of the bearer, adequately spaced according to the thickness of the stock

Our yard looked tidy and when claims arose we sent photographs to our suppliers around the world who, surprisingly, often did not care, and then wondered why we were not satisfied with their goods.

By the winter of 1947, Timbmet was able to offer dry English elm coffin boards, which sold very well. We continued drying elm on a larger scale successfully for many years. We purchased and "sticked" the boards in the summer and we were able to sell the dry and semi-dry coffin boards the following winter. ["Sticked" is a technical term for placing thin laths between the boards to allow air circulation.]

As turnover grew, the company required skilled measurers and graders. Oxford was not a centre for the timber industry, but we managed to train three people, and put an intelligent piano porter in charge of the yard. He was Fred Haywood who lived in nearby Farmoor and was for many years employed at Russell Acott Ltd.

We fenced in our part of the yard against the wishes of the landlord but the bankrupt premises of Chawley Works was the target for local petty thieves stealing the second-hand bricks, timber and tin sheets from existing sheds. We were fortunate in having a stalwart friend in Sergeant Seymour who together with two police constables lived in three houses nearby. They walked their Alsatian dogs in the yard in the evenings and at weekends.

At the beginning the Timbmet offices were based at our home, 18a St. Margaret's Road, Oxford where we employed two lady clerks. Early in 1948 my parents bought a converted large house at 110 Banbury Road and the ground floor became the Timbmet offices until 1963 when we moved to a small purpose built office at the yard in Cumnor. For about ten years Timbmet employed a very conscientious young lady who learned very quickly and was capable of coping with shipping documents as well as all other office routine. For family reasons, she moved to New Zealand, and unexpectedly turned up for a visit just five years ago, causing tongues to wag!

Restricted imports allowed from Slovakia

While building up the yard trade, Ludwig managed to persuade the Board of Trade Timber Control to permit Timbmet to import beech from Slovakia, then part of the liberated Czechoslovakia. The authorised purchasers were the National Stock Authority. He went to the lower Tatra mountain area several times and inspected parcels of beech. In all instances they were quality approved on arrival, and full payment was made by the Board of Trade.

As we were not members of the Timber Federation, we could not repurchase the stock for our UK trade but there could not have been many small timber merchants whom the Timber Control entrusted with overseas purchases. Mr Ron Vickerstaff, who was seconded to the Board of Trade from Denny Mott & Dickson, was a great help to my father. I know how highly he spoke of Ludwig after he died. By then DMD belonged to the Mallinson group.

In January 1948, my father was in Slovakia inspecting and purchasing a large parcel of beech, but he did not want to leave until a letter of credit arrived at the local bank. Barclays refused to forward the draft because, according to them, the village did not exist. With good presence of mind, I dashed off to the school of geography, part of the new Bodleian Library, and explained my plight. They kindly uncovered a large wall map of the area, confirmed the existence of the place and gave me a letter verifying this. In less than an hour, I had managed to persuade the bank to pay. There are not many places in the world where one could have done this.

In March 1948, the Czechoslovak Communist Party overthrew the coalition government and a very radical communist regime took charge of the country. President Eduard Beres was forced into exile. Jan Masaryk, foreign minister and son of the first President of the Republic, jumped from the window of the Foreign Office and died instantly. Ludwig did not return again to Czechoslovakia.

The repair of war damage in the UK gathered momentum. The Board of Trade began to issue limited import licences to build up stock in non US currency only. There was no need to buy through an accredited agent or to be a member of the Timber Trade Federation to be allowed to import timber. The timber agent who was a member of the TTF could not sell to a non-member or a consumer. It was up to the daring businessman to assess the risks involved.

The destruction in Europe was still largely unrepaired. The central part of France was comparatively unaffected by the fighting and was rich in forest resources and, with the infrastructure undamaged, was a likely place for oak and beech supplies.

Ludwig in France

Ludwig took the opportunity to explore the region and made a few purchases. As confidence built up between the suppliers in France and Timbmet, business became more regular. However, my father never fully trusted the French and always inspected each parcel piece by piece. To speed up volume and allow himself a short respite during the day, he took with him an intelligent employee, Vick Watkins, who used to work at the Shurmer Furniture Factory in Oxford, to help him make the inspection. Before he left, he ensured that the goods were clearly marked and hammer stamped. If no goods wagons were immediately available, he made sure that railway consignment notes were completed. Lunchtime drinking, so natural for the French, was the downfall of many British buyers. He sometimes enlisted the good offices of the local gendarmerie to ensure that the right parcel was loaded on the rail wagons allocated for our goods.

By 1949, the supply of hardwoods was almost adequate for the still reduced manufacturing capacity of the furniture and joinery industry, and the smaller timber users, involved in coach building (for lorry and bus bodies), making domestic wood products, toys and heels for shoes, etc. The Board of Trade started to be more generous with consumer licences so as to gradually reduce the huge national hardwood stocks drying at many different country locations.

For the first time we found it harder to sell all the raw material. We were able to purchase from private sources both in the UK and in France. Large volumes of beech were felled in Germany as reparations. The work was supervised and largely undertaken by the Canadian armed forces timber corps. Beech must be quickly converted and dried so as not to go doaty, that is, when rot develops in the form of black spots and the timber deteriorates quickly. Unfortunately, the milling and drying capacity in England was inadequate to cope with the huge volume, and consequently much of the timber was wasted unless it could be used as wood for fuel.

We had by this time around fifty suppliers of home grown timber and many other saw millers who delivered fresh sawn elm, oak and beech, converted to our own particular requirements. Ludwig demanded a high standard and the native timbers were not always such good quality as the European. Claims did arise, but most were settled amicably. In the much larger forest areas of Europe the choice was easier. Until recently no grading rules for British timber had been compiled.

A part of our supplies was purchased in the round and sawn at the mill, or alternatively transported in the round for conversion at a trade sawmill. Once a log was bought it was marked and the quality became the buyer's responsibility, so that no further claim could arise.

At the same time Ludwig and I had to travel to make our name and sell the air dried and partly dry stock to the users. This became much harder than in the first three years when good timber was scarce. The stock in our yard was of higher quality than in most of our larger competitors' inventories. We had to find the small number of buyers who appreciated quality and understood waste factors, but even so most of these furniture manufacturers only wanted to pay a very little extra for the superior merchandise we had available. This struggle has continued in our trade since its very beginning, largely because timber is a product of nature.

In about 1949, we appointed our first sales representative, Mr Godwin, a pleasant middle-aged gentleman with a sound knowledge of timber. He started to make regular visits in the High Wycombe area and gradually widened his calls around the Home Counties and into London itself. Many factories and workshops were concentrated in the east end of the city.

Dan marries

About the same time, I met a young lady from London at her uncle's house in Oxford and we got on well together. After a few months of courtship, we became engaged, and on 6th August, 1950 we were married. Rosie's parents helped us buy a nice house in north Oxford where we lived for the first twenty years of our married life. To economise, as we did for many years, we spent our honeymoon in rainy Llandudno. We watched the sheepdog trials on top of the Orme, saw the first spruce plantations in North Wales and visited the historical townships of the principality. We were impressed by the low church preachers giving their sermons on the rainy promenade. Looking back, perhaps we should have gone somewhere warmer and more romantic; on our return journey, we found the sun at Stratford-on-Avon, so we lingered and I did not report back to duty until Monday morning. I got a very severe reprimand from the governor.

CHAPTER 9

1950-52
Expansion of hardwood importing;
and a turning point

A round this time, Ludwig realised I could not be in the yard and on the road at the same time. Perhaps he also appreciated that I ought to be at home with my wife a little more, but never after seven in the morning or before eight o'clock at night. To supplement my services, he advertised in the trade press and interviewed a number of applicants; and offered the post to a young man from the east end of London called Larry Smith who, apart from his army service, had spent all of his working life at Wm Mallinson & Sons of Hackney, London. Wm Mallinson kept the largest variety of hardwoods in stock from all countries of the world. They also had a veneer warehouse nearby and these premises must have been an Aladdin's cave of exotic veneers and the highest grade of hardwood stocks, where architect and client could choose their requirements on the spot and all in one place.

Larry had joined the firm on leaving school. He must have had an apprenticeship in the practical timber trade while working in various departments, and being bright he learnt a great deal. He had missed post-war opportunities for promotion due to priority being given to ex-officers; he joined us very willingly, and Timbmet bought him a house at 16 Hawthorne Close, Botley. He had recently married and had a young baby son; he was also connected to a telephone at home and given a bicycle, as well as the yard keys.

Transport

As a rule, general haulage companies disliked transporting timber because compared to other commodities it is bulky cargo as well as of comparatively low value. At the start we worked with J. Scott Transport, the largest in the Oxford area. Their depot was off the Banbury Road, behind Summertown Shopping Centre, down Mayfield Road and opposite Summerfields preparatory school. Walking down there a few months ago, I saw it has all been redeveloped into small flats and maisonettes. There may be one building left, now residential, which was the transport office; and also a retaining wall. One can hardly imagine how long vehicles manoeuvred in and out of their yard and the surrounding street. Scott Transport was nationalised by BRS [British Road Services], together with other local haulage companies, and a large depot opened with full workshop facilities at Long Lane, Littlemore, Oxford.

Quite early on, even as tenants, we needed sand and gravel for binding in roads at Chawley which we built from low grade broken bricks. We hired rollers and JCBs from Smith Bros at Bletchington, an old-established firm of sand and gravel merchants, who also had a general transport fleet. On the staff was Bill Herbert and his 12-ton loading capacity 'Giant' ERF motor lorry: he was a priceless individual, and we always hired him to take green timber from the sawmills to our customers. At first I helped with grading and loading at the mill, and later Bill wrote our delivery notes, copied from the supplier's particulars. He was trustworthy and discreet, and he worked well past his retirement age.

Dennis Belcher cycled from Longworth for interview on a Sunday. My father liked the look of him, and so he was engaged as our first lorry driver. I gave him a lift home in the car; and my father bought our first lorry, a brand new 8-ton Bedford, for Dennis to drive. He was a widower when in 1989 he married my secretary, Marion Briggs, herself a widow: Dennis was born in Longworth. He passed away in 2002.

Werrell's transport, a solid little company, was around the corner. At first we did not hit it off together, but Werrell's always had car components to deliver from Oxford to the docks and, where possible, we helped them with return loads of timber.

Our earliest close partnership was with Amey's transport, part of the Amey Roadstone Group. They had a good fleet of 8- to 10-ton lorries and were based at Wootton, near Abingdon. These vehicles were ideally suited for the deliveries of coffin boards to the north west and north east of the country. It was quite a relief when they had enough fuel allocated to them for general work; up until then, we had been compelled to deliver coffin boards and other orders by rail from Oxford goods station, often using closed goods wagons which were not easily loaded. The wagons from the northeast stank of fish, so we had to provide liquid refreshments for our men on the way back from the station to the yard to keep the production going to load all the trucks allocated to us by the end of the day. It often made a dent in my then meagre weekly wages!

Specialist grades

As mentioned earlier, the high standard of quality Ludwig set for the Timbmet inventory enabled us to sell to only a minority of cabinet makers. The majority of them bought various "selects" grades, rather than a full FAS ("main" grade) or true prime quality.

The largest consumers of hardwoods in the immediate post-war years were furniture manufacturers who were providing the requirements for domestic, government and commercial users. Significant quantities of hardwoods were traditionally consumed in the UK for the construction of public buildings, ecclesiastical woodwork, schools and hospitals. At first native woods were used, but by the turn of the 19th century Far Eastern hardwood species had become popular in England, not only for the marine business but also for the top end of the housing trade.

After the Second World War, specialist importers bought West African solid hardwood logs which had to be sawn and dried in England. They were mainly medium durable, ideally suited for furniture, windows and doors. Import of these logs increased gradually over the years and a few European companies established sawmills in West Africa. The earliest were subsidiaries of the United Africa Company [UAC] and Glikstens, who were very well known importers; they sold through English agents and members of the TTF, but as were not members we were unable to buy these supplies direct.

Timbmet started to make visits to the larger builders who usually had their own in-house joinery facilities. This meant supplying less than a lorry load to one customer: in other words, smaller quantities, often selected to a cutting specification and delivered close to the lengths and widths required, with the least possible waste, in a good clear grade with as few faults as possible. Because of these requirements, we had to learn new ways of buying, selling and distribution. With all his practical knowledge, Larry proved to be the ideal yard foreman.

In good times, hauliers prefer not to be forced to distribute part loads, so it became necessary to start our own distribution service. We chose two more 8-ton Bedford lorries, but from the beginning did not anticipate that we would need a maintenance department. The local franchise was with the nearby City Motor Company, who had premises on Botley Road, with weekend servicing facilities. I do not remember now how much we paid for the vehicle, but I do know that I often passed a tent and tarpaulin maker at Caversham, Reading by the name of Carter: I bought the first lorry sheet for our Bedford at a reduced cost of £8 from the owner's son. We must have impressed one another because we kept in touch for many years afterwards.

Growing demand for African and Far Eastern hardwoods

To purchase the additional quantities required for the joinery manufacturers in the building industry, we needed supplies of African or Far Eastern hardwood. At the time, the Korean War had started and there was a large demand for quality durable timber for use in the Far East.

During the 1939-1945 war many cargo ships had been destroyed by submarines on both sides, so a shortage of freight space arose due to extra cargo and troop movements required during this time. In Africa, the fledging shippers had very few scruples. If a ship arrived in a port, it was loaded with logs, often with complete disregard to the quality and species purchased. As the cargo had to be paid for before the goods were landed, many importers were never compensated for their losses: some of the larger timber agency houses had more reliable connections but the risks were still considerable.

From about 1948 onwards, Ludwig did mix a little in trade circles. He also visited the offices of the TTF from time to time when in London; and the committee eventually permitted Timbmet to become a probationary member for twelve months. We filled in forms and had to provide accounts and personal references.

During this period, we could purchase our requirements from agents accredited to the TTF who generally represented the better producer and were more trustworthy, and if a claim arose the agents did their best to resolve the issues. We had to buy £200,000 FOB [free on board] value during the twelve month period. On the whole, the timber agents were most helpful to Timbmet: they were hoping for a new permanent customer. Mr Charles Griggs, of C. Leary & Co, advised Ludwig to top up the volume required by purchasing a small volume of Burma teak, and a larger quantity of Burma gurjun. Gurjun is a timber similar to Siamese yang, Philippine apitong or Malay keruing, but much milder in texture. The gurjun was carefully put into stick for air drying, and sold gradually for structural purposes. We wish we had it today for barn restorations.

As yet we had no market for teak. The top class builders involved in royal palace restorations, Whitehall buildings and similar contracts, had not yet heard of us and it took many more years to become customers. Once again we put the teak carefully in stick for drying in a damp spot of the yard and allowed the 'Chawley weeds' to grow around it. Our market came a few years later once the Middle East countries had joinery, woodwork and furniture made in the UK. The private boat building industry also needed teak, and we were able to supply very dry naturally seasoned timber in large quantities. Due to the lower value of our currency, we made good profits on this stock; and Dan Kemp even signed a certificate to a Middle Eastern buyer to the effect that this teak was not grown in Israel!

Turning point: membership of TTF

We were finally admitted as full members of the National Hardwood section of the Timber Trade Federation in May 1952. Ludwig was exceptionally pleased as now he felt he was accepted by the trade establishment in the UK, his country of adoption. We do not know what some of his competitors thought. Without membership of the TTF, Timbmet could never have progressed so fast. At about the same time, the Board of Trade Timber Control wound up its operations. Most of the stock was sold and the last remnants, mainly of poor quality, auctioned, and the temporary staff returned to their previous employers. Apart from currency controls, business was fully free again as it had been before 1939.

The Monopoly Commission was established in 1950 and looked into the affairs of various industries. In October 1951, the Board of Trade referred the TTF to the Monopoly Commission; and in 1953, it was recommended that the approved lists be abrogated. The president of the Timber Trade Federation and his honorary officers at the time decided that all sections would comply rather than incurring the risk of the imposition of a government order. The old trade practices continued in use for some time, however. The agents did not sell to the inland merchants and consumers and, in turn, the importers did not buy direct. No doubt there were firms who were non-members who imported their own and sold to whomsoever they pleased. Some of these were manufacturers who purchased their raw materials from abroad.

From this time onwards Timbmet seemed able to trade with every one. The Federation never interfered and we were left to our own devices. At the time, we were still a very small company and the majority of business was in home grown hardwoods.

CHAPTER 10

1953-1962

Trading on a more level playing field

Our lease at Cumnor had expired. My father tried to renegotiate and offered a considerable increase in rent. The Earl of Abingdon's land agents would not or could not agree to anything, although they were willing to take the rent without being able to offer security of tenure. In 1952, fortunately for us an adjoining field, west of the site, came on the market. It was just less than three acres of land with a good frontage to the main Cumnor Hill. The site had had red ribbon outline planning permission since 1935 for a petrol station and a car repair shop.

The land belonged to a local shoemaker in Oxford, Mr Morris, and he offered to sell the freehold for £1,300. He accepted £1,250 and the transaction went through smoothly; the solicitors' inclusive fees were 20 guineas (£21). The field was purchased by my mother: nicknamed 'Granny's Field' it has been retained and is still named 'Granny's Field' to this day. This acquisition provided us with emergency storage ground.

We had temporary planning permission, renewed annually, from Berkshire County Council for the storage of timber at Chawley Works, our rented premises. When the site was purchased in May 1956, planning permission was granted for the next three years.

Imports of Japanese oak and elm

We needed Japanese oak to balance the inventory for the joinery and coffin board industry. This was a mild species grown on the lower slopes of Hokkaido Island, one of the most northerly inhabited islands of Japan. The four seasons suited the growth of mild light-coloured oak; the timber was precision produced and the saw milling and grading excellent. The specification was slightly smaller than for the best European oak. The timber was air dried for a few months to ensure its delivery in good condition after a six-week sea voyage. When available, we also bought smaller quantities of Japanese elm and minute parcels of ash and lime. Each board was stamped and branded by the shipper and, until the American army completely withdrew, marked 'Made in Occupied Japan'.

Most British timber agents handled this species as Japanese business was well regulated and organised, and had the financial backing of well known Japanese international trading houses who were mostly also bankers. It was surprising how quickly Japanese business returned to normal after the war.

We also imported Japanese oak and elm coffin boards as well as coffin moulding stock to Liverpool and Glasgow. We had private wharfingers there who looked after the timber under cover for us if it was not sold during passage to the UK. Ludwig opened accounts with nearly all the sizeable coffin manufacturers in Lancashire and Yorkshire: these firms produced the majority of coffins for the whole of the country. Ludwig made several visits to Scotland and gained customers easily. One of them was the late Phillip Watson, of Gordon Watson (now part of the House of Fraser) who was particularly kind, and provided him with a driver and car whenever he wanted to visit his competitors. Mr Crawford of Fyfe Douglas & Co of Glasgow, today part of the Glasgow Co-operative Funeral Department, was a tough customer, but once a deal was struck, was always a kind friend. These two men introduced Ludwig to leading builders in Scotland. A number of post 1950 churches built in traditional style have the pews made of oak that was dried at Cumnor, with seats made mostly without a joint in lengths or widths.

Growth of overseas trading

Various UK and Dutch timber agents introduced us to 'reliable' African log shippers. Some of them already had European partners living part of the time in the producing countries; and we, like other log importers in Europe, had numerous disappointments, losses and unpaid claims.

Foy Morgan, who were leading timber agents later merged with Price & Pierce; Foy Morgan did not want to have any connection with Timbmet, even though we became members of the TTF. Ludwig offered to pay in advance and put a cheque on the table, and they reluctantly agreed to supply high quality utile logs. For the coffin trade, we needed quality whitewood. Obeche logs were best suited being of large diameter and good long straight boules, ideal to cross cut to coffin lengths and produce nice traditional lids without a joint in the widths. The logs from the

Cameroons were most suitable, slightly heavier in weight, firmer in texture and a good creamy colour if shipped quickly after felling.

Before the international agreements in tariff and trade were ratified, Great Britain gave preference to imports from its dominions, colonies and dependencies. The logs grown in the then French Cameroon were transported across the River Calabar to Nigeria and shipped as being of Nigerian origin, free from 10% import duty. For some years, tropical hardwood imports to the UK from Africa came principally from Ghana and Nigeria. Eventually shippers from the republics of Ivory Coast, Cameroons and Congo adjusted their prices to compete.

When the two agency houses merged and were known as Price Morgan, we became large customers: the Timbmet account manager was John McKee, whose father David was managing director of D James Webster, a very old established timber importer in Liverpool. Until he retired, his brother David was also involved in the agency business. John married a young lady whose father was a private merchant banker from Vienna. John understood the continental mentality and appreciated Ludwig's business principles. He and I got on very well together and he persuaded the senior directors to grant Timbmet credit far in excess of insurance limits. It was only many years later that I got to know the chairman.

Everyone in the trade was very surprised when John left at a comparatively young age and emigrated to Alberta, Canada to become a farmer. Before leaving the UK he confided to me that the real reason was for the family to escape death duties as his father-in-law was very wealthy. Flatau Dick was at the time an unlimited partnership representing several good hardwood producers as sole agents in the UK.

The Mim Timber Co, near Kumasi in Ghana, entrusted all of their Western European sales to Flatau Dick. At first it was logs and flitches but from 1960 onwards it was also sawn timber from their new sawmill in West Africa. The owners of Mim were the late Oscar Charmant and his family who originated from southern Slovakia. Ludwig must have been in regular contact with them. Oscar's father was a leading advocate who represented Hungarian minority interests at the peace conferences at Versailles.

The border lines were finalised at Trianon in 1919 for the countries which were created out of the Austro-Hungarian Empire. Mr Charmant had recommended that part of the proposed southern region of Slovakia should remain part of Hungary. Unfortunately, his view was not accepted and the family, to say the least, was made very unwelcome in the newly created Czechoslovak republic. They may well have been forced to sell their woodland and farms at low prices; they emigrated to England around 1922, and earned their living in the timber industry.

Just before the outbreak of the war, the Charmant family established Victoria Sawmills, with a large sawmill and kiln complex in Hayes, Middlesex. Timbmet made good use of the service they provided. Mr Oscar Charmant had his office at Hayes and after my father passed away, and even at very short notice, I could always have a salad lunch with him, and give him my 'shopping list'. Most of the time I got what Timbmet required. Occasionally Flatau Dick would feel that I was given preferential treatment, but Timbmet repaid the company by taking into stock unpopular items of species that were temporarily out of fashion. We had the storage at Chawley to accommodate it. Sometimes the quantities were fairly substantial but Mr Messenger, the finance partner at Flatau Dick, managed to make arrangements for bills of exchange for Timbmet.

Giles Sim, of Churchill & Sim, introduced Timbmet to the Yugoslav beech producers Sipad in Bosnia and later to the oak sawmills in Croatia: these were all state controlled enterprises. The above named agents helped us to build up our business: they trusted the Kemps and provided additional financial support. We also purchased from smaller agencies at reasonable rates of interest.

Insurance became more important as Timbmet owned larger quantities of stock. Ludwig got to know a sub agent for C E Heath & Co. and we stayed with them for about twenty years. It became fashionable to make changes so we followed suit but now, fifty years later, we have returned to our original brokers, who now trade as Lambert Heath. Ludwig was a very demanding employer. Although he wasn't keen to pay overtime, he generously rewarded those in need. He also started a pension scheme with the Yorkshire General which included his manual workers.

Selling

With these additional connections established, and the war ending in Korea, timber supplies became plentiful. New sawmills established in the Far East and West Africa were producing additional quantities of good quality lumber.

Timbmet, as always, aimed to increase its market share in the UK. Mr Godwin, our only sales representative other than myself, travelled the whole of the south of England and gained many medium to larger sized builder customers who usually had their own joinery department. We served the furniture factories, mainly the companies employing up to 200 operatives, and different craft firms. The very large firms of mass producers of domestic furniture were often particularly difficult to please.

By 1955 we provided about 30% of the hardwood needs for the coffin industry in the UK. Chipboard began to be used, slowly at first and mainly for cremations. Remploy, the rehabilitation workshops, and Papworth Industries were employing many war disabled. We managed to satisfy the former with native timbers, and the latter with Japanese oak strips, boards and squares for table manufacture.

Magnificent quality ash grew in parts of England. Because the aero industries did not require this material in volume, we managed to buy prime freshly sawn stocks which we air dried: we offered this to many large coachbuilders for the manufacture of bus bodies, but mostly we could not get past the door. We were concerned that the stock might deteriorate however well it was stored out of doors.

We then tried the Midland car works and some of the smaller quality sports car manufacturers, without avail. However, the Morris Traveller's car division at Coventry often had some difficulty in getting enough 4" thick planks for the back pillars, where light coloured large logs were needed to produce the curved components. We had the stock available and, after numerous calls, persuaded the purchasing manager of Morris Minor to visit and make an inspection. They fully understood that the first order delivered was of exceptional specimen logs, but we managed to follow on with an average of good quality ash to their satisfaction. A month later, on the front page of the Gliksten magazine, a photo appeared of these logs which Glikstens had obviously claimed to be their own supply. All our employees were a little upset, but we decided to lie low because all that really mattered was the gain of a new substantial customer for ash and a share in the business with a major competitor.

Compensation and the Chawley purchase

After years of negotiations and a full court hearing at the British Foreign Office in May 1953, my parents were allocated approximately £48,000 from the Czechoslovak fund as part compensation for the loss of their property and assets. They held the land deeds as evidence of full ownership. The amount was shown in my late father's will, and estate duty to the value of 10% was charged. It was only many years later that a bill was passed in the British Parliament exempting foreign compensation for assets lost due to the Nazi atrocities from any form of taxation, but this law was never made retrospective.

In about 1956, the liquidators of the Chawley Timber Brick and Tile Works started to look for a serious buyer for Chawley Works. The negotiations may not have been conducted quite straightforwardly. The most serious contender was the Amey Roadstone Company. The Earl of Abingdon's family was represented by Withers, a leading firm of London solicitors; the late R B Cole, senior partner of Oxford solicitors Cole & Cole negotiated on behalf of Timbmet. [His son John is the present non-executive chairman of the Timbmet group.]

We finally managed to outbid all other contenders, probably because we allowed the thatched cottage, at the south eastern end of the property, and the house, at the western end of the works, to be excluded from the sale. These houses were occupied by two old serving employees of the brickworks. I believe we may have also given up half an acre of land for the cottage and offered to put in drainage.

We also agreed to continue to pay an annual levy to the local parish to redeem the right of the local poor to graze their cattle on the land; no one could point out which field the right applied to, but the sum was very small. The Church Commissioners eventually surrendered these rights to all landowners in perpetuity in return for a fixed sum of money. No doubt they made better investments with the proceeds. Ludwig willingly and gladly paid R B Cole 1,000 guineas (£1,050) for completing the deal. This was an appreciable fee at the time. The only thing we ever regretted was our kindness to our immediate neighbours.

CHAPTER 11

1956

Development of land at Chawley

The cost for Chawley Works was £16,000. When the deal was completed, an auction sale was held for loose items stored on the land. As the light goods had been stolen long ago, only a few derelict rusty steam engines were left which did not fetch a king's ransom at the time. After this, we arranged for a company of experienced steeplejacks to demolish the three tall chimneys, and thus removed a genuine eyesore from the horizon, which was perhaps the only time our neighbours appreciated Timbmet!

There were a number of somewhat derelict buildings on the site which we put to good use. We repaired what buildings we could and made them safe. The most valuable was a timber framed building with preservative treated softwood poles to which were fixed tin sheets. The roof was of similar construction. The building was about 60 x 30 x 7 metres high and situated in the south-eastern corner of the yard near the thatched cottage. Formerly this was the Earl of Abingdon's sawmill.

The main conversion machine was a 6ft diameter circular saw set in a deep pit and powered by a steam engine. This was a very ancient dangerous piece of equipment but none the less large trees had been regularly sawn. The oak came from nearby Wytham Woods, and the elm from meadows in the surrounding countryside. Much of this had been used for estate maintenance, some was air dried and sold to the trade, and the lower grade utilised for the trolleys that transported the clay from the pits and for pallets on which the bricks were dried. They had built their own wagons. Timbmet filled in the saw pit and used the shed for very badly needed storage for dry timber.

Close to the existing garage was a similar building used by the brickyard for the repair of traction steam engines. It had not been used for a long time as the pit was filled with broken bricks and gravel, and this became our first vehicle maintenance workshop.

A brick building measuring about 40 x 15 metres is still in use today as our re-sawing mill. [The annexe built on to the side became our first canteen called Fred's café.] By the entrance on the left, where the sharpened saws are stored, was the 'office' from where we communicated with head office at 110 Banbury Road. The original use of the building is unknown but from 1939 to 1945 Morris Oxford car radiators were produced there for the limited car production allowed during the war years.

Nearby there was a tall storage shed which had not been used since about 1930 when the brick works went into liquidation, and was no longer safe. I assume this was where the bricks were formed before they being put into the kilns for curing. There was a deep basement to house the many belts needed to drive the machinery; the remains of the blacksmith's shop were also nearby. The building, erected in 1879, collapsed during a heavy snowstorm a few years before we became the owners, which was fortunate for us as it prevented anyone putting a preservation order on it. We donated several of the unbroken pitch pine beams to the restoration of the 'SS Great Britain', and also gave iroko for the repair of the hatches.

The main brick drying kilns, low brick buildings, were in the area nearest to the front of our premises. Working in such high temperatures must have been a back breaking job. We gradually demolished the various structures as we developed the yard, and used the material for road building. Should Inspector Morse have been around then, he might have found the kilns useful for one of his murder plots! A small statue of the Earl of Abingdon, which was originally on the gable of one of the buildings, broke into pieces as the building collapsed. The broken pieces disappeared and were only returned to us a few years later. We asked the Ashmolean Museum for their help in restoring the statuette: this was readily given and today the repaired figure stands in its glass case in our reception here for all to see.

By now in the year 1956 our annual turnover had risen to around £200,000, equivalent in value to £3,000,000 per annum in 2005. To put this into context, an example is that in the mid-1930s the freight from West Africa to England would have been just over £1 per cubic metre: in current value about £45 a cubic metre! The first slowdown in trade following the end of the war in 1945 occurred in the UK in 1958. Fortunately for us, the ravages of war were still far from repaired in Europe; this kept up the demand for timber products and prices remained steady. In the years 1950 to 1960, there was hardly any inflation and the pound sterling was still the principal world trading currency.

More staff employed

We had twelve men in the yard, and had acquired a second 10 ton capacity Bedford lorry, with two Scamell trailers. We took on a new lorry driver, Ken Cripps, who proved to be loyal, reliable and trustworthy. Our first representative had left us and another person, whose name escapes me, was on the road for Timbmet. About 15% to 20% of our turnover was also ex-ship direct to customers, and some English freshly sawn oak and elm also went straight to those who dried their own timber. This involved me in many early morning inspections and the supervision of the loading, mostly to hired transport.

Larry Smith managed the yard and transport. He was a practical timber expert and was skilled in timber handling without cranes or other mechanical lifting tackle. In the office we employed three young ladies but we had a constant turnover as the stork seemed active! I pleaded with my father to engage a male office manager and for a time he tried to find someone with the right background and knowledge living locally. Eventually he advertised the position in the Timber Trade Journal and interviewed several applicants; and finally he chose Leslie Boustead, who came for a number of interviews on his motorbike on Sunday mornings. On the last occasion, in early September 1958, he brought his girlfriend, Janet which was when I met him for the first time.

Leslie Boustead joins Timbmet

Ludwig offered him a post as office manager with Timbmet at a salary of £10 per week plus a £2 weekly living allowance. He was promised that after a short probationary period he would be offered a rent free semi-detached house to enable him to get married. Right from the beginning, Leslie proved to be very self confident, diligent and efficient. Timbmet fulfilled its promise, bought 16 Maple Close, Botley, and soon after Christmas 1958 Leslie and Janet married. Ludwig gave them an alarm clock as a wedding present! Leslie never ever needed to make use of it as he was very self disciplined and an exceptional timekeeper; and expected the same from all employees.

Leslie had left school after passing the GCE examination to work for the wharf manager of North Eastern Timber Co. which, at the time, was a sizeable hardwood firm in Hackney. He started as a tally boy checking the boards out of the barges, and progressed into the yard office. At that time he also attended evening classes and passed examinations for membership of the Institute of Wood Science. He did national service as a midshipman, and when that finished he joined a small importer, W C Marshall, whose premises were under the railway arches in East London. The owner very soon realised Leslie's capabilities, and left him almost single handedly to organise the yard and sales.

Ludwig's health

My father's health began to deteriorate from the summer of 1958 onwards. However, one Friday morning in June, he was summoned (it sounded almost like a royal command) to present himself at Morris Motors, Cowley, to meet John Lay, a senior buyer with the company. He went by taxi and, although far from well, seemed to have made a good impression. During the interview he was questioned about Timbmet; no doubt they were checking on information I had previously given them about the firm's ability to provide the service and to deliver their timber requirements punctually. The interview went well, and an account was promptly opened for Timbmet; and in the following week I went personally to collect my first order. It was one of the rare times that Ludwig ever seemed fully satisfied with his son.

Also at that time the Post Office and telephone service (GPO) vans were fitted out with timber shelves. Once accepted, and after getting to know the head of the woodworking department, business flowed smoothly for some time until panels and plastics took over from solid steamed beech and ash.

By curious coincidence, just a few weeks later, on the last Friday of July before the two week holiday shutdown, Ludwig had a similar call from Pressed Steel Company asking him, at only a few hours' notice, to call to see Mr Montgomery. The following interview and discussions must have gone well as the company opened an account with Timbmet. The orders were smaller and much more spasmodic, mainly for pattern making timbers with some also for maintenance requirements. These continued until patterns for them were produced in Germany.

In his mid sixties Ludwig still went to inspect timber in France, physically checking the parcels and receptioning (that is, inspecting and selecting the goods piece by piece.) He visited our northwest of England customers travelling by train; his last call was usually on Luke Howgate & Sons at Dewsbury. Even after Rowland Howgate's tragic death in a car accident, another member of the family would see him in the evening, negotiate the next deal, and then put him on the train home leaving York at 10.00 pm, due in Oxford at about 2.00 am. He would be back in the office by eight o'clock in the morning. On his arrival on one occasion the mail was not opened and ready on his desk, and I was severely reprimanded. I do not remember what had delayed me that day, but you will appreciate that I had a very hard master to please and nothing to him ever seemed impossible. Ludwig would not accept 'No' for an answer!

Ludwig's death and the end of an era

As the year progressed, my father became increasingly less interested in the day to day running of the business. He was unable to concentrate for any length of time, and in the spring of 1959 he had a heart attack from which he never really recovered. He was in hospital for the last month of his life, and in July 1959, passed away peacefully. Unfortunately no one was with him at the end as the nursing staff had told us to go home to allow my mother to rest. She had been almost constantly by his bedside and they did not anticipate anything happening that night. As we left he had seemed to be calm and resting peacefully.

I feel deep respect for this man who had the foresight in his younger years to think out his plan to move his family out of danger in the nick of time, and to have the presence of mind to carry with him his current income tax papers and deeds of the properties he owned. As soon as he possibly could he started to work in the timber trade again. Opportunities for developing business during the war were very limited due to government controls in this country.

TIMBMET LIMITED

DIRECTORS: L. KEMP   M. KEMP

Hardwood Merchants and Importers

TELEPHONE
OXFORD 58493
PRIVATE LINE 5594I

TELEGRAMS
TIMBMET OXFORD

Our ref. IK/VT

110, Banbury Road, Oxford.

18th September 1958.

L. Boustead, Esq.,
113 Cadogan Terrace,
London, E.9.

Dear Sir,

I would like to acknowledge the receipt of your letter
dated the 15th instant and find that everything is in order.

You will commence duties as stated by you, on the 13th
October.

Regarding holidays, you will of course be entitled to
the statutory paid holidays.

You may like to know that we have had an advertisement
inserted in the local paper for accommodation, and will advise you
when offers have been accumulated.

Yours faithfully,
p.p. TIMBMET LTD.,

Director.

Leslie Boustead's letter of employment

Steam vehicle of the Chawley Timber, Brick & Tile Co. c.1900

CHAPTER 12

1959
Dan takes over

The death of my father put extra responsibilities on my shoulders. When I informed our solicitor, Mr R B Cole, he advised me to arrange for my father's funeral, and in the long term to care for my mother, and to devote my best efforts to the business which had meant so much to Ludwig.

New responsibilities

I soon had a phone call from the manager of Barclays Bank, at the Old Bank, High Street, Oxford and made an appointment to meet the manager, Mr I F Bradburn. Our discussions went well and he assured me of his full support. I promised to keep him regularly informed of Timbmet's progress and to consult him whenever I felt he could give me advice or guidance. To my great surprise, as I took my leave he made me stand to attention and requested that I should keep the Jewish Sabbath as my late father had. I affirmed this without the slightest hesitation, which pleased him. Sadly, however, some twenty years later I started to work on Saturdays and I have regretted this ever since.

My father believed that a private company, even if limited, is the personal private property of the owner(s). He would not show the Timbmet accounts to the bank, although obviously they could draw some fairly accurate conclusions from the banking figures. However, Ludwig had to bow to their demands to have his house deeds as security for the loan of money to Timbmet. At the time smaller companies did not have to file their annual accounts at Companies House. The bank contacted me a few weeks after my personal interview and asked me to produce the 1958 Timbmet accounts; I agreed to do so then and in the future, providing that they returned the deeds of 110 Banbury Road to my mother. Eventually they agreed to this. At the time I felt that a house on Banbury Road was of greater value than all of Chawley Works.

Later, as I got to know him, I found out that Mr Bradburn was a deeply devout Christian and a great believer in Jewish tradition as well as the

Old Testament. He was the church warden of St. Mary's, the city church, and was the last person to live in the bank premises in Magpie Lane.

The timber agents we traded with promised me their support and help. The only firm who wished to interview me was Flatau Dick & Co. at 9 Camomile Street, EC3. They were important timber agents who were representing some of the best hardwood shippers in the world. I called there as requested and met Mr Douglas Walton, with whom Timbmet conducted day to day business, and the financial partner, Mr Messenger. I managed to assure them of my ability to continue the business. I was also looking for one or two capable experienced men with hardwood trade experience to assist me in the steady growth of Timbmet.

I fear that reading this account of Timbmet's early beginnings may give the impression that all was easy going, when in fact just the opposite was the case. Only a few long-serving hands, who are now mostly retired and elderly, would be able to recall the early difficulties we faced for some years until we were accepted by the top quality joinery and furniture manufacturers; and shows how much a handful of loyal employees contributed alongside the old and young Kemp to make Timbmet such a great success and the envy of the trade.

A prestigious contract

Benfield & Loxley, established about 1800, was at the time one of the leading college builders. In 1960 it became known in the trade that they had gained the contract to refurbish the oldest part of the Bodleian Library that is Duke Humfrey's, Selden End. A great deal of stone and woodwork was required, but at the beginning the firm was not very friendly towards us. I did my utmost to remedy this with the directors, and at the same time Leslie Boustead was doing his best to make friends with the joinery manager, Ewart Taylor. As a result, we won the order for well air dried English wainscot oak, to be selected board by board at our yard, at an average price 38/6d per cubic foot.

The Bodleian

On the day appointed for a meeting, Benfield & Loxley's managing director and their joinery manager turned up at the yard. After they had inspected our oak timbers for three or four hours, heated arguments began over their quality. I kept pointing out that the quality requirements even for such a prestigious contract were too high. We stopped work at their request, and they told us that the architects demanded that Benfield must only employ their own skilled craftsmen on the job with no sub-contractors. Benfield & Loxley agreed to this, but with the promise to delete from the contract the proviso that they purchase the raw materials on the open market, and not from the nominated suppliers. In the event, they compromised slightly on small defects such as an occasional pin knot and a little live sap, and continued selection. The joinery for this contract was fully assembled off site and left to settle for about six months before it was finally installed into the building.

The main library building, which dates from about 1400, was erected in double stone. In 1696 King William III introduced a window tax. During the rebuilding and restoration in 1961, it was felt that by reinforcing one thickness of the wall and removing part of the other, one could adequately stabilise and make space for a narrow staircase to reach the landing, rather than having to climb by ladder. Two imitation circular oak windows were created without glass and looked very impressive. The very wide panels were the only items from the large quantity of joinery used in the refurbishment which shrank a little after the library was reopened and the central heating turned on.

I was promised that Benfield & Loxley would not object to Timbmet advertising the work done using our timber, with photographs provided by the contractor. Benfield's undertook to do their best to ensure that neither the University authorities nor the architects would not raise any objections.

During the lunch break, I phoned Leslie Boustead who told me that the area salesman from Wm Mallinson, our competitors, had come to the door enquiring whether Timbmet had got the order instead of them. This was the first time, as far as we know, that an architect nomination in a bill of quantities was rejected by the builder who won the contract. As time went by, due to increased building costs and because of inflation, we were able to gain work where architects nominated other timber suppliers.

A lesson in joint advertising

Halls Oxford Brewery had its own joiners' shop. A Yorkshire manager, Mr Kibblewhite was in charge; his deputy was his nephew and we received our orders regularly. They were very demanding as to the quality of the oak they would accept but we came to an understanding about their requirements, agreed prices and managed to satisfy them. They needed exceptionally wide unjointed boards for bar tops as well as $2\frac{1}{2}$" and 3" curved oak for the windows of their off-licences, which later became known as the Victoria Wine Company.

When one large public house in particular had its first major refit since the war, I requested Mr Kibblewhite Senior to allow Timbmet to advertise in the local press. He became rather abrupt, as follows:

Kibblewhite	'Son, you get our business?'
DK	'Yes, sir.'
Kibblewhite	'You get paid?'
DK	'Very promptly, sir.'
Kibblewhite	'Then be satisfied and p*** off!'

Today we ourselves cannot cope with customers who want to advertise jointly with us.

Some years later when Timbmet became more prosperous and the borrowing needs larger, Leslie B and I were occasionally invited to lunch at the Old Bank to meet some of the regional directors from the Thames Valley area. We were entertained on the first floor in a large front room furnished as the original dining room of the Thomson family who had been leading bankers in Oxfordshire until 1900, when they had sold the business to Barclays Bank.

At that time a number of regional bankers in the south and southwest of England merged to form an enlarged Barclays Bank. Sir John Thomson, the last director of the Bank, a prominent citizen in the locality and Lord Lieutenant of the county, would occasionally and unexpectedly join the guests for lunch although long after he ceased to be a director. On one occasion he did so when I was present; I was introduced to him and my occupation given. He very quickly asked me about my trade, and wondered whether as a family business we owned land and forests; I had to disappoint him especially as I was not interested in hunting and shooting!

About ten years before the Bank closed the doors of the Old Bank building, the mahogany dining room furniture was removed, perhaps to be returned to the family. The room was given modern furnishings and sub-divided in a way that allowed two functions to be held separately with each part retaining the windows facing the entrance to All Souls' College.

The Old Bank was sold in 1998 and the new owners gutted and refurbished the whole interior: it is now a modern upmarket hotel with the top floor bedrooms giving a wonderful outlook over the colleges and spires of Oxford.

Minty Furniture of Oxford manufactured solid oak extending bookcases, which they sold principally by mail order through newspapers in the northwest of England. Timbmet by this time was a large buyer of Japanese oak, and this helped us to obtain the right quality of 1" FAS short boards in the length and width they required. We managed to negotiate a contract with them. The timber was despatched in shipping dry condition, and we had the oak kilned at Greenwich sawmills to a maximum moisture content of 11%. There were many arguments on this point and on the quality with Mr Fred Beckett, who was the works director, and a local Oxonian. I came to know the managing director, Mr J Bowles; and as I got on better with him, we managed to iron out often non-existent and trivial complaints and gain ongoing regular orders. On one occasion, he teased me by saying, 'Young man, you could even sell ham in a synagogue!' and I replied 'This is a great compliment sir!'

CHAPTER 13

1963-1964

Many malicious rumours circulated about the future of Timbmet as a result of my father's death at the comparatively young age of 69 years. Leslie Boustead and I took no notice of these, and the stories were gradually disbelieved. We continued to trade successfully without having the experience of the old timber man to guide us in day-to-day decisions. My mother grieved long and bitterly after my father died. As her flat was above the office, it was possible to help and assist her, as well as keep her company, without losing too much time in normal business hours. Although it was my greatest wish to transfer the office to the yard, I did not rush matters so that I could offer her comfort. My wife was of great help and had a lot of patience. We lived barely one mile from one another.

An unwelcome setback

Unknown to me my parents had known a Dr Schoenberg from Vienna. He was legal adviser to the Bunzl family who owned pulp and paper factories in Austria. They had a lot of foresight and pre-1939 had established a subsidiary factory in England. (Bunzl plc now operates in thirty countries as food packaging suppliers.) It seemed that Dr Schoenberg had had permission to have some personal clients apart from his principal employer; and after my father died, I was invited to meet him at the Bunzl offices in London. After a short discussion, he handed me a prepared draft contract of employment as managing director of Timbmet. I protested immediately as the contract contained unwelcome conditions, and I felt that no one other than myself would be more honourable and fair to my mother and my brother, who at the time practised medicine in Singapore, having finished his military service in the British army.

After many weeks of frustrating negotiations, I was appointed to the job without any conditions or contract and with just a promise and a firm handshake. For a time it left a bitter taste. I promised to report to Dr Schoenberg personally twice a year or, if any problems arose, to contact him for advice. Hacker Young were authorised to do likewise and to provide statutory accounts at regular intervals.

About five years later, Dr Schoenberg relieved me of any obligations to visit him personally. This gave me a lot of satisfaction. I disliked, on entering his office, to be greeted by a large crucifix on the wall and a Madonna on his desk, most unusual symbols in the city office of a public limited company in London, yet I can only praise his fairmindedness and the respect he showed me.

Dan officially takes over

To help me conduct the business efficiently, I had to take on more staff. An advertisement in the TTJ for an experienced salesman brought a number of replies. I interviewed each personally and chose George Clarkson, an employee of Goldblatt & Sons, who were beech and hardwood importers in Edmonton, North London. He accepted the position and served Timbmet loyally and efficiently for about twenty five years until a spinal injury prevented him from carrying on. George was appreciated wherever there was an owner, buyer or an honest company purchasing officer: he was unable to tell a white lie, and this was a highly rated quality even twenty years ago. He lived in Enfield, Middlesex and represented us in most of the south of England area, including Central London; he worked a six week cycle which meant he spent nearly half of his time away from home. Regular hotel accommodation was booked for his visits in Southsea, Leicestershire and Norwich. Although he was unable to cope with the 'giants' in the furniture and joinery industries, Leslie and I took on and enjoyed the challenge with the buyers of these companies. George and his wife Ruth live in retirement at Milford on Sea.

Due to increasing business, Leslie Boustead and I decided to find another salesman to cover the West Country and South Wales. We chose a slightly older man, Tom Bunting, who had spent some years with Claridge of Enstone in Oxfordshire and Honiton, Devon. He had an exceptional knowledge of native hardwoods, and served Timbmet for slightly more than twenty years until at 65 he expressed a wish to retire.

During 1950 and 1960 inflation was very modest and therefore any increase in turnover was a genuine increase of sales, often to new customers in the UK. The first postwar downturn in trade in the UK occurred in 1958-1959 but fortunately only lasted for a few months. It did not affect world timber prices as the countries on the European mainland were still much further behind in their rebuilding programmes than the UK, so the Timbmet stocks did not lose value. By 1961 we had recovered from two years of static turnover and began to expand again.

New office building

We requested my mother, Margaret Kemp, director and majority shareholder of the company, to give us permission to build a new office at Chawley Works. We had explained to her on numerous occasions the disadvantages of the office being separated from the yard, leading to long phone calls with urgent orders; as soon as she agreed, we asked our architect Mr Harvey to design a suitable modest office building on one floor, adequately reinforced to take a first floor at a later date for future expansion. Berkshire County Council, together with the Cumnor Parish Council, managed to raise objections, but eventually in late autumn planning permission was granted. A G Carter of Headington, Oxford was awarded the contract: the builders struggled through a wet autumn and a very bad winter but nevertheless the office was completed with very little delay. We moved in on Friday afternoon 15th March, 1963 and as a result efficiency in the office and discipline in the yard were greatly improved.

Plans for a major installation

Ludwig and I had verbally agreed previously to erect some more shed space at Chawley. We both appreciated that our customers were beginning to expect us to have ready kiln dried timber in stock for prompt delivery; the big firms already had their own kilns, normally of brick construction and with fans and motors supplied by Wells of Sheffield.

At the time, we were not quite ready for this expenditure. Brick kilns with a traditional boiler house were old fashioned, and the new oil fired air heated kilns were not yet fully developed. We watched such experimental kilns, built by Cubbage, operating at Cattle, the wood turners, in Gerrards Cross, and on a larger scale at Stockwells, the beech importers at Stokenchurch.

By the time the office was ready, Berkshire C.C. had granted us permission to build this, our first modern shed; and we awarded the work to the contractors on site for a cost of £12,000. The 12,000 sq.ft. building (shed 2) is situated on the eastern side of Chawley Works and constructed from steel stanchions and aluminium rails to which impregnated softwood cladding was fixed. The building was ready in the autumn of 1963 and proved a great aid in increasing our business and being able to serve our customers with ready kiln dried species, partly in logs and lumber.

Timbmet's first crane and driver

As our turnover increased, some world countries started to ship bundled stocks, rather than loose boards spread in the holds of cargo ships. In order to speed up the unloading of lumber at our yard, we hired a lorry mounted crane from Amey's on a day-by-day basis. Once we had this facility, every other gang wanted the crane to help with lifts of fresh sawn logs etc, so we decided to engage a lorry mounted crane and driver on a contract basis.

Ludwig had arranged for a hydraulic crane to be demonstrated at Samuel Elliott & Sons, Caversham, Reading, the prestigious ship furniture and top quality joinery manufacturer. I do not think he intended purchasing one, but he aspired to meet the management of the company; and undoubtedly was disappointed that only the sales manager of Coles Cranes, and a foreman of Elliott's, looked after us.

Although our coffin business diminished gradually, overall our hardwood business grew, with an ever wider range of imported species and grades. Due to this change in trade we found that we did not have enough skilled personnel in our yard. We realised that to ensure that we could attract the right person on a long term basis, accommodation would have to be provided. At the time the company's resources were heavily committed, but it happened that my father-in-law had passed away and my wife had inherited a sum of money. She used part of this to purchase 48 St Paul's Crescent, Botley, and let the property at a reasonable rent to the company.

We advertised in the TTJ and several young men applied, all with reasonable references and trade knowledge. LB chose Mr Wallis, nicknamed Wally, from Sherry & Co. of Homerton, East London. He got on well with Larry Smith; they were two of a kind, but after two years he insisted he had to return to London as his wife had not been able to settle in Oxford.

We then received an application from a Welshman in Cardiff who wanted to join us to improve his position. 'Taffy', the only name I can remember, was even more suitable as he was of potential management material, but just a year later all our efforts failed to keep him at Timbmet. Once again it was his wife who in this instance wanted to live in the circle of her Welsh family. He returned to his former employer, Robinson & David, but later lost his job in a company takeover. He kept in touch, but Leslie would not have him back.

John Blizzard

We must have taken a large order for $1\frac{1}{4}$" TT air dried beech which was much bigger than our stock, or one that our regular French supplier could make available to us in the short term.

In the UK there were always merchants and stockists who stored their timber on public wharfs, and we were offered a parcel of landed stock at Bull's Bridge wharf on the Grand Union Canal near Ruislip. I went to inspect the stock; the wharf manager pointed out the parcel and left me to it. I always told a prospective seller that he did not have to meet me, as I would make up my own mind as to whether the timber was suitable for our purpose. I was looking for a parcel of $1\frac{1}{4}$" light coloured beech, well air dried, reasonably free of stick marks, full cut and flat, and fairly free of heavy end splits. I climbed a pile, and on top was a man measuring an order ready for despatch. The total quantity available was much larger then we had been offered, probably brought over from France by barge. I watched him measure the load and I liked the stock and the measurer: he introduced himself as John Blizzard. After a brief conversation on his background and trade experience, I invited him to come to Oxford and we met two or three times. I offered him a job as a senior measurer with a rent free house, and he willingly accepted. John's wife Lavinia liked being in Oxford. She held several senior positions, one for many years with the Oxford University Press; and they didn't feel that an hour's drive from their families in West London was a great distance to travel.

On an opposite pile at Bull's Bridge was another measurer, a young lady called Edna, nicknamed the "blonde bombshell." She was a very fast worker and had a reputation for bad language and drinking! I think she might have been the better choice for our men but I did not dare employ her.

Out of interest, Bull's Bridge Wharf is now a very large and prosperous Tesco store, situated on a picturesque site. I have no doubt it earns more profit in a few months than the owners of the wharf made in seventy years of timber storage and handling.

John worked for us loyally for many years finishing as buyer of home grown and European hardwoods. On retiring he asked if we would be prepared to sell the house to him at a reasonable figure; which we did, and he modernised at his own expense.

Postal deliveries

It did not take us long to realise that the postal deliveries in Cumnor were a little slower than those in Oxford city. As almost all written communications came via the GPO, it mattered to a young business to get the shipping documents, offers from shippers and payments from customers as quickly as possible, and therefore we used the telephone extensively, as well as telegrams and later telex, and finally email as soon as it became available.

We asked the letter sorting office at Beckett Street, Oxford if we might be allowed to collect the mail early each morning. To our horror, we were told that the city delivery area ended at the south-eastern corner of our yard, Hurst Lane and that we could collect our mail from Cumnor village post office. This was no help at all, as the local postman would have delivered just as quickly on his bicycle. In the end it took an appeal to John Patten, our local MP, to help us to have a PO box. Thus started a new routine: Leslie, another yard employee and I took it in turns to collect the mail at about 7.30am daily in rain, snow, or sunshine.

Religiously LB and I, and some years later Adrian Sumner, would open, sort and discuss the contents of the mail together, making many decisions on the spot concerning company policy, purchasing, and pricing, etc,

I always knew the overdue accounts as for many years I had a list typed for me on yellow paper by Dulcie Fereday, later to become Adrian's mother-in-law. I enjoyed announcing the receipt of late payments and passing on the information to the salesmen in the office.

Adrian Sumner

Adrian Sumner joined Timbmet shortly after leaving grammar school in 1962. Over the years through diligence and loyalty and gradually acquiring practical knowledge of the timber trade, he became sales manager, assisting myself as a buyer, and eventually purchasing director of the Timbmet Group.

Although it may seem strange and unorthodox, this *modus operandi* continued unbroken for almost forty years. For thirty of those years Leslie and I, then later the two of us with Adrian, discussed company policy daily; after Leslie's death Adrian and I continued this together. What we were able to gather in a short space of time was of enormous value. Even when we reached an annual turnover of over £30,000,000 we still had plenty of time during the day to receive sales calls and spend time with visiting customers; and we also assisted our sales staff with the larger and more complex quotations.

1963-1964

Bodleian Library restoration 1961: old air-dried English oak

71

CHAPTER 14

1964-67

In 1964 Leslie Boustead attended Oxford Technical College to gain the membership of the Institute of Chartered Secretaries. This meant six years of evening classes, with a half-day release in the last year. He had much encouragement and help from one of the lecturers for whom he had a lot of respect. Seven students started the course but only Leslie and a determined disabled young lady made it to the end. We were all very proud of him. It gave him much extra confidence, and he gained a good deal of respect in our industry.

He also managed to become an advocate in the local magistrates' courts, defending some of our very able yard men, who on some nights used their strength and muscle inappropriately!

In 1966, my wife Rosie joined the Timbmet team on a part-time basis, to help LB with the payroll; Rosie used a manual Kalamazoo system. For a time the yard employees were paid weekly in cash which meant filling pay packets, a very laborious job. We managed to calculate all overtime worked up to and including Wednesday, and paid out on Thursday afternoons. Rosie worked in a corner of Leslie's office and kept everything locked in a very small lion safe. She had to retire in 1993 due to suffering severe osteoporosis.

It is only since LB passed away that Timbmet has had a Human Resources [HR] department. Rosie had dealt with most of the employees' personal problems, calling on Leslie for help only with any that might have legal implications. Later this role was taken over by our company secretary, Geoffrey Clough. In the early days I had been helped by Sergeant Seymour, our local police chief, through whom I contacted the local priest. I was indebted on occasions to a Roman Catholic Jesuit called Father Hickey, who lived with other clergymen nearby.

By 1966 our turnover reached £500,000 per annum. Our two full time salesmen were very stretched and could not cope with meeting all our potential customers. We had an application with good references from a Brian Harvey, so we arranged for him to call on customers, mostly in the centre of the metropolis where the sun did not often shine. To our surprise we found that his main attribute was to constantly create new jokes of all kinds, and he tried to trade his jokes for orders. Many buyers briefly enjoyed his company but they seldom gave him any substantial business, so we had to part company with him. He was replaced by Peter Pearce, a native of South London, who remained loyal until his retirement, and was a steady quiet person who did well calling south of the River Thames, all the way to the south coast. For the first time I began to realise the difference between the personalities, and the accents, of those born north and south of the river.

Widening of contracts

Even in the early days, Ludwig had tried to approach government departments and national industries but it was not surprising that he was unable to gain 'access' to the corridors of power. He had success with the partly government- funded furniture factories who were employing disabled personnel; we traded regularly with, and to the full satisfaction of, Papworth Industries near Cambridge, the sister firm Enham Industries near Andover, and also with branches of Remploy in South Wales and the northeast. Many long term orders were agreed, at keen margins as there were no financial risks. It was only many years later that we became approved suppliers to the Ministry of Defence and other government departments.

The Royal National Lifeboat Institution renovated and modernised their existing fleet and ordered new lifeboats, which were all still built from timber and used very large quantities of African mahogany logs. They purchased parcels of logs and had them cut and converted into thick planks of up to 9"; they were put in their Isle of Wight store yard for long term air drying before being allocated to the yards. We also supplied logs to the RNLI specialist builders, Groves & Gutteridge, and others. LB looked after this business wearing his midshipman's hat!

Geographically, F Minns & Company of Botley were our nearest potential customers. They had a large joiners' shop on land now occupied by an administrative office of Barclays Bank and Morgan Cole the solicitors. The joinery director was Mr F West: we were seldom able to please them. I felt this might have been caused by Ludwig's personality, which clashed with Mr West's, and a few months after my father's death, I made another attempt. I arranged an appointment and Mr West suggested I call at the end of the working day, as he loved to spend time arguing. He told the strangest story he told about my father, as follows:

There was an exceptionally good quality parcel of dry prime log sawn oak at the top of the yard, all thick planks well sticked and covered on top, and he wanted to buy some of this stock -

LK: 'I have no wish to sell but you are welcome to have your requirements from other good parcels.'

West: 'Why not?'

LK: 'There was a man once who had a private cinema and enjoyed screening and watching films at the end of his day. Likewise, after work I like to go up to the yard and admire some of my best butts of oak.'

We shall never solve the mystery of why an international businessman could have made such a statement. Thinking long and hard about it, I recall that in pre-war Europe the technical ability to kiln thick oak was not properly known. To have heavy planks of hardwood dry in stock meant many years of foresight and of capital outlay: if one missed one year's autumn cut it might take a long time to balance the inventory. For this reason such dry stocks were very valuable and, even in hard economic times, they commanded a premium. I doubt whether Mr West would have wanted to pay the price Ludwig asked for his "super prime" butts.

An architect designing a building and incorporating quality internal and external fittings in hardwoods, and needing planks 65mm or thicker, should plan well ahead of requirements, almost from the time the foundations are laid, just like the good wine needed for the toast at the topping-out ceremony The lead times for very special requirements are very much shorter today, but so often too little time is allowed and sometimes the final end product is not up to the very high standard agreed in advance.

General discussions with Mr West went on rather late and, when he and I parted, we found the front high double gates locked. We had no option but to climb the gates to get out. It is true to say we never enjoyed such a good relationship with Minns & Co as we did with others in Oxford.

Sale of land at Cumnor

In 1964 we were approached by Berkshire County Council to purchase from us ·536 of an acre of land near the thatched cottage belonging to the

Wickson family. This piece had an outline pre-1939 planning permission for housing. They wanted to erect two pairs of semi-detached police houses overlooking the yard towards the Hurst. The idea appealed to us as we thought we would give us all round permanent, built in security. It took a little time to persuade my mother, but eventually she agreed.

We suggested to BCC that each party should nominate a respectable firm of estate agents to jointly agree a value. This proposal was readily accepted and in early January 1965 the land was sold and conveyed to the local police authority at a price of £6,700. Both parties were very happy with the arrangements.

Later, however, when we applied to build another shed and there was a public enquiry to determine whether Timbmet could build kilns on the site, the police authority raised objections as it would disturb the sleep of their men when on night duty. To add insult to injury the houses were never built. Some years later, when the piece of land was sold and planning permission obtained for three detached private dwellings, the land fetched £30,000 in an auction sale.

Britain's economy falters but Timbmet keeps developing

At this time Britain's balance of trade with the world was in continuous deficit. Inflation was rising and unemployment, for the first time since the war, increased considerably. In spite of this "little" Timbmet prospered year by year through distributing its products to ever larger parts of England and South Wales and thereby enlarging its customer base. We engaged and trained extra personnel for the office and yard operations, and added two lorries to our fleet. Most of the credit for teaching and training must go to Leslie who had great flair and aptitude in this respect.

By now one lorry mounted crane was not enough to cope with the work so we hired a second one but later decided it would be more economical and practical to purchase our own. Several machines were demonstrated at our yard, and we decided on the 6-ton Jones telescopic, self propelled machine made by the British Hoist and Crane Company. It was left to me to obtain the best price possible and I probably made two trips to East Ilsley, Berkshire, where the factory was situated. I managed to gain a small reduction and one or two minor extras to the machine free of charge.

On the last visit, I was told that, by coincidence, two gentlemen from Bowmaker were on the premises on other business and had asked if I would like to meet them. I agreed, and then and there we negotiated a two year hire purchase deal at a very advantageous rate. Undoubtedly they had checked us out beforehand! Up to this point, we had bought all equipment for cash. This machine could operate in narrower aisles and slew much more speedily than the lorry mounted Coles cranes, although perhaps the Jones was unable to lift quite so high. The price was just over £6,000.

We were constantly running out of undercover storage space for seasoned and kiln dried wood. We got Mr Harvey, the architect, to design another building similar to shed 2, with some slight improvements and incorporating a SEB electric sub-station to ensure an adequate power supply for the future. It took some months before planning permission was granted, but it was all done by private negotiations with some give and take.

CHAPTER 15

Devaluation shock

The economic clouds over the country grew darker and darker, and the general outlook was poor. For Timbmet at that time, however, the sun seemed never to set over Cumnor.

Britain was heavily in debt and the balance of payments almost out of control. The World Bank sent representatives of the IMF to England to meet with the government of the day, the Prime Minister, Mr Harold Wilson, and the Chancellor of the Exchequer, Mr James Callaghan. Due to the uncertainties the price of gold started to rise. The US treasury and the governments of other countries were unwilling to see gold rise above $35 an ounce. The alternative would be to borrow more from governments abroad, but only short term money was on offer.

The Chancellor opposed devaluation, but Mr Wilson and other ministers decided to "defend the pounds in our pockets"; and on 19 November, 1967, devalued our currency from $2.80 to $2.40 to the £ sterling, a cut of just over 14%. The announcement was made over a weekend so as not to create an undue run on the currency, stock market and commodity exchanges.

I was personally shocked although not fully surprised. I felt this step was a terrible humiliation for our country although not entirely our own fault. Sterling's role as a pegged reserve currency had made UK exports uncompetitive, and led to a manufacturing slowdown. The unjustified wage claims by the trade unions did not help matters.

I pulled myself together and decided to keep my appointment for Monday morning at Pontrilas Sawmills, Pontrilas, Gwent. It was a cold, damp and foggy morning. I kept my eyes on the road and concentrated on driving. At Pontrilas, I selected a few oak butts and, as usual, looked in on a few surrounding home grown sawmills and small English timber merchants who were nearby in the Forest of Dean. On the same day, five chair manufacturers, needless to say not regular customers, found their way to our yard wishing to purchase mainly beech stocks, as it was obvious that prices would have to increase fairly soon. Foolishly, we gave them all a little benefit hoping that these companies would support us in the future.

For hundreds of years most international business outside North America, and possibly also South America, had been conducted in £

sterling. By honouring these in the future, all our suppliers with unfulfilled outstanding contracts would lose the difference created by the devaluation of the currency. The phone rang from all over the world. Everyone wanted to come and renegotiate. We managed to compromise with most of them, but some contracts were cancelled by mutual agreement. A few of our Ghana shippers were able to be more generous than others as they were mostly tied to Britain and traded in sterling.

The most difficult company was J Lalanne of Paris, who were owners of timber concessions in large sawmills in West Africa and the Congo. Monsieur Mathieu came over to see Leslie and me to renegotiate; and we spent an afternoon, evening and late night together, arguing the pros and cons as perhaps only the French can. We did not finish until we were asked to leave the lounge of the Randolph Hotel at about 2.00am.

The next morning, at our office, we had a telephone conference with Lalanne's agent in London and their head office in Paris. Lalanne's supplies were excellent and we needed their timber on contract. We were able to agree that Lalanne contributed only $1\frac{1}{2}\%$ towards our extra costs; and the agents contributed $\frac{1}{2}\%$ of their commission.

From that time onwards it was evident that a great deal of confidence in our currency and our government had been lost. Most international trade started to be contracted in US$, or in the currencies of the country where the goods were purchased. If sterling was used it was always coupled with a currency clause.

Devaluation brought a new aspect to the log trade between England and the European continent, especially once we were all in the European trading area. Traditionally there had always been some log experts who traded in specialities. They travelled the length and breadth of England looking for the highest class butts in most species of hardwoods that were free of defects, of good grain and colour, and sometimes with unusual imperfections. These were offered to the veneer manufacturing trade. When a butt was very exceptional, the cost of freight was immaterial, because if such a log were converted it would yield veneered leaves of a very rare pattern or grain, and such flitches would command very high prices. Occasional disasters did happen, but on the whole these experts knew their business and enjoyed their occupation

The biggest advantage in our industry was for the European veneer manufacturers, as they gained a good source of logs at very competitive prices. Having joined the Common Market the English veneer producers suffered severe competition from Europe. The devaluation of the currency proved impossible for the majority to continue trading.

Plans for further building

The country was in recession. Leslie and I thought long and hard but decided to go ahead and build shed 3 of similar standard and specification as shed 2, again with a reinforced concrete road running through the building and, on either side, the soil levelled and consolidated with hard core. When we presented a simple business plan to Barclays Bank with a view to borrowing the money, we were met with a very firm refusal. The government had ordered the Bank of England to restrict the overall volume of money they and other financial institutions could lend to industry. They gave instructions that a larger percentage of their capital was to remain liquid.

I remembered how easily Bowmaker had lent Timbmet the money to buy the crane, so I approached their local representative as to whether there would be money available for our project. His answer was that their business was to lend money for the purchase of plant and machinery, but that he would phone the regional office at Southampton for advice. I was then asked to call and see the local director: the visit went well, and I was offered the money on condition that we surrendered the deeds of our home, which had been paid for by Rosie's parents, as well as the house John Blizzard lived in, which had been paid for by a legacy from Rosie's father. The loan was to be repayable in instalments over the next two years. When I explained to Rosie, she fully understood the implications, but agreed as she could see the future benefits. We kept up our repayments to Bowmaker. How they covered up lending on a building rather than plant, we shall never know.

We kept growing, and by 1970 our turnover was £650,000 which at 2005 prices would be £6,000,000. After the end of each trading year in June, we sent our financial records in a large trunk to our auditors, Summers & Co. in Fitzharding Street, W1. They checked the books, and a few weeks later a senior clerk would come to Oxford to discuss any errors and adjustments with Leslie and me. One afternoon about September or early October 1970, I went on my own to call on Edward Greenbury, the junior partner, for our annual meeting to finalise the accounts for the year ending March 1970.

Dock strike

At the time the country was in the midst of a national dock strike which had been going on for some weeks and the Government had declared a state of emergency. With the help of our forwarding agents, W Hall & Co, we tried devious ways to retrieve some of the cargo diverted to European ports, but without any success

While I was with Mr Greenbury an urgent phone call came from Leslie informing me that W Hall, our loyal agents, had found a wharf in the Thames estuary willing to accept a small cargo vessel which they felt sure would be able to unload the timber and deliver it to transport, but with the help of unregistered labour. Mr Graham Combes, the owner of W Hall, persuaded us that if we were ready to take the risk and pay a substantial amount to the ship's owners, they would ensure that all our parcels of timber lying at Rotterdam would be gathered quickly and brought back to England. The risk was that if we were found out, the timber would have to be returned to the Continent and additional charges incurred. It was up to us to make a quick decision. I was in the ideal spot. Edward Greenbury decided to ring Graham Combes to hear the offer for himself, and after a short discussion we agreed to proceed, and left Leslie to make all the necessary arrangements.

After Mr Greenbury and I had completed our discussions, I left his office and walked toward Oxford Street. By the time I reached the shop window of Lilley and Skinner, it suddenly occurred to me how serious the consequences could be for Timbmet if things went wrong. If we were caught getting timber unloaded by unregistered dockers in England, the union might refuse to deal with our cargoes in the future. Fortunately for us, all went smoothly and we had the advantage of having some of our timber back quicker than the competition.

About a week later the strike was finally settled, but it took many weeks for the huge volume of diverted cargoes to be returned to England. The following years brought more strikes: the Continental ports made the most of our misfortunes and the diversion costs were exceptionally high. The Timber Trade Federation, together with a large insurance broker, established a mutual self-help fund. All members paid in a little extra for the marine insurance to cover the eventuality of strike diversion costs (DITA). Thankfully, in recent years we are receiving refunds of previous premiums paid.

*****

Kiln drying was done by various contractors, most of whom took on more work than they could cope with, so very little arrived to an arranged timetable We talked to Edward Greenbury, by then the budding star at Summers & Co, our auditors (who later merged with Hacker Young.) He helped us to produce a business plan to put forward to our banks. Mr Wilson called for an election; the Labour Party lost and the new Conservative Government came into power under Mr Edward Heath.

We decided to work with Leslie Cubbage the managing director of Cubbage Kilns in High Wycombe. By 1970 the kilns were fairly well developed and several batches of his air heated, oil fired kilns were working at larger furniture manufacturers in England and Ireland. Cubbage bought most component parts such as motors, fans, humidifiers and boilers, etc., from other producers.

There were also several kilns at Stockwells, beech importers at Stokenchurch, which we often visited and thereby gained confidence in the way they functioned. Early on a misty evening, 31st December 1970, Rosie and I were returning from a family lunch in London. We were well dressed; I was wearing a blue overcoat and bowler hat. As we were passing Stockwells, I couldn't resist looking in. On top of one of the kilns was young Brian Stockwell; nearby was an aluminium ladder. I dropped my hat and climbed up to see what he was doing. Obviously surprised to see me he explained that the air vents were not opening properly and that he was trying to make a modification. Poor Rosie, as on other social outings, was not very pleased to say the least, but by now she was becoming used to it.

Postal strike

On 20 January, 1971, the British postal workers went on strike: this lasted seven weeks, but they did not get the full extra money and conditions they demanded. The strike must have cost the economy many millions. At that time, direct debits to banks, BACS, and CHAPS (direct credits) were not widely available, nor were facsimile (FAX) facilities. For us in the timber trade it was a nightmare, as shipping companies insisted on original bills of lading, although they relented towards the end.

We sent invoices with the delivery drivers and also requested customers to hand their payments to them. Our representatives collected cheques on their rounds and made special calls. On some days we sent two drivers on Leslie's favourite motorbikes to make journeys more economically. Rosie went to Paddington station twice a week to meet our southern sales rep who handed her all the cheques he had collected. She had a cup of coffee with him before taking the next train back to Oxford. In the evening I used to meet Tom Bunting, our midland representative, who lived in Charlbury, north of Woodstock, at one of the pubs, and brought back his batch. It is surprising that hardly any records appear to exist of this strike, and not many older people seem to remember the great inconvenience.

CHAPTER 16

1969-72
Starting with a compromise

Cubbage helped Mr Harvey to design our kiln base (including shed 4) on two levels in order to save excavations. The design incorporated a flat area for twelve kilns, ten of 1400 cubic feet capacity and two of 700 cubic feet capacity. Behind the short kilns was space for two oil tanks. Because of the exposed site, we decided to double insulate the aluminium walls, as we had experienced very low temperatures at Cumnor during the winters of 1947 and 1960; as extra protection, and to save fuel, we planned to erect a roof above the kilns. The 1400 cubic feet capacity kilns were to be 42 ft long, and this helped to utilise the space as we were able to make up many different combinations of lengths in S/E [square edged] lumber, as well as log sawn material of 10 ft-16ft, or more.

In late 1969, due to the continuous expansion of the business, we engaged Mr Don Rogers as yard manager to assist our senior foreman, Larry Smith. He was recommended to us by friends in the trade, and had had a mechanical engineering background through his army service and for a number of years had also organized the extraction of logs from the sizeable timber forests in West Africa. He had the ideal qualifications to help us with our latest development plans.

Compulsory purchase order

Early in 1971, we had details ready and submitted an application to erect and operate timber drying kilns together with a large storage shed at Oxford. A few weeks later, we had a request from Berkshire CC to purchase 13½ acres in Hurst Lane, part of our estate at Cumnor. Timbmet refused: we had no wish to sell, as the land formed part of our overall business strategy. Also, with the degree of animosity shown to us by our neighbours, we needed to retain our land, if only for shelter. We were then served with a compulsory purchase order, and instructed our solicitors, Cole & Cole, to represent us. Presumably they requested a public enquiry, and this was eventually heard at Abingdon Magistrates' Court in April 1972. Lengthy preparations went on beforehand including consultation with a barrister. On the appointed day, the two sides were represented as follows:

For Timbmet:
>   Mr S De-Piro - Instructed by Cole & Cole
>   Mr P Finemore - Partner of Cole & Cole
>   Mr J C Smith - Partner of E J Brooks & Sons, Land Agents
>   Mr A E Harvey - Architect
>   Mr D Kemp - Proprietor

For BCC and Vale of the White Horse District Council:
>   County Solicitor
>   Assistant County Solicitor
>   Senior Planning Officer
>   Junior Planning Officer
>   Two representatives from Cumnor Parish Council

The Chairman was an Inspector from the Ministry of Town and Country Planning. Some people were unpunctual which delayed the start of proceedings.

The Timbmet representatives were permitted to explain why the compulsory purchase of land would be harmful and damaging to the company. They gave an outline plan for the future of Timbmet:

> That Timbmet should be able to dry hardwoods scientifically in modern kilns which would ensure less waste, thus saving precious foreign currency, hardwood being an essential raw material for the building and furniture industry

This statement was accompanied by plans, graphs, drawings and letters of support from customers, the Timber Research Organisation, the Building Research Institute and the Timber Trade Federation.

After we had finished our submission, the representatives of the BCC outlined their objections.

1. The requirements of the educational authorities was to provide additional land for sports and recreational facilities, depending on the number of pupils in the Matthew Arnold School
2. The plan that the school was to expand into a large comprehensive with over 2,000 pupils

3. The shortage of other land in the district meant that the south-eastern part of our premises was about the only suitable area which could be adapted for these purposes.

Parish Council representatives used the opportunity, on behalf of the residents from a wide area, to put forward objections which included smell, smoke and additional traffic hazards. Mid afternoon the case was adjourned until the following day. I felt depressed and miserable. The Timbmet advisors agreed to meet in the morning, half an hour before the official start of the public enquiry.

As I started to drive back to Cumnor, I had a brilliant idea. I went straight to Westminster College, then a Methodist teacher training establishment situated close to Matthew Arnold School. At this time of day I was most fortunate to see the deputy headmaster without an appointment. He was willing to listen to my case and seemed sympathetic: and gave me permission to inform the Inspector that they had more than enough sports fields, and would be willing to share with Matthew Arnold. This made me feel a lot better. I broke this news at our morning mini-conference before proceedings started and the barrister conveyed the information at the start of the hearing.

It was my turn to stand in the dock and be cross examined by the county solicitor. I had been well briefed weeks beforehand by my advisors and I did not allow myself to get confused by rapid questioning. Likewise, Mr De-Piro had the opportunity to examine the evidence of the Berkshire County Council officers.

By late morning, the inspector adjourned the hearing and called for a private meeting between the two senior representatives of Timbmet, Mr De-Piro and Mr Finemore, and also the county solicitor and planning officer. The rest of us stood outside the court, and I chain smoked nervously. Before the hearing continued, Mr De-Piro advised me to compromise. He said that I had given an excellent account of myself and if the Minister himself read the transcript of proceedings, he would see how inadequately prepared some of his solicitors were. In spite of this he thought we would lose our case.

The Inspector suggested that we ask to retain $2\frac{1}{2}$ acres of land as a protective zone from neighbours, dog walkers and mischievous children, etc. and surrender the rest. Mr Smith and Mr Finemore agreed that this would be a wise solution. The hearing was resumed and the offer put forward. The Inspector was willing to recommend this to the Minister and felt confident that this proposal would be acceptable.

About eight to ten weeks later we were given the official decision. The area compulsorily acquired was to be as proposed. Compensation for the land was set at £4,000 plus £500 towards legal expenses; and a good strong chain link fence was to be erected by the Council to keep out intruders.

About £50,000 was spent levelling and draining the land. The Council would not give permission to build changing facilities for the children, as the land was designated green belt. As we had predicted, neither the teachers nor the children were prepared to walk approximately one third of a mile from the school up a muddy footpath to the playing fields.

The school was never fully enlarged to become a comprehensive. About ten years later, we regained the land for £20,000. The BCC borders altered and Cumnor became (and is still) part of Oxfordshire. When the dust settled, we continued to negotiate with the Vale of White Horse planning department for:

1. The twelve kilns
2. A transfer well; and
3. A new shed on two levels for the preparation of the timber to go into the kiln, and extra storage of dry timber

Following written representations, these proposals were eventually granted on appeal in October 1972. There was now nothing to stop Timbmet growing and becoming one of the premier hardwood companies in the UK.

Financial backing

As soon as the planning permission was confirmed, we approached the bank who already had our detailed plans. Mr F Croxson, the manager of Barclays Old Bank, contacted district head office, and the bank granted us a five year loan for our project. I signed a £180,000 loan (in 2005, almost £2,000,000) with a shaking hand on a plastic table in my modest office (even though I had a good desk, as well as a attractive bookcase by Gordon Russell.) By then Leslie had been appointed Company Secretary, and he co-signed with me.

We did not go out to tender for this development, but appointed Messrs Kingerlee, the builders, to develop this phase for us on a negotiated basis. We enjoined Ridge & Partners, quantity surveyors, to be extra careful and act fairly for both parties. We wanted the kilns erected as soon as possible as we were convinced that they would offer better service to our customers and show us an increased margin. We also firmed up the order with Mr Cubbage for the kilns, and after several joint meetings established a progress chart, which forecast the contract to be completed by the middle of September 1972. There was a lot of excavation to be done; clay had to be removed and a very sound base had to be laid. A loaded kiln bogie of green timber, in some species, could weigh up to 50 tons.

The scissor lift; and giant gantry crane

The timber sticking (placing the softwood laths between the boards) was done with the aid of a hydraulic scissor lift. The timber packs were placed by an overhead electric gantry crane onto a sidewalk (platform) that could be raised and lowered to enable the men to work comfortably and safely at the right height. Not having to lift any excessive weights over their heads when building the piles helped them and also minimised the bending when unloading the dry timber. This was quite a precise operation as the stickers had to be in line one above the other and the kiln bogie square to be safe and enter the kiln with the least waste of space.

The whole building, measuring 240ft by 52ft, was straddled by an overhead five ton capacity gantry crane made by Carruthers in Scotland. This had total mobility in the length and width of the building to allow us to stack the shed to the full height, without the need for access roads for fork lifts and mobile cranes.

We were advised the date of delivery for the gantry. Everyone from the office cheered loudly when the lorry turned into the gate as they knew how much assistance this would provide for the men in the yard.

CHAPTER 17

1971-72
Home affairs

In 1972 the trade felt we should be represented in the hardwood section of the association in the Timber Trade Federation. A vacancy existed in the London Timber Trade Association and we were offered a seat on the committee; but Leslie and I thought hard and agreed that neither of us should accept high office until Timbmet was well established, with good strong management. We had already seen two other small firms fail due to the proprietors spending too much time on trade committees; and one of the owners was highly decorated by the French government for promoting trade between the two countries. I decided it would be better to let Leslie join the committee, as I hoped this would give him more confidence, enabling him to meet leading personalities in the trade.

Within weeks we were offered a place on the National Hardwood Importers section of the TTF. Leslie served loyally for many years, and took a great interest in trade affairs. Sometime later, he was offered the post of vice-chairman which automatically led up to the post of chairman. Leslie politely declined as per our original agreement. During the early days, Peter Salgo, director of Montague Meyer and also a committee member, was very kind and helpful to him in many ways; Peter was a qualified advocate with a very fine brain, and advised the trade on legal matters.

The year from 1971 to 1972 was a turning point for Timbmet. The Conservative government of Mr Edward Heath encouraged expansion and enterprise. There was money available for building industrial property, as well as loans and mortgages for the construction of private and council housing. The banks' 'corsets' were removed allowing them to lend more freely.

We used every opportunity to make use of the existing favourable conditions to enlarge our business customer base and turnover. Above all we could show we were very profitable, which helped to gain the full confidence of our bankers. Inflation began to increase but we, with others, did not see the risk; we bought landed stocks and additional hardwoods arriving ex-quay. We put this timber into stick for air drying and made very big profits the following year.

Our turnover hovered around £90,000 monthly, close to an equivalent of £1,000,000 in 2005, and looked like rising as we had the right stocks from good shippers, reliably air dried together with some kiln dried available off the shelf.

Dividing responsibilities

To remain efficient, we decided to divide some of our functions, and appointed managers. Timbmet had finally found a good works manager, Don Rogers, with timber and logistic experience, who had worked in Africa in very primitive conditions and, during the rainy season, in very muddy terrain. He was determined to make our yard easier to operate during the winter.

We also took on Richard Clapham, who saw the kiln project through right from its inception. He was proud of the plant and equipment put into his care. Richard had come from Magnet in Essex, who closed their door-making factory and consolidated their production in Keighley, Yorkshire. He was offered a position at their new plant, but wanted to remain close to London to keep in touch with his family, especially his parents. He attended night school and studied timber technology and woodwork; and in later years he also became our Technical Manager.

We were running four of our own Bedford lorries, with seven trailers, two cranes and two side-loaders. In addition we used British Road Services, particularly for our North Midland and Welsh runs. They provided empty fifth wheel coupling trailers, which we would load and sheet with their tarpaulins. We would give them notice of our loading and they would collect at the end of the day with one of their tractor units and return to their large depot at Long Lane, Littlemore. The goods normally left the following day to our customers but during main holiday periods, and just before Christmas, there may have been one or two hiccups. By and large the BRS Oxford depot was well above average, and gave a good service.

The occasional swear words were inevitable in the industry, but I could give back 'pleasantries' when absolutely necessary! Sid Tuckey and Bill Clapperton were my main contacts at BRS. I learned routeing from a very humble and capable traffic clerk who knew almost every hamlet in England, and taught me the routeing for our own transport. No extra charge was levied for multiple drops; e.g. the Oxford to Leicester price applied for, say, five drops in Leicester, so an odd mistake within a town was not costly.

For a time we worked with Frank Grounds Transport. They delivered car components which were made in the Midlands to the Cowley car plants, mainly with 10-ton lorries. Two or three drops back to the Birmingham area were available, particularly for a quick turnround round the same day. If they failed because of time the goods were unloaded at their West Bromwich depot, and the odd order disappeared into their warehouse graveyard! We had a similar arrangement with Walsh, an East Anglia haulage contractor whose lorries were big; our orders were less so, and after a few months our trial partnership was brought to an end.

Eddie Stockford joined us in 1962 as a labourer; he was always eager to learn and became a measurer and grader. Larry Smith had an endless amount of trade knowledge but no patience to teach; John Blizzard was much better, and by 1970 we had several others trained, so we decided that Eddie should take over transport and keep an eye on cash collections. To this day he is still carrying out these duties and, with the help of electronic equipment, looks after twenty three vehicles of different sizes.

Our lorries were looked after by the main Bedford dealers on the Botley Road in Oxford, in close proximity to our yard. City Motors did all our maintenance; they worked seven days a week which was essential for efficient truck operating. Small niggling breakages were looked after by a mechanic who came in three nights a week and at weekends. Bumpers, mirrors, bulbs, small dents and holes in the floorboards were all in Eddie's domain and also maintenance of or minor repairs to cranes and side-loaders.

To improve our service and reliability, we decided to engage a highly skilled, all round commercial vehicle fitter with a knowledge of mechanics, hydraulics and electrics, a rare combination even thirty five years ago. Jim Pitts did not disappoint us; he is still in our employment and became maintenance manager of our fleet, plant and buildings. We met Jim while working on our lorries at City Motors and he has proved invaluable in many crises over the years.

Travelling around the country

I was responsible for all the timber purchasing. Almost 100% was imported or native hardwood. I found the home-grown buying most interesting and stimulating, especially when buying butts in the forest and away from any telephone; I enjoyed the hours spent outdoors in all weathers as it was exercise, although not comparable to a structured physical workout in a gym, or playing badminton or similar. Many sawmills had closed, and the government became stricter with their forest policy and concentrated on replanting the huge volume felled during the war. Most sawmills wanted to sell the best in the round for a quick turnover and return of capital outlay; the mills only had second quality for fencing and similar.

As Timbmet expanded, I needed more help with the home-grown buying, and we had a ready made person for this post on our staff, John Blizzard, and he was pleased to accept the position. For a time we went out together and his practical knowledge of sawn timber and keen intellect enabled him to easily grasp the job. Although a real Londoner he seemed to have a good approach to country folk with a farming attitude to life.

My object was to relieve myself of some of the tasks and to have, with Leslie, complete oversight of the future conduct of the business. I have tried to maintain a very strict routine throughout my working life. Going out socially during the week was a rare event.

I could write pages of tales from my experiences on the road buying home-grown timber, some very hilarious. I would like to record a few.

The Linnell family, home-grown saw millers, were (and still are) special friends. When Victor's daughter, Joan, married on a Wednesday it was impossible not to attend, so after a short morning at Cumnor I went home and picked up my dear wife who was dressed in all her finery. We attended the church service and lunch, which we both enjoyed.

To round off the day we called on two of our home-grown sawmill suppliers in the county, as so often the owners lived on the premises. I was surprised that, when they saw my wife, we (or at least Rosie) were not invited to the house. It was always useful to make such calls, as often there was round log stock in the yard, and the saw miller, rather than ask his customer to visit, would wait for someone to come and make an offer. This type of business called for regular travel which often wasted a lot of time in finding one's requirements. In good times or bad, prime butts in all species maintained their value as there were only a few in any one parcel. Usually on these visits I nosed around as far as I could, as most saw millers did not wish me to see any of their very best veneer logs. On this occasion, we discussed any timber tenders outstanding in the area, and no doubt talked about one's families and the political issues of the day, and then departed. No one had taken any notice of Rosie. A few days later when one of our lorry drivers called to collect fresh sawn oak, he was gently called aside and asked the question, "Who is the lovely young dish Mr Kemp is driving around the countryside with these days?" Our driver answered very confidently, "You can be sure it is his wife... She is a lovely lady." They must have known where we came from. It was surprising that this family was not invited to the wedding as both the families knew one another well.

Sometimes I used to go valuing home-grown timber in the evenings in summer, on bank holidays and in the Christmas and Easter holidays with one senior gentleman who was most respected in the home-grown trade. I am sure he hardly ever bought any of these lots, which were sold by tender; he just wanted to know the value of the parcels and judge what to offer to owners of estates who sold him the timber by private treaty. For me it was a great opportunity to judge the quality of standing, and sometimes also felled, logs. It may have been time consuming, but this person was exceptionally experienced, and a good teacher.

Another small mill owner, Mr Barr, of Hungerford, who never modernised, and had a most dangerous site due to neglect, used to sell his best oak logs at stump. He was fortunate that most of his raw material requirements were available close to his sawmill. He invited me, and no doubt one or two others, to inspect a parcel which I only realised later was not his to sell, but was up for sale to the highest bidder.

He asked me to call at lunchtime. On arriving at the mill I saw him sitting in his car eating his sandwiches. On these occasions I also took a lunch box and a thermos flask: I got them out and went to his car. He invited me to have lunch with him and offered me the front passenger seat. He said "Don't open your flask, have a drop of mine." He promptly refilled his screw top and offered me the tea to drink. I did not hesitate although he had used the same cup before. This seemed to mean a lot to him.

After lunch we drove in his old decrepit vehicle to the site. I chose the logs I wished to buy, determined the lengths and girth and suggested a price piece by piece. As I left him he told me that he would contact me, as he was unable to conclude a deal on the spot. I found it strange but it didn't take me very long to realise that he was using me to value the timber. He then either offered the sellers the value I had made for my selection, or 70-80% of what I was prepared to pay for the best logs, depending on the value of the residue. If the estate accepted the price, I also had a deal; if not, it was a wasted half-day. We were once invited as a family to his home for a Sunday tea to meet his wife and sons, who were table tennis fanatics. He owned a large good arable farm, a much bigger enterprise than his neglected unmodernised sawmill.

As in all trades there is always a minority of less scrupulous individuals. Some sellers would leave the logs purposely where they were felled rather than gather them to a clearing in the forest, or to the roadside, where they could be easily inspected and accurately measured. Placing the tape by sword under the log to obtain true girth was only possible where the ground was reasonably clear, otherwise some bark or twigs would be included which naturally would enhance the measure easily by 5-7%. One had to use one's hand to pull this rubbish away to get the tape taut around the boule. In some parts of southern England there were snakes but most of these were not harmful.

Often a butt, not absolutely straight grown or with other imperfections, such as knots, would be laid best face up hiding the twist or other defect. Wherever possible, particularly for the very best logs, it was advisable to purchase only after the butt was lifted off the ground for all round inspection. This was not practicable on many sites.

Once when I was young I saw a log at Monmouth sawmills lying near the entrance. The butt was 21' long and of large diameter. I was still young and inexperienced. The owners demanded an exceptional price, which I decided to accept. I measured the log in the mud along with two or three other butts. These were all delivered to Greenwich sawmills, Marlow, Bucks, where at that time most of our native logs were stored and sawn, Mr Rigby, the manager, duly reported to my father that I was careless, and may have been misled. In any case, my father used to drive to Marlow regularly in the summer months on a Sunday afternoon to inspect my purchases. He took my mother with him and they had tea at one of the many cafés in the area.

On Monday morning my father expressed his displeasure in great anger. He declared that this log would remain unsold in Marlow to constantly remind me of my stupidity and failure of duty to Timbmet. It was not to be sold in his lifetime. The log remained there for over eight years during which time most of the sap decayed until my father died.

Around 1960 H J & G Wright, builders, of Great Missenden, had to strengthen and restore the Norman tower of the High Wycombe parish church in the town centre. We had the enquiry, and I told them this most unusual story and invited them to inspect the log as it was nearby. The contractor and architect were pleased to find a dry log which, if cut into big beams, would not warp or twist when installed in an old stone building. The sections required were so large that the twist in the growth did not concern them unduly. They wanted the sections free of heart shakes (that is, faulty timber at the centre of the tree), and allowed us to cut sill sections, from the middle. Nothing was wasted except the dead sap. Due to inflation over ten years we gained on the overall transaction, even allowing for ten years' interest costs.

I always tried to utilise my day fully, but sometimes the short days did not allow enough time for a thorough inspection in full daylight. It happened two or three times one autumn at Vastern Sawmill, Calne and Wootton Bassett. The owner, the late Mr Barnes, called me a 'moonlighter'; quickly I responded, "This moonlighter always pays his bills and trusts you as sellers." This went down exceptionally well and cemented an already good relationship existing between Mr Barnes and Timbmet.

The Andover Timber Company was a big sawmill; they cut large quantities of home grown hardwoods and put the best butts into stick for air drying. One could always find partly air dried and fully air dried stocks at their yard. They cleverly mixed the qualities in each pile, thereby creating average quality lots and insisted on selling each complete pile of logs with no individual selection offered. As with most saw millers, they always sold the full veneer quality in the round. At times when their log stock was too big, they would sell a quantity of sawmill logs in the solid.

On one very icy morning in winter, they wanted to sell a parcel of felled oak butts and other timbers. John Matley, director of the Andover Timber Company, phoned to ask me to come over to Andover and make an inspection. He said he would take me in his car to the site, but did not want to reveal the address. I thought it strange, but I was interested and turned up as arranged. It was a treacherous journey; this was in the early postwar years when cars did not have the de-icing and heating facilities as they do now. John Matley drove to Stratfield Saye, the Duke of Wellington's estate, south of Reading. The road signposts were very clear so I knew where I was. (They had been removed or demolished at the beginning of the war so as to make it harder for the enemy if they had succeeded in invading this country, and had just about been restored all over the country.) It was very slippery underfoot, but the logs were properly laid out so that any major faults would have been seen under the ice cover. I made my purchase, subject to final measure, which was to be delivered to Marlow sawmills.

We were both very cold and I suggested that John stop at a café or pub on the return journey. He said he could not, but I would be very welcome to sit in his office and eat my sandwiches, and the staff would give me as many hot drinks as I wished. He would go home for his lunch and meanwhile I could look around the yard and inspect his sawn stocks in case I found something of interest. The prices were generally higher than we could afford as most of Andover's customers were consumers. I found his behaviour very strange; but he explained that his family were members of the Plymouth Brethren and they did not eat even with other Christian denominations, but only amongst themselves. On further questioning I found that there existed small hotels where they could holiday with others of the same religious body. He expected me, as a Jew, to understand that both my religion and his tradition discourage mixing or socialising with others, due to the fear of intermarriage. I was still a bit upset at having to waste time on dangerous roads.

I must have covered several hundred thousand miles on my travels to find English timbers in the southern half of the country, which included parts of East Anglia, the North Midlands, Wales, Devon and Cornwall. Fortunately I never had a car accident. However, once a pile of elm coffin boards fell on top of me in a very poorly equipped, neglected sawmill at Lyneham, Wilts: I was in great pain but managed to keep my boots on and drive slowly back to Oxford. The following day I went to hospital where I was diagnosed with a fracture and my leg was put in plaster. This was about eighteen months after I got married and it worried Rosie a great deal She phoned her family that night telling them of my accident and two days later there was a knock on the door. My father-in-law was on the step, having come by train from London to see with his own eyes what I had really done. His remarks and use of language were so unlike him that the two of us could only laugh our heads off!

CHAPTER 18

March 1972: West Africa

Now that I had a reliable overall manager in charge of the yard, I started to think of overseas travel to meet some of our suppliers. I had been to France once or twice, and now I wanted to become familiar with other producing countries.

After many requests from our main shippers to come and see "how it's all done" and some discussions with a few principal agents in London, through whom we purchased the majority of our supplies, I chose to travel with John McKee of Price Morgan. He was a junior director of the company, very experienced for his age, and highly respected in the trade; Price Morgan represented J Lalanne, who were our most important suppliers on the Ivory Coast, and so typically French in many respects - that is to say, very touchy and often pretending to be offended. I was convinced I could cope with all the others on my own.

Ghana

I met John at Rome Airport. He had spent a long relaxing weekend in Italy with his wife before beginning our tour. We flew by Ghana Airways to Accra, where we were met by one of Price Morgan's principal shippers, Bibiani Lumber. It was always useful to have someone known locally to take you through the immigration and customs procedure. We spent the night in a hotel at Accra; it was customary in the early days to pay a courtesy visit to the Ministry of Forests which we did the following morning and we then proceeded along the scenic coast road to the port of Takoradi. The roads everywhere were in much poorer condition than they are today.

It was generally recommended that it would be politically expedient to be as neutral as possible. In the absence of reasonable hotel accommodation, I stayed at the house of Brandler & Rylke, a large firm of log shippers with whom in fact we did hardly any business. Our log requirements were always at the top end of the market and not in shipload quantities. John stayed in the town house of the Bibiani logging company, his largest Ghanaian shipper; the owner was very close to the ruling family, the Ashanti tribe, who were a great political influence at the time.

I was comfortably accommodated. A European shipping manager and his family were living in the house. For my special dietary needs, I was given a variety of fresh flat fish cooked in butter, far more than I could cope with and left some over. Later when I was shown around the house, including the kitchen, I found the servants sitting on the floor eating their food native fashion: I was told that they would prefer their own, rather than my European style cooked food!

Brandlers provided me with a car and driver, as John McKee spent his time with his principal shipper, Bibiani. I remember visiting British door manufacturers, two large sawmill complexes, F Hills of Stockton-on-Tees, and Briscoe of Denmark, who later became EAC and are now Ghana Primewood Products. One had a dark red shipping stripe and a gazelle as a shipping emblem, the other company a green shipping mark and a beaver. They were both well run, producing upper end FAS to an equal standard bordering the former prime empire grading rules. As far as was possible in Africa, everything was kept in good order with spare parts to hand locally. Both companies exported large quantities of square edge lumber and, in addition, veneer and A/B quality solid logs which had the outside end diameters clearly marked with their colours.

From there I went to Sekondi, a suburb of Takoradi, where I enjoyed a late lunch in the home of John Bitar, then already one of the largest Lebanese timber producers in Ghana. He lived next to the mill; I remember his showing me his plant and yard. When I commented on some bad sticking, pointing out that a little more care would alleviate complaints, and some obeche which was already discoloured after a very short period in stick due to neglect, he appeared offended, but in reality it was only pretence. Their enterprises have grown and expanded and they are now probably the biggest producers in Ghana today. John Bitar is about 90 years old and has finally retired to the Lebanon; and the companies are well run by his two sons, William and Ghassan.

I spent another night in Takoradi and on the second day visited smaller shippers. I did not visit Sambreboi, on the west coast, which was the main mill of the United Africa Company. They did not offer any advantage over the other sawmills and by and large their FAS was always nearer the lower end of the grade. This was also the case with Gliksten's production (now called Suhuma Timber and owned by JCM) at Sefwi Wiawso. I also felt that I must not upset my loyalty to Mim Timber Co. who with their agents, Flatau Dick, gave Timbmet exceptional support right from our very modest beginning.

UAC had several specialities. One of them was square logs. The smaller ones were adzed (dressed with a special tool for cutting away the surface of the wood) in the forests and then sent to the port. The larger logs were brought to the mill and the outside of the logs sawn into lumber until a reasonable square was left. These were mixed with the smaller squares for export and they contained the full heart. Some buyers thought this was an advantage but I could never see the gain, except that they were charged less for actual measure, not hoppus (log) measure. The current owners of the company are Samartex who are important suppliers to our business.

It was politically expedient to visit also the Ghana Export and Timber Marketing Board. They controlled the export licences and selling prices.

On the fourth day, John took me in Bibiani's vehicle up to Kumasi, the main timber producing town, which was about 100 kilometres north-west of Takoradi.

First of all, we paid our respects to the shipping office at Mim Timber Company in Kumasi. They controlled all the timber and logs which were transported by road to Takoradi: the road was in bad condition and sometimes in the rainy season the timber had to travel to Accra and then by coastal road to the port of Takoradi.

From Kumasi, there was a railway line to Takoradi which operated an elegant night sleeper passenger service reminiscent of colonial days, with carriages not unlike the Orient Express. The railway carried a lot of logs and timber to the port and there were never enough heavy goods engines in service but somehow the timber reached its destination!

To keep myself as impartial as possible, I had to stay at the City Hotel. In those days the accommodation was very simple, with no air conditioning. Men could not be in the bar on their own; John was able to stay in the Bibiani guest house. The following morning, he picked me up early and we travelled about 80 kilometres south-west to the village of Bibiani to see Mr Ben Kufour. I toured the large sawmill and afterwards had a late lunch at his large new mansion, which was built in the French style. I was always accustomed to taking small gifts wherever I travelled, in the form of coasters of Oxford or English landscapes and, for the more important, small items of Wedgwood china. We were both shown into the salon before our meal and I was amazed to see this large room decorated in blue and white, with sofas, and side-tables laden with sizeable pieces of Wedgwood. My small offering was insignificant and almost an embarrassment!

Over lunch, Ben asked me what I thought of his mill and I said that I liked what I saw, as by then I had visited a few mills in Ghana, but I went on to say, "Even a blind man could distinguish your production." He asked me to explain and I told him that I thought his saw sharpening was inadequate and that he wasted a lot of timber. Fortunately all the lumber we had from him was exceptionally full cut to allow for the uneven surfaces (ridges). Naturally, he was most upset but asked why this should trouble me. I told him that recently I had had to deal with a complaint rejecting his lumber. This had been from a large softwood importer at Southampton, not fully conversant with hardwoods. In order to prove my point, I loaded myself with as many pieces of timber as I could carry and without saying anything to the customer, walked as fast as I could in the direction of the sawmill. I requested them to plane the pieces to 2" thickness. They obliged in spite of having to stop production. The finished pieces were still hit and miss 2" proving that they could still finish at $1\frac{3}{4}$", fully planed. There was no claim except for the extra time involved putting the timber through the planer twice.

After a leisurely lunch, John and I left, and went back to Kumasi. A few months later I received photographs of the new saw sharpening equipment installed at Ben's mill. He had obviously taken note of my comments!

The Kufour family were closely related to the Ashanti King, and Ben made arrangements for John and me to have an audience with Opoku Ware II. We were privileged to meet him and to have a short discussion on how our two countries could co-operate better, especially in timber exports. On the last lap of the journey to the palace, our car was accompanied by two jeeps with armed soldiers. In 1972, ten years after Ghana's independence, the leading tribe still had a great deal of influence over the national government.

I spent three days and two nights at the Mim Timber Co, which was about 70 kilometres from Kumasi. I was collected and driven in one of their 4-wheel drive vehicles. The journey took about two hours: and this was one of the best roads in Ghana. Mim ensured that at least part of the route to the port that they generally used was in good condition.

On arrival, I was greeted by Dieter Rotzel, the German managing director, whom I found to be exceptionally capable and efficient. It was an honour to be accommodated in Oscar Charmant's bungalow which was simple but comfortable with air-conditioning, although it was primitive and noisy.

Mim cared more for their workers than other companies did; everyone was well looked after, and lived in wooden mini-bungalows. There was a good elementary school and hospital on the site, and a nice Catholic church in the village. Generally, as one travelled through the country, the villages where the missionaries were living were always tidier, and here life seemed better in general: apart from the church there was always a school, and the children were dressed either in yellow, green or white depending on the denomination of the mission.

I spent the evenings with the local managers, and I also had the opportunity to be with Desmond Charmant, Oscar's son, who was married to two Ghanaian ladies, but had a full western outlook and kept himself informed of world affairs. He was familiar with the political situation in Europe, particularly the last hundred years of the Austro-Hungarian Empire. He had copies of the 1919 Treaties of Versailles and Trianon, which were written in French, affecting the finalisation of the Slovak borders with which his grandfather had been involved as a barrister.

My principal object was to tour the sawmill, but I also spent time in all other departments. I saw the production of timber from the log intake to the loaded lorries taking the finished product to the port. Needless to say I was very impressed; everything was tidy and in good working order. To achieve this they had a large number of expatriates of western European origin, with at least one person for each department.

The forest allocated to them was exceptionally fine with well grown trees. I visited part of the logging operations, something I had never experienced before. At that time they did not have to transport their logs very far to the mill, which was always a great advantage. In some way it is not surprising as the sawn product was excellent: they provided an extra large specification, 7' and up, 7" and up, with an average of at least 12' by 12"; and for a good friend like Timbmet, it could even be better - that is, except for afrormosia, walnut and mansonia.

All timber was carefully put into stick for air drying before being measured and bundled for export. Like others, they sent the lower grades to Malta, Cyprus, Greece, Egypt, Morocco and Tunisia. Their FAS grade was nearly always equal to prime, but if they had more coarse grown trees, particularly in utile which was a big part of their production, they also sold an export grade. I had the good fortune to visit at a time when there was no demand for this material and I decided to spend time inspecting the stock thoroughly and found it to be adequate for our requirements. So I purchased a large quantity, which came in particularly useful in 1973, when demand for timber outstripped supplies.

Desmond Charmant frequently went on holiday to Switzerland. The Swiss landscape and architecture influenced him, and he created a little area around the sawmill and surroundings like a Swiss village. At the end of my stay, I said my goodbyes to the most senior personnel, which included one Danish manager, Mr Kronberg, who had spent a lot of the time with me at the mill, and they took me back to Kumasi. The Mim Timber Company is known today as Ayum Forest Products, a much smaller company, mainly slicing and peeling veneers.

I must have spent another three days visiting both large and small sawmills in Kumasi which was the most important timber producing area in Ghana, close to the major forests. At one of the smaller mills, the manager was John Baldwin whom I had met in England at Lancaster Sawmills, at Newent in Gwent. He spent a day with me and I was provided with a car and chauffeur for the other two days.

One of the most important suppliers was the Naja David family who had a modern sawmill and kilns, and also produced veneers. This business continues under the title of A G Timbers. Another important timber supplier was A E Saoud Brothers and, as far as I know, this business has closed. We had good supplies from a small German owned sawmill: this company was A Laing, whose director in charge was Mr F Blanke.

A number of the smaller mills are no longer in existence and overall the production is now less than it was thirty years ago. Timbmet also had useful suppliers amongst the lesser known producers.

The Ivory Coast

John and I flew to the Ivory Coast to continue our journey. We checked into the hotel Du Parc at Abidjan from where we made daily trips into the interior to visit sawmills. The country was developing well under a very firm and revered leader, President Felix Houphouet-Boigny, who kept all factions united until he died in December 1993. He also built a new capital city in the centre of the country called Yamoussoukro and spent a very large sum of money building a replica of the basilica of St Peter's in the Vatican.

Our main suppliers were Messrs J Lalanne Group who had their head office in Paris where all the business transactions were done. They had a sister company called SEPC. Maurice Binlich and Amoury Legras together built up a large international business; Amoury was responsible for obtaining a large, very valuable piece of forest land in the Daloa area. Lalanne, like Mim, built schools, hospitals, roads and other infrastructure as part of the deal with the government.

On the first evening John and I were taken to the modern part of the city where Maurice had a very elegant flat in a new apartment block close to the lagoon. We enjoyed a very delicious French style meal. Madam Binlich acted as hostess and a number of senior managers of the local head office and sawmills were present. Maurice commuted regularly between the Ivory Coast and Paris, whereas Amoury lived on the coast so as to look after the businesses.

The next day John and I went to Bingerville, west of Abidjan on the inland lagoon from where it was possible to load timber direct to barges. It could then be transported to the oceangoing cargo ships in the main port. This mill was entirely steam powered and the engines were kept in immaculate condition. The mill mainly produced a very mild sapele which Timbmet marketed by the native name 'Aboudikru'. In the coastal region there were also stands of makore logs, which were of exceptional size and quality: because of the smooth grain, this timber was ideally suited as a substitute for ebony. The makore was much heavier than utile or sapele and would be adequate for today's fireproof regulations. It never became popular in England because the dust created by machining caused irritation to the eyes, nose and throat. The only firm in England who used large volumes and manufactured quality furniture was the Stag Furniture Company in Nottingham.

The next day, we flew in a small company plane to their main concession and large sawmill at Daloa. As we approached, we could see small fires burning. It was explained to me that the local farmers plant crops between the trees and then after the harvest burn the land to clear it from pests. I was assured that there was a camera fitted to the undercarriage of the plane filming the area and guards would be sent out to warn the locals to stop this practice.

We landed on the airstrip near the mill and were given a very extensive tour of the sawmill operation which was as quality conscious as Mim, but smaller. They were producing one or two additional species of timber which were of interest to Timbmet, and not available in Ghana.

There were still good forests surrounding the mill. It seemed that care was taken not to deforest the area too much. We were taken by jeep a few kilometres and stopped in a clearing with a large timber building. A native woman carrying two baskets of freshly baked French baguettes came from nowhere! From the opening of the building you could see the heat coming through the doors. She went inside and opened the flaps, which were designed to give some air flow; she quickly laid a table outside, and the managers unlocked gas fridges containing a variety of French cheeses and meats as well as bottles of light wine. We enjoyed a short lunch and spent the afternoon walking through the forest. The shipper outlined the felling programme and explained to me their future conservation plans. I was able to ask questions and they were all answered in great detail.

We returned to the plane late in the afternoon for the journey back to the capital. On the way we ran into heavy rain, wind and thunder and had to land on a bush airstrip, near the provincial town of Gagnoa. It was a quite frightening experience, and we may have killed a few chickens. The pilot made arrangements to take us to a modern local hotel, surrounded by illuminated mini lakes which made it look quite pretty, but while we slept we had visitors: the frogs from the lakes hopped in unexpectedly to keep us company!

By the morning the storm had subsided and we flew back to Abidjan. We had missed our dinner invitation with Yve Herve and his wife who lived on the outskirts of the city.

During the day from the hotel I made contact with other shippers to arrange further visits which I had to do on my own because John was only allowed to sell products from the Republic of the Ivory Coast ex the J Lalanne group. In the afternoon Amoury took us for a short trip in his yacht around the lagoon to see the beauty of the area, which was never fully developed for international tourists, with the exception of the French. In the evening we went to our postponed dinner with Yve and his wife. It was a much more modest affair than Maurice's. The main speciality was lobsters which I almost refused but I decided to be polite. I watched how the others tackled the fish and followed; I'm sure the hostess must have realised something was unusual but she did not say anything. At the end of the evening, just before we gave our thanks and left, we were asked to take a passenger back with us to the hotel, together with his cooking utensils. They had hired a chef from the hotel we were staying at to cook this delicacy in my honour!

It was my fiftieth birthday but I did not dare to tell anyone, as I was afraid of having to consume too much alcohol! Michel Lalanne came from the Republic of the Congo to meet me. We had breakfast together at the hotel; he was anxious for more business between our two companies. He was in charge of Boissangha in Brazzaville. Most veneers to the UK came from Ghana and the Ivory Coast where they were lighter than the timber in the Congo Basin. It was virtually impossible to sell the darker afrormosia in this country until some years later due to a drought in the Volta region of Ghana, when huge forest fires destroyed most of the trees of the light afrormosia. The freight costs from the Congo were higher than from West Africa.

For the rest of the day, at my request my hosts, arranged for me to spend time on the Plage to watch and grade round logs for export. I spent the day with the chef des grumes [in charge of the grading of logs, and their export], a large burly Frenchman with powerful features, wearing an Australian bush hat. I was suitably attired for the heat and kept up with him, climbing over the logs looking for faults, checking and measuring both ends, determining the grade and watching him advise his 'boys' where to cross cut, paint and number each log.

The European continent bought largely solid logs as opposed to lumber. The importers in France, Holland and Germany purchased a single species in thousands of cubic metres. Provided the measure was correct, they did not check the quality in such minute detail as in the UK, where only small quantities were bought and the preference was for mostly S/E lumber.

I said farewell to all at Lalanne & SEPC who made my stay so interesting. I remained booked into a hotel, at times travelling with recommended Ivorian taxi drivers to various inland sawmills and on long trips to potential or existing suppliers. I got by with my limited French. Most French companies are known by their initials, so full names escape me; and since my visit, ownership of some of the mills has changed. However, Philippe le-Flanchec, Thaney (owned by SCAC, a very large oil and coal supplier in metropolitan France,) and the proprietors of CIB remain vivid in my memory. In addition they had considerable timber concessions on the Ivory Coast and greatly supported the ATIBT [Association Technique de Bois Tropicale.]

I spent three days with my friend Tony Maughan of Charles Boss & Co, very well established timber agents. He was well connected on the Ivory Coast. We travelled by road to San Pedro, the developing new port in the west of the country, and visited several mills in one village. The local chief, part owner of a supply sawmill, gave a party in my honour and slaughtered a lamb in my presence, which was then roasted on a spit. It also transpired during the afternoon celebrations that one of the chief's wives had just given birth to a new baby, so in fact it was only a shared honour!

ADK'S, the shippers', Lebanese owner was a very lively person who liked the London night spots at weekends, and used to come, with Tony Maughan, to settle claims on Sunday mornings. It was hard going at times; he wanted lots of strong black coffee, toast and hard boiled eggs which I gladly provided to get some settlement and maybe also to close some kind of deal, even of dubious value. It pleased Tony, and did not waste time on a weekday. ADK had access to the last national forest hitherto unexploited, near the borders of Liberia.

Summary

To summarise my visit to West Africa: I visited Ghana and the Ivory Coast on this major tour. I went to Ghana only once again, in 1990, on a four day official TTF mission to discuss the utilisation of secondary species. It was only after 1995, when our purchasing department was enlarged, that regular visits to West Africa were undertaken.

In 1972 there was hardly any secondary production. The very low grade timber was sold to the local population, and the third quality to some developing nations. A great deal was burnt to run the plants and also a lot of fire wood was needed by the local people, as they had no other means of energy for cooking etc. The companies spent large sums of money on modern equipment to improve and speed up production. Kilning was in its infancy; the need to deliver dry timber to the market place was not yet really understood by the mill owners. For instance, at Mim secondhand kilns from Korea were used without any operating controls, yielding very poor results. All their other plant and machinery was modern and well maintained.

The only component factory at the time was in a village close to the main timber plant where a Danish company, Mim-Scanstyle, with key European staff, was producing chair parts for Europe. It seemed that in West Africa the expatriate management remained in their posts for many years with their wives and young children. The older children were sent back to their home countries to be educated.

I established many deep and lasting friendships on this trip with the top and middle management on the spot. My detailed interest in production, local life-styles and ecology, etc. formed the basis for some very strong bonds. The main purchasing of West African timber was from head offices that were often in mother countries, and mostly negotiated with their selling agents and shippers who visited their customers. I may have been in France once or twice, to meet the owners of the businesses. Some of the larger shippers, however, would not sell direct, only through their agents.

I was able to renegotiate contracts if market conditions changed, to postpone shipments, alter specifications and adjust payment terms, etc. Over the years, misunderstandings did arise, sometimes even quarrels, but on the whole the producers liked to work with Timbmet, especially as we never reneged on any agreements. The fact that we did not mix much with our competitors also assisted confidentiality. It is unlikely that LB or I would have spoken in public or private regarding any confidential arrangements.

Our messages to the coast about the quality supplied were not always appreciated, especially some in poor French written by my wife! The word 'bananas' describing a parcel of bent logs, went down very badly and took some time to be forgiven.

I feel sure that Timbmet received the best available qualities of hardwoods from West Africa at competitive prices. They were not always the very cheapest, but the terms and other conditions we enjoyed far exceeded that of the major competition.

Sadly, my best friend, Oscar Charmant, was killed in a car accident while spending the winter 1974-1975 in Africa. Though badly missed, as he was a mine of useful information, this did not make any difference to relations between Timbmet and the Mim Timber Co. Ten years later our needs had more than doubled with the result that our purchasing volumes were similar to those of the big three. I am sure we did have advantages one way or another. Our large yard, able to accommodate quantities of hardwoods for air drying, and Timbmet's willingness to share the risks with shippers must have played a part in our success story.

CHAPTER 19

1972 and 1973: two busy years

I returned home after three weeks in West Africa, my longest absence from work ever, and found everyone in good spirits. The business had not suffered and all the staff had worked well together without me.

1972 was a very good trading year. Mr Heath's government made credit available for many large construction projects, and building societies had money available for mortgages. The Treaty of Rome enabling us to join the EEC was signed on 1 January, 1973. Not many of us fully understood the implications. For the African tropical hardwood importers and users, it opened up new supplies of similar species and new timbers became available, duty free from the ex-French and ex-Belgian colonial countries, e.g. the Republic of Cameroon and the Congo. The changeover developed gradually, and in 1973 these additional quantities enjoyed a good demand in the UK.

We at Timbmet took advantage of all available opportunities. We built additional hard core roads on the premises; we also improved the drainage system on site, mostly using our own labour under the direction of our works manager, Don Rogers. This meant we were able to accommodate the additional quantities of hardwoods for which space would be required for the impending economic boom.

Our West African hardwood imports increased. Victoria Sawmills at Hayes closed soon after the death of Mr Oscar Charmant; the site was sold for redevelopment as the family had no interest in the business. It was a very sad day for Timbmet: the management had always looked after us, and it also meant we had fewer kilns to rely on.

Handling and storage space

As the trade became very busy, there were times when we were unable to place solid logs directly to a sawmill without incurring a double handling charge or demurrage at the docks We even used Valentine Wood, at Silchester near Reading, one of the most inefficient places in Europe. As a last resort I contacted Mr Davies, director at Gliksten hardwoods, and explained my plight to him. The next day I had a telephone call informing me that we could land several hundred tons of solid logs at their wharf and they would process them for us. Gliksten had a very nicely laid out yard on the canal at Stratford, E15, with adequate room for all their operations. At that time they still operated four large band mills on two shifts.

Looking back, one wonders how they had the spare capacity in a boom period. The most likely answer is that gradually more and more users utilised S/E lumber rather than solid logs in the UK. To me it seemed a strange and curious arrangement for the 'minnow' to be served by the giant! Although I delegated a good many of my duties to others, I still continued to mark my own imported logs for cutting. On a number of occasions I went to Glikstens, arriving just after lunch to inspect the Timbmet logs, and was always courteously assisted by a very able mill manager, Mr Ted Brooks. When I finished mid to late afternoon, I was surprised that once or twice I was invited into the board room for tea; I felt honoured. I was obviously very curious to find out as much of their business as possible, and they must have been surprised to see a proprietor of a medium-sized importer doing this task himself. On one occasion, I was warmly greeted by the chairman of the parent company himself, Mr Alan Groves.

The Seymour (Schreiber) families came from Eastern Europe in the mid 1930s and established themselves at Cocking in Sussex, milling homegrown timbers. After the war they bought a site at Rotherhithe where they built a new sawmill and installed two large band mills and a battery of six kilns on a very small plot of land, just over three acres. It was a success story from the start with the cheapest lighterage anywhere in London. They featured this on the front page of the Timber Trade Journal, with a photograph taken from London Bridge. It was a very effective advertisement. I'm not a jealous type but perhaps on this occasion, I was very envious, although a little later I felt somewhat ashamed of myself.

Renting kiln space

By 1972 Vitak also built a sizeable kiln plant at Belvedere, Kent. Many different firms used the service. LB and I decided to try and book a minimum of ten kilns with them for our use on an annual basis. We were confident we would need the drying space even though our kilns were near completion. We continued to use theirs very extensively even after we opened our Bicester site in 1980. Ron Clare, the kiln manager, was efficient and together we were able to plan our requirements two or three months ahead. It worked reasonably well. Parcels did get mixed up while in their care, but if you were strict, you got a substitution of someone else's stock in the same species. Bill Richardson, the foreman, a very colourful character, robbed Peter to pay Paul. I hate to think how it all landed up when they finally closed down and we were no longer involved. The kiln programme and progress was discussed over the phone every Thursday afternoon at 3.30pm.

John Bitar in Oxford

In 1973 Easter and Passover fell at the same time. I knew my good Lebanese friend, John Bitar, was on his own in town staying at the Waldorf Astoria. I offered to visit him on Good Friday morning to which he readily agreed. I told Rosie: she was not very pleased as she had hoped for help from me to prepare a Passover meal that day for friends and visitors. When I explained my reasons to her for the journey she relented and asked me to try to be back quickly.

I travelled by train to Paddington and took a taxi to the hotel. John was waiting for me and we settled down to a leisurely coffee. I started my personal questioning. "John, are you on your own here over Easter?" He replied yes, he was. I said "Do you mind my making you a proposal? Perhaps you know it is also Passover tonight. Nevertheless may I invite you to come to Oxford? I know there are rooms available at the Randolph Hotel. Stay there, join us for meals and spend the days with us. We shall make it as stimulating as possible. And the Passover rituals may be of interest to you."

He thanked me very politely and I could see the twinkle in his eyes. He took out his wallet from his jacket pocket and put on the table three sets of tickets, and explained that he had invited a French couple living in Takoradi who were presently on leave in Paris to come over to London and spend the weekend with him. One set of tickets was for the opera, one for a symphony concert and the other for the ballet. Inwardly I felt relieved as it could have been a strain to mix our friends with a complete stranger! I hurried back on the next train and did my best for Rosie in the kitchen.

At the time of such grave timber shortages no other of Bitar's English customers would have thought of doing likewise. John was a highly educated man, tall, elegant and exceptionally well-dressed and well-mannered, whom one could have taken to any high society event.

A few weeks later he tried to gazump me. He offered us via C Leary, the agent, a parcel of avodire, a white hardwood which did not grow in large quantities. I accepted the offer but John Bitar refused to confirm this. Forty-eight hours later the same parcel was offered by Flatau Dick at a higher price. I made a counter offer, and told them that I had already bought the parcel. They disbelieved me, but promised to come back in two days' time if it was unsold at the full price.

They came back to me and I said I made the counter offer on one condition: that they put on the telex "Greetings from your Jewish cousin." This did not conform to normal business practice, but I insisted on it and they finally relented. The offer was accepted, and John Bitar knew what I meant. From then onwards many of the other Lebanese traders in Ghana referred to me as their Jewish cousin!

1973: A visit to Yugoslavia

The whole of the Yugoslav timber trade was nationalised: it comprised Export Drvo in Croatia, Yugo Drvo in Serbia and Sipad in Bosnia. The principal agent representing Yugoslavia was Churchill & Sim and the partner responsible was Giles Sim. We purchased beech even when still on a government licence; he paid regular visits and I suggested that I accompany him on his next trip, to which he readily agreed.

We went at the end of May 1973 for a whole week and landed in Zagreb on Sunday afternoon. There was time to do a little sightseeing and we went to the old city. I was taken straight back to my childhood and felt I had returned to my home town. The public buildings and churches were in the same style and architecture as in Bratislava, in the baroque of Austria-Hungary. I was pleasantly surprised that young people were coming into the church, presumably for a short prayer, although they were looking around them before entering, hoping that nobody would recognise them.

Early on Monday morning we visited the offices of Export Drvo who controlled the oak production in Croatia. We met Mr Vrban, the sales director, and were introduced to other staff. After short discussions we were provided with a driver and car for the week.

Giles knew the main sawmills and we visited about eight of them. The productivity and general morale was low, but there was some very good timber available. They produced only in the manner they were accustomed to, and there were no specialities available. Because of the state of the machinery, which could not take heavy or large butts, the long clean lengths that we required were mostly cross cut. We had the ability to choose our sawmills and got to know the management a little. There was generally a lot of respect for the agents and Giles personally: surprisingly, as he was a highly educated and 'posh' English gentleman, whereas the Croats at the sawmills were quite the opposite.

The timber in the middle of the country was of mixed species, primarily oak and beech. The administration for Yugo Drvo was done from Belgrade where two very efficient late middle aged ladies were in charge. From our experience it later became evident that they ensured the mills kept their promises. The majority of our purchases came from a large sawmill complex in Novi-sad.

We spent the last two days in Bosnia-Herzegovina, who had the largest volume of timber, mainly beech. We saw some of the primitive and slightly more advanced sawmills which produced large volumes of beech in all grades, steamed and unsteamed. The English market bought only the top grades; the lowest grades were used either for home consumption or sold to the Middle East, mainly Egypt. There was no choice of mill and it was all marketed under the 'Sipad' brand.

We visited the head office at Sarajevo, which was the capital city of Bosnia. It was a newish large office block where several hundred people, mainly male, worked in close proximity. All looked like Slavs but I realised that amongst them there were many Muslims, Catholics and Serb Orthodox as well as a handful of Jews. They all seemed to be working and living in harmony; but one could not visualise what would happen later.

I was aware that a very famous illustrated Hebrew manuscript existed somewhere in safe storage at Sarajevo. It was the Passover Haggada written in Spain in the 14th century. I asked someone where it could be seen, but I was told that only President Tito could authorise this! Walking the streets in the evening we were shown the crossroads where the Austrian Crown Prince Ferdinand and his wife were murdered in 1914 on a state visit. This was the last of a number of political events which finally led to the First World War.

Everywhere we went, we were provided with simple, clean and adequate accommodation. The food was very basic, particularly for a non-meat eater.

111

On my travels, I tried to find out more about working and living conditions in Yugoslavia. The difference in take home pay between a labourer and senior management was sevenfold and strikes were forbidden. In Oxford, disputes were constantly disrupting production at the car plants, threatening our exports. I thought that if we, in the UK, could adopt some of the better practices seen in Yugoslavia, a happy medium could be created and life would be better in all sections of our society, with the prevention of much industrial unrest. Giles was public school educated and a true blue Conservative, so naturally he disagreed with me.

Our new kilns completed

In the summer of 1973 we were getting very excited at Timbmet as the builders had finished their work on the new storage shed and the light building covering the kilns. Also ready was the sunken well, in which the traverser car travelled carrying the bogies laden with the timber to be kilned to their respective drying chambers; and again, when ready, back to the shed for de-sticking. The main work left for Cubbage was to complete the aluminium conventional oil-fired and air-heated kilns, and to install the platform scissor lift.

Early in July, just before the main holiday season, we held a great evening party. We raised the scissor lift to table height and covered it with paper tablecloths. We self-catered the usual goodies and nearby had several crates of beer. We invited all our customers from the three surrounding counties, including some firms from whom we had not as yet done any business. We must have had over three hundred visitors that evening. There would not have been a kiln plant for many miles around, apart from in High Wycombe.

While it was still daylight we toured the installation and explained how the kilns would operate, the ancillary work that was required to run efficiently, and the sticking and de-sticking procedure. It was a warm moonlit night with some cloud. Our guests chatted with us and to one another; and it was well past eleven o'clock before the last person departed and left us to clear up. Imagine the publicity value measured and compared to the time, effort and cost! The evening was talked about in the trade locally for some time afterwards.

The great day of the opening was in the second week of August 1973. This was Dick Clapham's finest hour, and we were all very proud of our achievements. It was a low key affair and virtually all our employees of all ranks attended. My mother, Margaret Kemp, cut the conventional ribbon and Gill Farrington (née Manion), a very shy young lady at the time, handed her a bouquet of flowers. Happily, Gill is still a very valuable member of our team. We had a few short speeches from LB and Don Rogers, and then the usual refreshments. We also watched a first kiln being filled, the doors closed and the motors started. It took a few more weeks for all of the six kilns to become fully operational.

Our joy was not to last for long as industrial unrest in late autumn compelled the government to declare a three day week, with enormous power cuts for the industry and domestic users.

The Board of Trade, with the electricity boards, set up a tribunal to determine which industrial processes were essential to function continuously without interruption. Brick making and cement manufacturing certainly got exemption very quickly, as did other processes. The Timber Trade Federation's case for kiln owners seemed very low priority.

With such high borrowings on our investment, we were concerned about our future so I decided to defy the law. If the kiln was shut down for one day in the middle of the drying period, the timber would reabsorb all the moisture resulting in a complete waste of energy. To kiln successfully, it has to be an uninterrupted process. LB and Don were not easily intimidated, both of them having very strong personalities. Nevertheless someone must have influenced them to contact me to explain the risk I was taking by not shutting down at the appropriate times.

I insisted that we continued, as I was sure we would get exemption. Still they were not satisfied. I said that if Timbmet got prosecuted I would, as head of the company, have to bear the consequences. I added that if I had to go to prison, I would choose Aylesbury, "as there was a Jewish assistant governor there who would make me comfortable and provide me with kosher food." They left silent and disgruntled. Not many days later owners of timber drying kilns, like others, were permitted to operate normally.

The wonderful trading conditions suddenly changed. The government had problems to settle with the trade unions; and Mr Heath was forced to resign. With the help of one or two secondhand generators and battery lights, we managed to get most of the essential work completed in the dark, but the outlook for Christmas was bleak.

We did not have many large timber contracts left on our books, as we had overbought in the previous year. Unlike other companies we cancelled very little from reliable sources. One large afrormosia contract on passage from Mim gave us concern, as because of the current political situation I felt we did not want to be heavily indebted to our bankers. E Gomme (G Plan) were still busy exporting their modern furniture. I made an appointment with the chief buyer and was very harshly received; he certainly needed the thinner stock, but in order to obtain payment in seven days I virtually had to capitulate to his terms. It meant cash in hand for January 1974, although we had to call twice for the money.

When the goods were ready to be despatched ex-ship, Gomme had no space to take delivery. The buyer asked us to arrange temporary storage. We obliged and brought the afrormosia to our yard against the customary rent and handling charges. By late spring much of it was still at Cumnor. We made an offer to repurchase the balance, as it stood, still un-kilned, and in good condition. Mim as usual pre-dried and put the timber into thin sticks for shipment. Gomme accepted this proposition.

*****

It gave me great pleasure to see how the company had succeeded and grown in the last ten years. Our good reputation for quality and service had spread far and wide and by now we regularly delivered to the north of England and the Scottish borders.

I was most pleased that our loyal workers who had acquired skills and worked a little overtime weekly, were easily able to obtain mortgages, get married and start families. My own family and I moved from a three bedroom to the four bedroom house, with more modern facilities, where we are still living.

CHAPTER 20

1974: An uncertain start

The year started with great fears for the immediate future. The strike ended in mid January and full power services were restored, but many people who had been laid off were not immediately re-employed. Some building projects and public works were postponed and bankruptcies were on the increase. Most timber importers, merchants and traders enjoyed a profitable business period from the autumn of 1972 to October 1973. We fought one another for the smaller volumes that were in demand; we kept reducing prices and gave longer credit, etc. The majority survived: we just gave away the good profits of the previous period.

Gathering resources

We had an NCR '32' Accounts machine on order and took delivery. It was a primitive forerunner of more advanced systems in the future. I found out in later years that we at Timbmet were behind the times in computer use and never caught up fully until 1995-97, under the guidance of Mr John Dobson, our present finance director. We were also slow in concreting the yard. Some customers who visit us now ask jokingly 'Where are the gum boots?' when visiting our premises in winter!

By being very much involved in the day to day conduct of the business, however, Leslie and I had a very good knowledge of the vital statistics needed to steer the ship on an even keel. We were fully confident that we could publish an aerial photo of our premises and survive any interest this might bring from the Inspector of Taxes. It brought doubts from some quarters as a few competitors claimed the piles in the picture were not genuine but superimposed! It helped us to gain new consumer customers, but only gradually as many companies were loath to change suppliers.

We had a good stock reserve air drying which meant that we would kiln mostly from partly air dried stocks, with around 30% moisture content. This helped a steady turn around from our kilns. The African interlocked grained hardwoods benefited from pre-drying and kept in better shape than if kilned from shipping dry, or fresh sawn.

Some shrewd decision making

Mim requested Flatau Dick to sell larger volumes of their production in the UK. Early in March a circular from Montague L Meyer was sent to most importers offering 10,000 cube of prime, shipping dry, Mim production, utile in 700-800 cube bills of lading. I was not surprised that they could not attract even a reasonable counter offer. Timbmet did not need the stock or the expense of purchasing the parcel; nevertheless, we did make an offer and after a few days it was reluctantly accepted. They expressed some doubt about Timbmet's financial strength as we had hardly ever traded in any volume with them, and I suggested they ask their head office to check Trade Indemnity, as I was sure they would quickly receive an adequate report. The local director was back within three hours, and happy to conclude the sale as he did not particularly wish to yard the stock.

I was able to prove to Mim and Flatau Dick that bulk sales of shipping dry lumber even of the highest quality is best marketed to British importers who are prepared to land the goods for air-drying and further processing before offering the stock on the market place. I think Flatau Dick understood my philosophy. British competitors were very jealous of Timbmet's ability to source a large part of the Mim production allocated for sale by them to the UK. We were able to purchase the good quality dimension stock in the principal red hardwoods which put us in a favourable position. We piled the stock out of doors in their widths, and sometimes also in lengths, which was cheaper than full lumber price, and often got a premium for the dry scantlings for skirtings, rails and flooring, etc.

A deputation of UK importers brought this to the attention of the Ghana Timber Marketing Board. The board instructed Mim not to sell any primary species in full specifications to Timbmet for six months. This seemed unfair and we felt badly treated. Mim no doubt thought likewise. We asked Flatau Dick to request that the Marketing Board allocate to us 500m³ of UAC plywood, silver grade, all to be 8' x 4' in various thicknesses for fairly prompt shipment. The obstacle was that Timbmet at the time were not members of the panel products association.

We were able to join the section very quickly and UAC sold us the goods for shipment in 4-6 months time. We had almost forgotten about this new venture, which arrived in good condition and was easily sold to our customers, as it was a well known leading brand.

In about April 1974, M Maurice Binlich visited England and asked to meet me with John McKee of Price Morgan. I readily agreed to an early evening meeting at the Bristol Hotel, London. It seemed that half of the European economy was beginning to slow down, and he made me some favourable proposals for my personal gain, which I rejected outright. Part of the conversation went:

DK	'Britain will be great again.'
MB	'Never.'
DK	'Why?'
MB	'The syndicates will not let you.'
DK	'I am convinced you will be proved wrong.'

M Binlich took this conversation badly and felt somewhat offended, and the meeting ended fairly abruptly. I did not meet him again for some years but the two companies continued to trade together. Neither John nor I realised at the time that "syndicates" to him meant trade unions.

Early Brazil: alternatives to African hardwoods

Sometime in 1974 John McKee, Price Morgan & Co and Michael Sharpe, of Churchill & Sim, each independently made an extensive trip to South America visiting timber producers in Brazil and Bolivia. They journeyed to the remote areas in and around the edges of the jungle. Travelling away from the main routes was tiring, arduous and often frustrating as well as time consuming. They learnt a great deal and seemed to have made the trip just in time. It seemed as if importers from other countries, mainly in Europe, were looking for alternatives to African hardwoods.

Brazil had a more progressive government, willing to make investments in two hydro-electric power stations, and to start construction of the trans-Amazon highway, opening the country to commerce.

The two men wrote a report on their personal experiences and, in places, it reads like Livingstone's description of Africa 150 years earlier! They were both quite sure that a great deal of progress would be made in a short number of years; and, with government grants, new sawmills would be built with the assistance of the World Bank and other international organisations who were keen to provide more employment. The USA began to show considerable interest.

They both listed two principal species, Brazilian mahogany (Swietenia macrophylla) and scented cedar (Cederela odorata). They also recommended another fifteen species for consideration. Some were very soft and light in weight, but most were heavy hardwoods over 800kg per cubic metre dry weight. Some of these are now very popular for decking.

Positive thinking: long term buying

We considered carefully and decided to purchase two species, the mahogany and the cedar. We agreed to invest £30,000 in total, two thirds in the mahogany and the rest in cedar. We purchased four thicknesses giving customers the opportunity to produce prototypes. On arrival we put the timber carefully into stick in an extra shady position in the yard for slow drying; we arranged extra sticking, end waxing against splitting, and covered it on top to save checking. We proudly surveyed the timber at regular intervals to see that it came to no harm. There was a long wait before we made anything of our investment, but we were convinced the day would eventually come!

Phoenix Hardwoods, part of Phoenix Timber Group plc, the large softwood importers, who installed the Mulberry Harbour next to their wharf in Rainham, Essex, decided to have extensive samples shipped of about fifteen species and, after evaluation and financial consideration, they bought two containers of twelve species. Unfortunately, as so often in England, they were too far ahead of time and had to auction most of it ten years later at ridiculous low prices as they are now available FSC certified from sustainable forests. A number of the timbers, such as jatoba and andiroba, are in regular use today with some of the heavy woods in flooring and for exterior cladding and decking.

CHAPTER 21

Trading with Japan

Reciprocating hospitality

Realising that the time would come when we would have to reciprocate the hospitality that I had enjoyed on some of my overseas journeys, I discussed this with my wife. She was a very good cook and hostess and willingly agreed. Our dining room furniture was 'best' government utility as permitted in 1950 when price and quality controls limited the design. We agreed to purchase a new suite. I wanted to go upmarket and chose a Gordon Russell Rio rosewood veneered table seating up to ten people, and two sideboards; they promised to excel themselves with the log for the table top. The chairs were in Indian rosewood, cheaper than the Rio. The trade price for me was £670 complete. I explained that we intended to entertain suppliers who could well show an interest and might visit the factory when in England.

My dear wife objected feeling that the expense was much more than we should spend; and our accountants would not allow us to purchase the furniture through the company, as it would give us a lot of personal benefit. I then involved my mother-in-law, who tactfully made peace between us and persuaded her daughter to agree to this expenditure.

Deputation from Ghana

Within a few weeks of delivery we had a request from the Ghana Cabinet Office for a party of ministers of the military government to pay us a visit. This coincided with the completion of a ground floor office extension, so before we moved in, we collected the dining room table and chairs from home and were able to seat and entertain the distinguished guests in comfort.

Trading with Japan; and a visit to Oxford

By 1974 Timbmet was probably the largest importer of Japanese hardwoods. About 85% was oak and the balance elm, ash and lime. We only bought stock from Hokkaido Island, the most northerly island in Japan, where the climate was similar to Central Europe, with four seasons each year. In addition we imported wide Japanese oak for the manufacture of high quality coffins. This product sold well alongside our English elm coffin boards. Very few importers visited the producing mills. The principal UK agents representing the shipper/exporters occasionally travelled to Japan, visiting the trading houses in Tokyo, who were often also bankers financing the mills, fixing prices and were responsible for the shipment, documentation and collection of payments for the goods.

The Japanese were good businessmen, tough negotiators and, on the whole, fair minded. Quality claims did arise but were mainly minor, often resulting from goods having been shipped inadequately air dried to withstand the six weeks' voyage. Perhaps it was that the producing mills had been too anxious to get payments for the merchandise from the export houses. Occasionally we had to resort to arbitration but the Japanese always paid claims promptly without having to apply for a court order to obtain settlement. We for our part made sure we did not resort to arbitration unless we were convinced that we had a just case.

One of our large regular suppliers was the Shin Asahigawa Co. By Japanese standards, this was a smaller international trading house, importing and exporting timber. To this day, Japan imports and consumes the largest quantity of timber per head of population compared with all other countries in the world. Wooden structures offer greater safety in a country prone to earthquakes.

The president of Shin had never been to England and requested Jack Furtado, of his UK selling agents C Leary & Co, at short notice to arrange an itinerary for himself and his party. Unknown to them it happened to be Easter week. Jack knew I would help if possible and would give up the bank holiday Easter Monday to meet and entertain the shipper. I willingly agreed, not realising that my few senior colleagues had long since made firm commitments to their families. I enlisted the help of Tom Bunting (our then midland sales representative) who was a good timber expert, highly intelligent and well informed, Larry Smith, who was the senior yard foreman (ex Wm Mallinson) with a good practical timber background, and one other person, whose name I cannot remember.

I made a good choice by contacting the licensee of the White Hart at Fyfield. He was the first landlord at the house in modern times. He had international catering experience in the large London hotels and he was willing to prepare a Japanese style buffet for our visitors in the pub's English medieval type surroundings.

The White Hart was built by the executors of Sir John Golafre, during the reign of Henry the VI, Lord of the Manor at Fyfield. Sir John had died in 1442 leaving a sum of money for the establishment of a chantry priest house to accommodate a priest and five almsmen. The building is partly on two floors. No doubt many poor travellers also slept there when passing through on their journeys. In 1548 the chantries were abolished and their properties confiscated by the Tudor government. At some stage St John's College acquired the property; they own a lot of land in the parish. In 1963 the building was modernised and many of its old features exposed. The oak arched braced roof is a particularly fine example of early English roof structure.

Our visitors came and we had a wonderful sunny spring day. We spent a good deal of time inspecting timber at our yard. The export manager, Mr Takahara, spoke reasonable English, and with the party was a Japanese journalist, based in London, who spoke excellent English; he acted as a general guide to the party. The president of the company was accompanied by his export manager and four senior employees, probably mill managers. It is sometimes surprising how timber experts can communicate with one another in trade matters by signs, body language and sketches, despite not speaking a common language.

Time went very quickly, and we adjourned for lunch. Our visitors were overjoyed with the table laden with Japanese delicacies and considered themselves very honoured by what had been prepared for them. After the food and drink was consumed, the Japanese journalist passed round "dirty pictures." This provided entertainment for some of the party, while the president of Shin, Jack Furtado and I discussed business matters and forward purchases. Tom Bunting made a useful contribution with his knowledge of the home timber industry, which was translated for our guests. Before they finally left Mr Hirato made a short speech and particularly thanked the landlord for the spread provided.

From this visit, we gained the ability to communicate our needs to Mr Hirato in Tokyo, which did not please their selling agents. By being able to give the finer details directly to the sellers, many misunderstandings were avoided.

A few years later, Mr Hirato was posted by Shin to Brazil and he offered us Brazilian mahogany and other species. The qualities were at the lower end and below our requirements, and after about 1980 due to high prices, Japanese oak lost its popularity in the UK. It had dominated the market for thirty years and was replaced by North American white oak. We gradually lost our personal contact with the Japanese.

CHAPTER 22

Tactical moves
1974-75

Ambitious buying and calculated risks

On 13th October 1974, I agreed to meet Philippe Netter of the J Lalanne group of companies who wanted to come on his own without John McKee or anyone from Price Morgan, their agents. We had ample notice, and also knew that the shippers had a large volume of lumber to sell as the European markets had slowed down six months after recession hit the UK.

In England the outlook for the following year looked more promising, so Leslie and I sat down together and worked out a specification for species and thicknesses in the timber species Lalanne wanted to sell. Some of the goods were no doubt already in stock at their mills in West Africa. The total came to about 5,000m³, mainly utile, sapele (the mild aboudikru) and iroko from the high forests, freer of calcium and lighter in colour; and also small quantities of logs, A/B grade in utile, iroko and walnut, only straight grown and of large diameter, free of bad heart and shakes.

We demanded a better average of lengths and widths, a large volume of ¾" and 4" thicknesses, more than we would need for our normal sales. All were to be extra full cut to lengths and widths, and on special credit terms. We had our programme ready a week or so before Philippe's visit. The thought of entering into such a deal began to worry me, and I developed severe back pain.

*****

I was born with a curvature of the spine. A great deal was done to help me as a youngster: special exercises, massage, and the wearing of a straitjacket, as well as lying suspended on my back and being supported by a canvas face mask at a 15° angle on a piece of blockboard to help straighten my spine. By my early teens, my back seemed fairly normal and in first years with Timbmet I did manual work as well, often receptioning timber purchases and helping out in the yard.

This recurrence was a shock to me. My doctor, whom I had not seen for many years, told me to take painkillers and grin and bear it! I told him what had been done to help straighten my spine, and he replied that had I lived in Oxford I would have been operated on at the Nuffield Orthopaedic Hospital. I think the pressure I put on myself over the intention to purchase large parcels of timber at the time when the "big boys" were de-stocking caused the pain to worsen.

Careful bargaining

On the appointed day, Philippe Netter duly arrived at our offices at four o'clock. As he seemed very young, I asked him whether he was authorised to make decisions on behalf of his company. He was, or pretended to be, very offended, but we made it up over a cup of English tea. I introduced him to LB and Adrian Sumner, our sales manager, and talked about the general business conditions in England and how at such times we need better than average parcels of timber as customers have time on their hands and could be extra "choosy" when, after all, they are only purchasing a natural product and not components or even a manufactured item. Just after five o'clock, Leslie and Adrian excused themselves and I was left to negotiate point by point with Philippe.

- The general quality
- All boards and planks to be full cut in lengths, widths and thicknesses
- The average lengths and widths
- All timber to be shipped or despatched in thin laths
- For African walnut, a lower quality and a higher sap content to be allowed.
- Payment terms

Timbmet wanted delayed shipments for late spring 1975, but Lalanne wanted to ship in January or February 1975. We agreed to this and, fortunately, the majority arrived at Easter. The greatest problems were the volumes of thin and thick board. I gradually gave in, as planned, to allow the shippers to feel they were gaining concessions. Anything he did not want to supply was deducted from the original volume, which did not please him.

The hardest bargain was over the prices Timbmet offered to pay. Lalanne needed the order more than I realised. On my part, it was a long term calculated risk. When finished, we put down the most important details on paper and each signed a copy. It was past nine o'clock. Late dining was unusual outside the big cities in England at that time. I was prepared for it and had made a provisional booking at a small Italian restaurant in Abingdon. We ate a reasonable meal, and ended the evening talking amicably about our respective families, our backgrounds and the future. I took him to Didcot station where he caught a late train to Paddington.

For some weeks a few more minor concessions were demanded by the Paris head office. The most difficult adjustments were on the sap content allowed on the African walnut (lovoa) which was most likely justified, and by the end of November all contracts were exchanged. Philippe, no doubt, was praised for achieving and concluding such a large deal.

Small parcels of this purchase started to arrive in January and February 1975, but the bulk was shipped to Avonmouth on the "Oranyan," arriving in Easter week. Rosie and I had booked an overseas holiday, so Leslie had the pleasure and honour of seeing the hatches opened. This was the largest single shipment to date to Avonmouth from West Africa. We managed to clear it all from the quay in the statutory time limit, some to trade kilns, and the majority to our yard in Cumnor.

A further tempting commitment

C Leary arranged for me to meet Philippe Le-Flanchec, who had a sawmill in Abidjan. Jack Furtado informed me that his company SEBC was closing for six months and that he wished to dispose of sawn stocks, so I agreed to come to London in the early evening. I did admit to him that I was in quite a lot of pain but he did not agree to come to Oxford instead. He phoned me again at midday suggesting that if I did not feel well perhaps we should call off the meeting. My suspicious mind sounded alarm bells: who else might get the bargain deal instead of Timbmet? I suggested I came by train and that Jack might be on the platform to meet me and put me into a taxi for the journey to the hotel. Jack, who was embarrassed, had to admit they were unable to get insurance cover from TI [Trade Indemnity] for this transaction. No doubt Price Morgan had applied for cover for the large deal the night before, in spite of previous assurances that they had no upper limit for Timbmet!

I phoned Donald Wright the senior partner of C Leary & Co and expressed my dismay. He apologised. His excuse was that he had been unable to reach the managing director of TI, who was abroad. He agreed I should come to London and he would endeavour to reach the MD and use maximum persuasion to extend the TI limit for Timbmet, if only on a temporary basis! I got to Paddington and a beaming Jack was on the platform. I could see from his face that the answer was positive.

Jack outlined the stock availabilities: nothing as exciting as from Lalanne. The quantities were smaller and the specifications fixed and could not be improved on, as timber for sale was already produced. The prices were reasonable and the credit terms exceptional. We had plenty of time for serious business discussions, particularly about trading conditions in Europe. By about 8.30 pm they seemed to be anxious for me to leave. As I made it appear that I was not in an exceptional hurry, they admitted that they were to meet Peter Jary of Boulton & Paul for dinner and a late show, and wished to change into evening dress. It was obvious that some long and wide utile and sapele were being kept back for him, no doubt some sill stock for window bottom rails and also 4" x 4" utile squares for newels for their Melton Mowbray factory.

I struggled home by taxi and train glad, as I told them, to get back to Oxford. In a few days I had come to terms with the calculated risks I had taken and felt calmer. Slowly my back pains receded. Fortunately it was not my heart, as this would have been more serious. A year later I looked back well satisfied with the decisions I had made.

1975: A retrospective look at Timbmet's standing

In late 1974 Mr Wilson won re-election by a very narrow margin. His Chancellor, Mr Dennis Healey, had to cope with a £4 thousand million deficit. Inflation was in double figures and high wage increases were permitted in the hope of economic growth. Nevertheless, the year started well for Timbmet and probably also for other old established firms serving the quality end of the market.

Looking back now I wonder what percentage of the hardwood industry in the UK Timbmet had gained in those last few years? It would take a great deal of time and research to establish meaningfully accurate figures. Unfortunately HM Customs' monthly statistics were never the most accurate; and since we joined the European community, the mandatory

Intrastat records have never been correct. It seems that goods were arriving from the EEC undeclared. In the period up to 1975 and for a few years after, three species formed the bulk of hardwood requirements at the cheaper end of the trade, but Timbmet did not handle vast quantities of keruing, ramin, or second quality beech.

There may be records for overall felling licences granted by the Forestry Commission for native hardwoods. As the trade was free from restrictions for the last twenty years there are no statistics available as to the approximate volume suitable for furniture and joinery as opposed to the lower end, for fencing, etc. We dealt in the best qualities, the prime part of the annual crop, purchased from native sawmills as freshly sawn or home-grown round solid logs which we converted. We then seasoned and kilned before marketing.

After a lot of thought and consultation of old records, I concluded we would have traded about 4% of the total hardwoods imported to the British Isles in 1974. What mattered most to us was the good name we enjoyed in the trade for quality and service at keen prices. The greatest satisfaction for all of us was how we gradually broke down the resistance of old and long established businesses to give us their trade. This trend continued year by year until some of the most conservative firms, used to manufacturing joinery for the ministries and royal palaces, entrusted us with their requirements.

*****

In 1975, for the first time since the end of the Second World War, the building, joinery and furniture industry in Western Europe slowed down as most of the war damage repairs were finished. There was surplus stock of dry S/E African hardwoods, mainly in Germany, and African species of logs sawn in France. These stocks were offered at a reasonable price, on behalf of continental importers, by the British agents who had offices in Europe: Churchill & Sim, Charles Craig and C Leary.

Klaus Block, metal, plastics and timber broker in Hamburg, handled considerable quantities of sawn dry hardwoods belonging to Danzer & Co., the well known veneer producers. Stocks in England were low due to British importers not buying for over a year. In particular the popular African species were only available for quick delivery in shipping dry condition.

CHAPTER 23

A trip to Yugoslavia

Expansion at Cumnor

We received approval for the erection of our vehicle repair workshop and sheds nos. 5-8, with a total floor area of 60,000 square feet, which meant making minor adjustments in the height and, above all, locating a supply of the coloured roof panels the Vale of White Horse D. C. demanded. We entered an agreement with Kingerlee to build all this over a period of time not exceeding five years, but allowing completion in three years by mutual consent. Jim proudly took ownership of his "castle" eight months later which enabled him to maintain the ever growing fleet of vehicles, cranes, side-loaders and company cars.

We advertised for sales staff and were fortunate enough to have applications from two capable people working as representatives for Turner Hunters, a subsidiary of Wm Mallinson. Both men had a good knowledge of the trade; Mike Mowforth took over the North Midlands and some of Cheshire and Lancashire, giving Tom Bunting a better opportunity to cover the Midlands in depth; and Vic Webb, a real Cockney, took on North London and Essex, which helped George Clarkson to concentrate more in the East Midlands, Norfolk and Suffolk.

Wrestling with computing

With the projected increase in business we started to look for a small computer system. A French company, by the name of Logabax (today trading as Olivetti Logabax), who had an accounts mini processor with a 32kb capacity that seemed just right for us, was recommended. Leslie spent many weeks meticulously writing up our office procedures step by step, working alongside two of their technical consultants. Gradually two of our office ladies received training in the use of the system at the Logabax offices in northwest London. Leslie and I were invited to the final demonstration and acceptance prior to delivery. The equipment arrived at our offices accompanied by two technical experts.

Unfortunately, we could not successfully operate the system which was disappointing, to say the least. Logabax kept rewriting the software, arguing that they had not had an accurate brief from Timbmet. Their practice was that in order for them to make a sale, they first introduced the most experienced staff to new clients; as soon as the contract was signed by the customer, they withdrew the skilled personnel before the full specification had been written or tested.

In later years, on all but the last purchase, the same people were never there from the start of the project until the completion, which created unnecessary problems and delays. The average smaller firm, overwhelmed by the big changes involved, do not study their suppliers' written contract in adequate detail. Also, it seems to be general practice in the trade to undersell the capacity the client needs to gain the benefit from their investment. We certainly could have never grown to our present size without the aid of technology. The only technical help Leslie had was from my brother-in-law, who was a consultant in the electrical industry. He probably blamed us for not educating ourselves earlier in modern accounts practice; and there were times when I felt like writing off our investment and starting afresh with a different firm.

Dan escapes to Yugoslavia

Whilst all this was going on I escaped for a few days on my next journey to Yugoslavia.

I continued to visit Yugoslavia with Giles (of Churchill & Sim) every two or three years. In May 1975 we visited two main oak supplying sawmills in Croatia including Novi Selec, specialising in wainscot butts, and then we continued to Dubrovnik where Giles had been invited to negotiate quantities and prices of beech for the coming season. The Sipad representatives liked to come down to Dubrovnik on the coast because even in May, Sarajevo has a very oppressive climate. We stayed at the 'Argentina,' a comfortable modernised pre-war hotel. At the time it was only for official visitors and the communist party hierarchy.

Giles and I met Mr Tratnik and a colleague from Sipad in the morning. After a short introduction and pleasantries it was politely suggested that I went for a walk in the town as they wanted to discuss the overall strategy without me. I had no option but to leave. I walked down into the famous walled city nearby where there were two rows of shops that were fairly empty of merchandise. I noticed a jeweller, which was surprisingly well stocked, and amongst the display was a tin amulet with strange, mystical lettering, probably Hebrew. The owner of the shop wanted a lot of money for it but I managed to persuade him to let me have it at a much reduced price, as I couldn't see that many people would be interested in it. I realised that it was a good luck charm, perhaps for a newborn baby. I still have it to this day, in our display cabinet at home, but I failed to show it for identification to a number of Jewish scholars of mysticism who occasionally visit Oxford University. Perhaps I should visit "Madonna" who may have the explanation!

I felt very uneasy to be away from the discussions and returned to the hotel before time. When I got to the foyer, the receptionist recognised me and asked me to join the meeting. Mr Tratnik and his colleague appeared to have a language barrier and seemed to be in a muddle. Presumably on other occasions a person with better knowledge of English had been present.

Laid out on the table was a large sheet of graph paper with the quantities they wished to sell in the UK market for the seven months to the end of 1974. This gave details of:

1. grades;
2. thicknesses;
3. short boards;
4. proportion of steamed to unsteamed;
5. proposed monthly deliveries;
6. percentage of log sawn mainly with one square edge;
7. suggested prices in pounds sterling coupled to a currency clause;
8. special discount rates to the biggest UK buyer.

It seemed clear to an experienced businessman what they hoped to achieve in sales, specification and monetary return.

My presence helped to diffuse misunderstandings. I translated into German and gave Giles's views of the market position in England. They must have appreciated the longstanding relationship between Churchill & Sim and Sipad, and ought to have known that Giles had made great efforts to successfully market the Sipad brand in the UK, and to respect his ideas. Giles couldn't understand why the Bosnians annually wanted to get a higher price, and demanded that they ought to make a bigger effort to improve their general efficiency.

After a short discussion, someone suggested that we have a break for lunch. This was readily accepted and they proposed we went down to the quayside and have lunch in one of the cafés. Before the food arrived, the local Riesling flowed freely as we toasted the timber trade, the health and prosperity of Yugoslavia, and Britain, and Marshall Tito. When the fish was finally served it was excellent. After a time I did not know whether I was a Gliksten or Timbmet employee, and the two Bosnians even less so! When we finally had a sweet course, it must have been 4.30 pm. I must have been very drunk; I was never a teetotaller, but neither was I accustomed to excess volumes! It was mutually agreed to resume our discussions after breakfast the next morning. Although it was not far to the hotel, we found a taxi to take us back: I didn't go to dinner that night, but slept it off.

I met Giles the next morning over breakfast and we discussed how we would approach the situation when we met the Sipad representatives. Due to the economic downturn in England, it was doubtful that Giles could sell the total volume they wanted in the current year, and even less likely at a higher price.

Sipad knew as well as we did that there was never enough $1\frac{1}{4}''$ (32mm) w/e available for the quality English chair manufacturers. Too many short boards were on offer for our market as was the case nearly every year. In a critical market the colour of the un-steamed should be extra 'white' if possible. I suggested that we point out the lack of discipline we had seen in the mills recently, which made it difficult to achieve our standards in spite of their having such good raw material. Sipad must be told of the thicknesses required for late autumn and early winter because after the best logs are sawn it is difficult to make any alterations in size later in the season.

As hardly anyone is safe in such political regimes, it was always doubtful how much of all this Mr Tratnik would be prepared to convey to his top management. My strongest and possibly my main argument, which was communicated to their head office, was that Yugoslavia was a very good customer of Britain. They needed some of the raw materials from our dominions and they were re-equipping their industries with British machinery. I knew the balance of payments was in our favour so I asked why they couldn't sell to us in sterling without the currency clause, as Yugoslavia was spending more pounds sterling in England than the value of their total exports to the UK.

We parted the best of friends. No doubt Giles knew what the shippers expected from him but we were both doubtful that British customers would be likely to have the capacity to buy the full quantities in 1974 as in the previous year. I gained a good deal of insight into the British Yugoslav beech trade. I also felt sure that from now onwards we would be able to buy Timbmet's beech requirements at the most favourable rates although we were not yet in the top league of buyers in England. I doubt if I ever revealed much of this to anyone except to my colleague Leslie Boustead.

Our flight back to London was due the following day, so in the evening I made Giles come with me to an open air concert in the old town. The Leipzig Gevand Haus orchestra played Beethoven's Fifth Symphony and the Trumpet Concerto by Leopold Mozart, father of Wolfgang Amadeus, with the trumpeters standing on the ramparts of the walls.

The computing system settles down

When I returned from my travels Leslie, with the help of one of the directors from Logabax headquarters in Paris, had managed to improve the computer software. The young ladies in the office had gradually become accustomed to operating the system and in general things were more bearable in the accounts department. The enlarged sales team worked well but it was thought necessary to appoint Mike Mowforth to succeed Adrian Sumner as Sales Manager. We realised soon after he had joined us that he had the right personality for the job and we felt also that he would retain his own customers.

We gradually gained a lot of confidence in Adrian who was a mature, well balanced young man and happily married to Lynne. He was reliable, had a good memory and willingly went out into the yard to observe operations and, if necessary, muck in! We decided to meet at lunchtime and confided in him our thoughts for the future development of Timbmet without offering him an immediate title; he became my personal assistant in purchasing and was in charge of the expanding shipping department.

Finance management

As demand improved in 1975 we were in a very strong position to meet the requirements of our customers and also to gain new accounts. Most of the large firms had reduced their stock in 1974 and some overseas suppliers stopped production; and Timbmet had a vast stock of air dried on the ground which could be finished quickly in the kilns.

While we enjoyed the progress and expansion of the business there were times when we needed advice. Problems did arise during strikes, and when credit restrictions were imposed by the Bank of England on joint stock banks, reducing their lending to commercial enterprises. Our company accountant, Edward Greenbury, always found time to discuss our problems and fears. He gave us good advice and often consulted his partners at Hacker Young on our behalf.

Different bank managers appointed at Barclays Old Bank, High Street, Oxford, varied in the amount of help they could give us. Sometimes they came from branches that catered for a majority of wealthy private clients rather than commerce, so their experience was more limited. Leslie and I met some of the directors of the Thames Valley board of Barclays Bank in Reading. They in turn introduced us to the newly formed Barclays Merchant Bank plc with premises at Gracechurch Street, EC3. I went to London twice a year to have discussions with the senior management. My principal contact was Mr John Stanton. The junior staff included several highly educated, capable young men, relatives of the original founding families who, a hundred years earlier, had given up their independent regional banks to form the national Barclays Bank.

These young "scouts" came to Oxford regularly to inspect our progress and we learnt from one another. They listened to us and sometimes expressed views with which Leslie and I did not agree. Politically they were ultra-Conservative. One of them, Oliver Stocken, was also a well known athlete and, I believe, marathon runner who, a few years later, held the top position in Barclays, Australia.

Another, David Salisbury, was instrumental in an outline proposal for Timbmet to be floated on the London Stock Exchange. I queried our size. Timbmet was not exactly a household word with investment houses, even less so with the public. I was told that they were planning six flotations simultaneously for mid 1976. All the other companies involved had a much larger capital base and together we would create an adequate interest for the issues to succeed. The bank was also prepared to advertise the background of all the firms for three months before the flotation, and this was unusual. Needless to say, my mother, a major shareholder of Timbmet, was not agreeable. Leslie and I were also against it. We wanted to develop Timbmet without bearing the responsibility to institutional or public shareholders, or the possibility of being swallowed up in due course by "larger fish." We continued to enjoy our occasional pub lunches at Cumnor with the junior ranks.

We were too small to interest Trade Indemnity at the London head office and had to be satisfied at being in touch with their Bristol branch. We negotiated for a long time for a policy that would protect us against an annual ceiling of bad debts related to turnover. This was supposedly unacceptable in 1975, but it is an option available now. At the time we felt that individual record-keeping customer by customer, and constantly watching their insured limit, was beyond the capacity of our small office staff. TI was keen to see how we opened accounts and controlled our credit ledger. Many Timbmet suppliers and agents insured their debts with TI, so our frankness with the underwriters helped us to obtain larger insurance cover for our shippers, even if the Timbmet debts remained uninsured.

A special relationship

We were loyal suppliers to Anglian Windows who were growing from modest beginnings to becoming leaders of the double glazing industry. We had great admiration for Mr J Williams, the founder of the business. At first our supplies were well air dried, ex-yarded stocks of African hardwoods, but by 1978 we were importing Far Eastern lauan for their requirements. In time, in order to retain our premier supply position we had to involve the East Asiatic Co., owners of the Luzon Mahogany Co. better known as LMC, in a joint venture. We disclosed our respective margins to Mr Williams, and provisions were made for currency and freight variations as well as strict payment conditions.

This arrangement worked well for a number of years. Our rivals tried very hard to spoil this relationship, but it remained invincible. In the best years, the annual turnover increased to almost £2,000,000. Great credit for this is due to Bob Spiers of EAC, and our Leslie Boustead. Needless to say, over such a long period of time disputes and friction did arise, but it was all of manageable proportions.

CHAPTER 24

1976

Arbitration and arbitrators

Leslie Boustead attended a half day seminar arranged by the TTF on arbitration in the timber industry. This was given by John H Jordan, an accredited member of the London Chartered Institute of Arbitrators. He was a most knowledgeable person and Leslie struck up a very useful friendship with him although there was a large age gap between them. John had retired early as director of a small beech importing firm and occupied himself as an arbitrator. The trade then settled its disputes regularly by arbitration rather than resorting to the law courts which also provided a platform for dealing with overseas suppliers over quality, and other issues. The London Institute was highly respected throughout the world, and John would advise us when to negotiate for an allowance or when it would be more appropriate to seek arbitration.

In 1975 we bought a parcel of Nigerian 'Lagos' mahogany, which had a good reputation for quality and texture. When the goods arrived a few months later, I could not believe my eyes: there was no doubt that there had been a deliberate mix up somewhere along the line. We informed the supplier of our intention to appoint John H Jordan as our arbitrator in this dispute, and requested the shipper to do likewise. Reluctantly, he agreed as advised by his British selling agent.

John was very correct. He did not want to see the parcel until the day both arbitrators had arranged to come jointly to inspect and adjudicate. They came, inspected, withdrew, privately discussed the pros and cons, and left. About three weeks later John asked us to pay the fees and upon receipt he would forward the judgment to us. We duly did so. We were shocked at the outcome: the shipper was declared in breach of his contract, but the damages awarded were negligible. We could not have got the difference from a salvage buyer in order to break even on the full value of the parcel. Arbitrators do not have to give a reason for their decisions. Hard pressed, John told us that when placing the order we should have taken greater care in defining the area in which the timber was grown. I thought Lagos meant the coastal area near the capital city, and the logs had a very good reputation for even colour, texture and having only a small sap ring. About ten years later we brought up the subject again when we met at a trade function. He told me quietly that the British government had requested the Association of Arbitrators to avoid creating additional friction between our two countries, if at all possible. During the bitter civil war, much blood had been shed and strife caused. Now, as is the custom, thirty years later the cabinet papers of the period were being published and include a reference to the issue of British relations with Nigeria during the war.

Generally speaking, if the shipper is not prepared to meet the claim as agreed by the arbitrators, the importers are entitled to obtain an award from the British courts. If the shipper still refuses to meet his obligation, one would have to resort to the courts of the land where the timber originated. This could mean a very expensive additional financial cost with no certainty of the outcome. Several times in such cases, I approached the commercial attaché of the embassy of the country where the timber originated, and in all cases, through presenting Timbmet's case, the embassy eventually persuaded the suppliers to pay the damages.

As soon as any shipper was notified of a claim, his first step was to blame the shipping company for allegedly stowing cargo on deck and not clearing the water from the bilges, etc. so we were accustomed to having marine surveyors visit our yard for their inspection of cargoes. One of the timber specialist firms was Johnson, Son & Mowatt; more often than not, it was a very mature Mr Castle who came. He was a typical Englishman and often reluctant to comment, but as I got to know him better he would explain whether he considered any damage or loss had occurred during the voyage. They often made enquiries with their agents at the loading port; they also checked on weather conditions in the country of origin and during the voyage which could have caused undue splitting or surface checking, or other damage, to the cargo. Many international shipping companies chose the London courts to settle any disputes, and their condition of carriage was endorsed accordingly on the bill of lading. British marine surveyors were in demand all over the world to assess damage to ships and cargo.

Plywood from Israel

By 1976 we were importing small quantities of Israeli WBP [water and boil proofed] bonded "Tabor" brand plywood. The goods were shipped on flat trailers of 26m³ each and these small quantities were an advantage from the start. The plywood had an excellent reputation, made from okoume throughout, or from African mahogany for the best marine grade. The production was of uniform quality, produced by several kibbutz owned mills and from two partly privately owned factories. The central sales agency "Israel Plywood" visited its customers regularly, accompanied by their British agents, Churchill & Sim. I got to know one of the sales managers, Chanoch Kovarski, who as a younger man had been engaged in producing the boards. We kept in touch and he informed me of any new developments or price rises.

We were buying CFG [Companie Forestière de Gambon] plywood from a French company based in Paris, whose UK agents were also Churchill & Sim. I was anxious to know Bert Springall better as he had an excellent reputation in the plywood industry and was highly regarded internationally. No doubt accustomed to trading in very large volumes he was not too inclined to spend time with me. However, he also represented the Israeli plywood industry, and one day in spring 1977 he said, "I will be in Israel in May, why don't you come along? I shall be partly on holiday and we could meet at leisure." Rosie and I happened to be thinking on similar lines but had not fully made up our minds. I said I would phone him back the next day. I consulted my better half and she did not need a lot of persuading!

A visit to Israel

Bert, together with Chanoch Kovarski, who was sales director of Israel Plywood, the export agency for both Kibbutz and privately owned manufacturers, met us at a posh restaurant in Tel Aviv. We spent some hours together and came round to talking about all manner of things. Naturally Middle East politics was on the menu. When it came to choosing, my wife kicked my leg under the table and whispered, "Don't order meat." I had never realised you could eat 'non kosher' in Israel.

Bert gave me the following advice: "You are trading successfully in a wide range of quality hardwoods. Purchase in addition quality decorative plywood and chipboard, and you can't go wrong. Leave the bulk plywood trade to the big specialist importers." Never was better advice given. Together we visited the main plywood factory at Afikim; and a year or two later when we were on holiday in Israel again, we stayed for a short time on the kibbutz and saw a little of life in a communal settlement. We also met a few families with whom we maintained contact. Bert and I had a lot in common and from our first meeting we spent time together socially, and often met his wife Olive. Adrian got to know him as well, and when Bert had to retire early because of ill health, he moved to Milford on Sea where Adrian and Lynne had a holiday home; I believe they played a lot of golf together.

Panel business

Bert introduced us to Charles Marien at Meerbeek. Marien was one of the oldest panel manufacturers in Belgium; it was a very family orientated business, and we got on well with Charles. Marien started this business peeling locally grown aspen ash and beech logs from the Ardennes forest and manufacturing woven baskets for the vegetable and fruit trade. They also grew large, sweet, red Belgian hothouse grapes which were famous all over Western Europe. For some years we received a large bunch of grapes for Christmas, delivered on their behalf from Covent Garden.

Leslie and I decided to give Adrian a free hand to purchase panels although obviously at the beginning we made decisions together since none of us at Timbmet had a great deal of experience in sheet materials. So Adrian was able to make his first trip abroad.

Our men took a long time to learn that you do not walk with dirty, hobnailed boots on fine veneered boards. We decided to have the boards packaged in small cartons as the Israelis did, but we often we had to pay a surcharge for the service. Even so on many occasions we had to break open the packs as customers would only buy as many pieces as they required for immediate use. Later we fitted out part of a storage shed with racks from which we were able to pick the loose sheet orders.

This business grew fairly quickly and we found we needed a second supplier. The local panel factories were overwhelmed with orders for the European community, which included office buildings being built in and around Brussels. We chose also to trade with De Coene Products and for a number of years dealt with Fred Belemans. In the last year before he retired, we purchased £750,000 of panel products from the company. His successor was Simon Gerring, who again will have retired by now.

Frederick needed a full meal at lunchtime, otherwise he became impossibly bad tempered in the afternoon. He appreciated that I could not cope with a full lunch as I would have gone to sleep but Adrian could manage the big meals. When Fred ate he wanted to concentrate and enjoy his food without talking to anyone. We found we could not provide a meal to his complete satisfaction on his annual visit as at the time there were scarcely any gourmet restaurants locally whose cooking was up to the highest continental standards. He, no doubt, put up with second best as our account seemed to be of value to him!

Furniture manufacturing: strips and squares

For many years Timbmet regularly supplied Japanese oak strips and squares for the manufacture of desks and tables for classrooms and other educational purposes. We had to buy well ahead of our requirements as we had assured Papworth Industries, at Papworth Everard, near Cambridge, of continuity of supply for their production. It was a great shock when, with very little notice, we were told the Ministry of Education had changed the timber to African mahogany. We pleaded for three months' delay before the change was implemented, but to no avail. We would not be able to maintain the business, as Gliksten hardwoods, with their own concessions and sawmill in Ghana, were able to undercut us. We had a fair stock of oak drying for this contract, all under cover in store at Surrey Commercial Docks in SE London. The timber took a long time to clear.

We were on very good terms with Mr Jack Cohen in Brighton, the founder of Jaycee furniture. He produced a good middle priced range of solid oak English style reproduction furniture. The company grew in size year by year and was one of the few in this price bracket successfully exporting to Germany, Belgium and Holland. Mr Cohen held seminars advising his English competitors to do likewise.

For a number of years he bought all his timber personally. We trusted each other, but we seldom met. We received his detailed requirements ninety days ahead of delivery, and we constantly updated ourselves with market prices and availabilities and nearly always got the bulk of his orders. The price negotiations and final specifications were discussed on the last Friday afternoon of each quarter of the year: we cleared our desk and laid out our stall, ready to negotiate over the telephone. Although some changes in design were made, the basic timber specification remained comparable.

As transport from Japan took six weeks, it left just about enough time to kiln the material in the thinner sizes, but not the thicker stock for which

the requirements were only small. The main difficulty was to find enough
1½" oak No 1 C & S grade, plain sawn for his tabletops. We had to buy a
lot of FAS to get the lower grade which was of much better quality than
today's American equivalent. Occasionally we were let down by our
suppliers. To help out, we offered Mr Cohen FAS without a price increase,
but he did not want to accept this. At times he preferred to stop the table
production for a few days, at great inconvenience to his customers. Once
we offered No 1 C & S quartered which created a hearty laugh. How
could I supply figured wood one week and plain sawn the next?

Jack Cohen was not in the best of health, so gradually he delegated
some of his responsibilities. He appointed a timber buyer, who very
quickly gave some of his business to the timber agents who started to
trade direct with the consumers. We tried to avoid giving business to
these firms but did not always succeed as they often represented the best
shippers. Unfortunately, Mr Cohen died at a comparatively early age, and
Jaycee was sold to Stag Furniture, and later to Bevan Funnell of Worthing.

Negotiating stocks

The loss of these accounts was a setback, and hurt our pride, but we were
determined to find new customers to replace the lost turnover. Our first
task was to try to renege on some of the contracts of Japanese oak in
specialised sizes. Timbmet has never liked to cancel a contract that was
not overdue since this is considered sharp and unethical business
practice. We tried to replace the cancelled strips and squares with popular
lumber sizes, which suited a more varied clientele, and we also sold off
1½" Japanese oak very reasonably. Both Adrian and I were engaged on
swap deals with shippers: he must have found this wheeling and dealing
strange as he was still very young and inexperienced.

A Danish contact

In the spring of 1976, I had a confidential telephone call from the East
Asiatic Company in Denmark requesting me to see Finn Grube who was
visiting England on a marketing study. I readily agreed; by now I had met
EAC home trained executives. They were usually well educated and,
above all, spoke several languages. They also had enough commercial

flair for international trade. Although their in-house school was perhaps not quite up to the standard of a modern business academy it offered a very practical training.

I spent some time with Finn and, at the end of our discussions, was convinced that EAC intended to set up their own selling organisation within the UK in the not too distant future. Up to now they had been selling their own productions and timber they purchased from various parts of the world via the traditional agents in England. I purchased 3000m³ kiln dried Luzon lauan to be delivered in three equal portions in February, March and April 1977. I requested that my offer be kept confidential, and he readily agreed. A few weeks later there was an announcement in the trade press that EAC were opening an office in London, to be managed by Finn Grube.

I concluded the final details of the contract in July 1976 for shipment on early 1977. By autumn, the news had been leaked out deliberately as Finn felt our large purchase would persuade others to follow suit. This parcel, although in parts only of average quality, was not all as clear grade as promised; however, it sold well and gave Timbmet a handsome return. Due to the volume available, it quickly made us the leading importers of lauan in the UK and we were the talk of the trade. It was one of the very few occasions in my long experience when an industry was prepared to pay a small premium for a superior product, giving preference to lauan over meranti.

Finn was still a young man and was the Middle East sales manager for EAC, based with his family in Beirut, Lebanon. In 1976 they closed the office because the political situation in the area had become too dangerous.

CHAPTER 25

1976
The home market

Don Rogers left Timbmet in 1976 to become the purchasing manager of Bridgend Timber who bought all timber requirements for the Christie Tyler group. A few years later he started his own agency business, Trunkstyle, specialising in birch and beech.

Howard Rogers, no relation to Don, joined us as works manager. He came from Gliksten, West Africa, where he had held a managerial position. Howard was strict but fair, and the men in the yard respected him; he was also a very loyal person and served us well. He died very suddenly on Boxing Day 1996 after the briefest stay in hospital. My son, Simon Kemp, also joined the family firm: he has worked in various departments over the years and has proved to be a very loyal and conscientious employee of Timbmet, and still is to this day. He has made many friends in all locations.

Mahogany for monks

It transpired that the Abbot of Prinknash Abbey in Gloucestershire wanted a grand mahogany table for all the monks to take their meals together. Strangely, he contacted the Commonwealth Development Corporation for advice, but it may be that he knew someone employed there or that one of the monks had been a missionary in Africa. The CDC in turn got in touch with the TTF, who always tried to recommend the nearest, most suitable stockists.

When contact was made with Timbmet and the desired specification given, the table was to be 36ft long by 3ft wide, and finished fine sawn to 3" thickness. This was obviously not a stock item! It took us almost two years to find the right quality log, straight grown with a tight heart, so as to produce the size in one piece. Leslie was very enthusiastic about this project. The two Ghana mahogany logs most likely to be suitable were landed at Vitak Timber Ltd sawmill, Rotherhithe, with the rest of the parcel which was all of superior quality. Leslie had called there and discussed the conversion in great detail and set a date: he personally wanted to be present when the cutting was done to ensure that the wide and long pieces were carefully handled, end cleated and end waxed.

At Oxford we were able to deal with the timber in one length. Our kilns were capable of drying almost 42ft in length providing we loaded at the end of the traverser, using two fork lift trucks and lifting in tandem. The planks were very carefully handled so as not to split them. Dick built other thick material around them of similar density to make up the kiln load and to ensure an even air flow throughout; the bogey was well covered on top with boards and on one side with hessian, and the stock was left to air dry for about twelve weeks before kilning.

Some structural alterations had to be made to the abbey building and entrance to get the "object" into the dining hall. Several of the monks were skilled craftsmen and did most of the work themselves. They also constructed very strong trestles in idigbo on which to lay the tabletop. The weight in itself would keep the big slab of mahogany in position. The CDC arranged to film the various stages of manufacture: they felt proud that all of this was to support the tropical timber trade, helping the standard of living in Africa. At about the same time a film was produced by the United Africa Company, showing the forest resource in their concessions in both Ghana and Nigeria, which they thought would last in perpetuity.

On the appointed day of delivery, we provided extra labour to unload and put the tabletop in position. It was heavy work without doubt. We were warmly thanked by the community of Cistercian monks and special appreciation was shown to Leslie for his personal devotion. To the best of my belief, however, he was never honoured by dining with them. I feel sure that the table is still in use to this very day. The monastery grounds and chapel at Prinknash are open to the public during summer months.

Contract labour

In addition to our own permanent labour force, we occasionally employed contract labour for sticking. They were mainly ex-dockers who used to carry timber from the hold of the ships to the quayside, piece by piece. They had to walk on roads made of scaffold boards, carrying the planks on their shoulders, and to protect their heads and shoulders they wore leather hoods. As more and more timber was bundled at the ports of shipment, fewer men were required as the unloading at the port of discharge was done by crane.

Alternatively, they would build piles in Surrey Commercial Docks, for storage by importers who kept some of their inventory at the port or at other wharfs along the River Thames or the Grand Union Canal; and when required these contractors would also put timber into stick conventionally by placing laths between layers to facilitate air drying. This is physically demanding work and requires more skill than is generally realised.

Timbmet also employed Roberts Brothers, Roy and Bill, from Edmonton. They had never worked this far from London, but used several of their men who lived in Middlesex, which made the journey to Cumnor shorter. As our turnover increased, we kept an ever larger air drying stock. By 1976 we had ten kilns in operation, with the last pair on order to be commissioned in the spring of 1977. We had a very large through-put from the driers as we filled them with timber invariably below 35% moisture content. This meant a lot of sticking and de-sticking. We decided to offer regular employment to two gangs of contract labourers, whom called "piece workers." In the docks the contractor was paid by each cubic foot handled, and for different operations varying rates applied, as originally costed by the Port of London Authority. We simplified things by paying by the piece and this worked out quite well as we did not expect the men to stick only 1" for a week. They would not have minded handling 2" for ever, middle weight, and middle rate. One had to be strict to ensure the men did the work properly. Our contract called for brushing and scraping the sawdust off from both faces!

Brooms were always near the men, but were not always used as well and often as required. Nevertheless, all visitors, whether local or from overseas, were duly impressed with the quality of the sticking on the bogies, or anywhere in the yard. Most of the log sawn piles were also impressive.

After a time, John Langston, leading hand of the Roberts Brothers, must have insisted that he became our sub contractor and we employed him direct. He seemed to have made his arrangements with the Roberts Brothers without involving any of us at Timbmet, and he continued here for about twenty five years. The work diminished considerably when we gave up buying home-grown oak and English hardwoods, as it is now possible for us to get most of our temperate hardwoods ready dry from Europe. Many African sawmills were adding value to their products by offering ready kiln dried. Mr Langston retired and we are still employing some of his labour today, a few of them having settled locally.

As our sales continued to rise, our kilns managed to provide us with only approximately 70% of our needs. The balance was kiln dried by contract kilning. Our subcontractors, who were often our competitors, did not offer the regular service as promised, but in some ways this was not surprising. When the demand was there they would fill their kilns with their own stock. Selling dry timber was more profitable than offering a kilning service. We started to look for other premises in the Oxford area, but the planners did not look very favourably at further expansion at Cumnor, although an appeal no doubt would have succeeded. At the same time our insurers expressed a wish to decentralise the risks.

The insurance company encouraged us to keep the two ponds at the top of the yard clean, in case of an emergency, and also asked us to dig ten smaller reservoirs to hold additional water, lining them with concrete. For good measure, Leslie asked Jim Pitts to buy a fire engine from an army surplus store, and we bought a mighty Thorneycroft with a Rolls Royce engine. The men had to have considerable training to operate the hoses in case of fire and acquire appropriate skills. Our Cumnor fire chief, Nigel Warmington, who was a part-time fireman in Woodstock, was not allowed enough time off during the working day to properly train the crew so the poor machine was allowed to go to rack and ruin, and eventually we sold the engine, the only valuable part.

British Rail

For many years we tried to become suppliers to various government bodies, principally directing our efforts to the purchasing department of British Rail, the Ministry of Defence and the workshops of the prison service. We managed, after a time, to satisfy the purchasing department of British Rail with our ability to serve them with dry and fresh sawn English hardwoods; and we also convinced them of the variety of our quality imported hardwood stocks suitable for passenger carriage building.

At last, in 1976, we were given the forms to complete the usual questions assuring them of our sound trading principles and financial standing, etc. We gave first class large private companies as referees. We were overjoyed to receive the appointment. The only personal visit we had was by a senior timber inspector from Swindon who was despatched from Swindon works by train to give us a physical look over. He came and was most impressed. I offered to take him back by car and bought him a light lunch on the way, which he was allowed to accept. We did a lot of business at fine margins for many years without having to worry about payments. We continued to battle away with the other government departments until we were eventually accepted by them.

Yugoslavia - and some research

In 1976 Rosie and I took our annual holiday in Yugoslavia. We spent one week at Lake Bled, and the second in Opatija on the Croatian coast facing the Adriatic Sea. We were fortunate with the weather and had reasonable accommodation but unfortunately the food was dull and almost entirely without variety. Due to the high price of oil, the government ensured that as little as possible of any commodity was to be transported from one part of the country to another, and this meant that any food and fruit available had to be of local produce. Private cars could only be driven on the road on alternate days based on even and uneven number plates.

In Opatija there were visitors from Czechoslovakia: they came in groups, under supervision. The Czechs did not like to meet foreigners and were afraid to talk, and we found out that families were not holidaying together. The condition of the foreign holiday was for one partner of a marriage to remain behind to ensure that neither absconded; and one or the other had to be highly skilled and a reliable party member!

Before leaving home, I went to the office and picked up the latest edition of the TTJ. In it was a short paragraph about a new MDF mill which had just been completed; the production line was from Sweden and local raw material was being used. Looking at the map, we found out that the factory was only 25 or 30 kilometres from the coast, so I phoned the management who agreed to see us. We hired a taxi and asked the driver to wait for us. On arrival we were requested to hand over our passports. They asked us if they could hold these and promised to return them to us, which they did. Rosie, although she did not show it at the time, was worried that they might not let us leave!

The factory was Lesno Kaminova Industria, Ilinska Bistrica, Croatia; Madam Trojst, the sales manager spoke fluent German and took care of us. She accompanied us and showed us around the plant. The thicknesses corresponded with the British sizes, but unfortunately the board dimensions were multiples of furniture sizes and door sections, which were of no interest to us as MDF in England was still in its infancy, used only in building construction. So we had a light lunch together in the canteen, and parted on good terms.

I brought back samples, prices and sales literature but because it was early days for this material, we never succeeded in finding anyone interested in it. Our staff were never encouraged enough to promote it. Timbmet kept in touch with the company, and a representative called to see us a year or so later, but it was still too early. They were not willing to produce a board size of 2440 x 1220mm, the basic plywood and chipboard sizes in the UK.

*****

1976 ended with a turnover of £5,452,000, which at 2005 values, would equate to £27,260,000.

CHAPTER 26

1977 and 1978

1977: changes in the US market

Due to the high price of Japanese oak, importers and consumers started to look at alternatives. The communist countries in Eastern Europe had never modernised their hardwood sawmills nor introduced modern kilning methods; Yugoslavia and Rumania produced fair quantities of mainly steamed beech, mostly on very archaic equipment, under full state control. English oak was mainly a specialist item for the restoration of old buildings, national monuments and churches etc, or new build in traditional style. The quantities available could not replace the volume of Japanese oak consumed in England.

In the USA some concentration yards, particularly on the north east coast, with modern grading lines and kilns, were at the same time looking to expand their businesses by exporting to Europe. Some of these companies also had their own sawmills. The long term economic forecast domestically did not appear very promising for the next four or five years. All these firms had exported small quantities to the UK before, often consisting of specialities only such as oak barrel staves, maple and ash billiard cue squares and prime maple for piano actions, etc. We had an interest in American red oak coffin boards as the Japanese variety was becoming scarce, and very expensive.

Old established British agents had connections with the producers in New England. From about 1974 onwards offers to supply were regularly received for most species. It appeared that firms from Liverpool predominated, probably because traditionally, and especially pre-1939, exporters from the USA came by ship to Liverpool to deal with their customers. American hardwoods were imported in large quantities to the UK from the beginning of the twentieth century until the outbreak of the Second World War, and the government then continued this trade by purchasing large quantities for national stock until about 1950. From then and for the next twenty five years, American hardwoods were out of favour.

USA hardwoods gradually became more freely available and, together with Japanese oak, predominated in the UK. The English manufacturer was dissatisfied with the grading of the USA material, and the majority of American shippers engaged on exports were compelled to supply above the minimum NHLA FAS grading rules to satisfy the market.

One of our early suppliers was the American Lumber Co. who had headquarters in Union City, Pennsylvania. The president was Mr Herb Asherman, a very astute businessman, who had created a large business by amalgamating and buying up country sawmills. He marketed all his products with a green diamond. We were unlucky as in the very early period we received two sub-standard parcels of white oak. The agents were Hunt Bros & Co who had offices in Liverpool: we must have written some very strong letters, and possibly also forwarded them direct to the shipper. Herb Asherman replied to Deryck Kermode of Hunt Bros that he had no need to get his wrists slapped by his master like a schoolboy! His excuse for the company not shipping up to grade was a shortage of logs and they hadn't wanted to be late in fulfilling his contract. Obviously they should have sought our consent before despatching the goods. I have kept the letter as it was very cleverly worded.

A difficult customer

We eventually reached a compromise and continued to trade successfully. Their lumber was very well presented. In 1977 we had another under grade parcel on our hands which was somewhat case hardened. The arguments went to and fro for a few weeks until Hunt Bros informed us that Bob Miller, the export manager for the company, was going to call on us and inspect, an offer which we were pleased to accept. Before he came, Mr Kermode informed us that Mr Miller was a very strong willed person and wanted to come on his own without his agent being present. This did not fully conform to custom, but it did not bother me.

Sometime in June 1977, at three o'clock, Bob Miller came through the narrow entrance of our offices. I happened to be passing and heard a voice shout, "Is there any one here ready for a fight?" Quickly I answered, "Yes, buddy, I am: ready to fight you physically and mentally just like Winston Churchill did – but a little civility doesn't cost anything. I presume you are Mr Miller? Good afternoon to you!"

Some verbal abuse followed and I shouted as much as he did. Our Howard Rogers came in behind him and, being a meeker person, was bewildered at the proceedings. (He told me afterwards he thought I had lost my senses.) Howard managed to calm the situation a little, and I invited Mr Miller into the office. After some refreshments, we put our case forward on behalf of Timbmet and suggested that we went to inspect the under-grade stock that was the purpose of the visit. He argued for hours justifying every piece, not admitting anything was wrong; he wore us out, including Dick Clapham, who tried to act as technical spokesman and mediator. Eventually, by late afternoon, we negotiated a small allowance but we were glad when he finally departed. This type of behaviour, and the constant battles rather than sensible commercial practice, very likely shortened his life. A few years later we heard that Bob Miller had had a massive heart attack and died, well before he was fifty: soon after his death the business was sold to Baillie Lumber. This episode must have affected my sensibilities, although I did not realise it immediately.

On a personal note

For many years I was secretary for marriages of the Oxford Jewish congregation. I could only register a wedding and issue a civil certificate with the permission of the rabbinate and the local registry office. On the rare occasions when a wedding was to take place we asked a Rabbi from a neighbouring community to come and officiate as we did not have a minister at Oxford. Even today the congregation manages with volunteers only carrying out congregational duties. In term time, the students participate. Two days after I had my meeting with Mr Miller I went to the Synagogue on Saturday morning. I fully realised that the young couple, who were to be married the next day would, as was customary, attend the Sabbath morning service.

To my surprise there were about forty visitors from the USA. The American bride and her English husband-to-be were graduates of Oxford University, and friends and family of the bride who had come over for the wedding were at the service. They brought with them the minister of their home parish, and he conducted most of the service and also gave the sermon. He spoke in a very self assured manner and reminded the congregation, half of them relatives and visitors of the bride, of the migration of impoverished and persecuted Jews two centuries ago from Russia to liberal and freedom loving America. He described the barren coast of New England where they had gradually worked to create a luscious paradise on earth. At this point I burst out unexpectedly and said, "Here comes another Yank to tell us how great they all are."

The Rabbi stopped his sermon; I apologised for interrupting him and pleaded with him to continue, assuring him that I intended to keep my mouth shut. I lowered my head in shame but he never lost his composure and the sermon and service continued to the end. Afterwards I gave the Rabbi and the family my most inadequate explanation for my spontaneous outburst of anger. They probably half-heartedly believed my story but on Sunday at the wedding the atmosphere improved. I was able to talk of how all our congregation worked voluntarily for the good of the community and I was one of the active participants. I also told them that my background was similar and how proud I was to have had the opportunity to settle in England.

*****

In 1978, our auditors recommended that we change the Timbmet financial year to 31st March to coincide with the Inland Revenue tax year, so we prepared the next accounts for fifteen months. Our turnover for this period was £9,008,500, which in 2005 value exceeds £30 million. We had had a profitable year. Encouraged by our success, we built part of the first floor of our offices and a bungalow for a caretaker having obtained planning permission for both a year earlier. When the builders completed shed nos. 5-8 they remained on site and carried on with these two comparatively minor projects.

*****

For some years we employed various well known security companies, but we did not have good service from any of them. We felt that to have one of our own employees living on the premises would ensure that the night patrols were being done properly. These firms hated being supervised and particularly disliked the long irregular hours I worked and that I came in over most of the national holidays. My slogan was "I come here to watch ze watchmen!"

A new contact

Adrian and I got to know Jack Furtado well when he worked for C Leary & Co. He decided to establish the agency firm of Lignum together with two colleagues and a South African finance partner. Jack had good connections with reliable shippers in many parts of the world. At the time we had a larger than usual demand for Canadian white maple, which he offered on behalf of two producers. I would not place the order until someone interpreted for me the grading rules relating to the colour, defining the meaning of No 1 and No 2 white maple. After a few attempts, and with the help of the NHLA, Jack gave a clear description of the grade. He thought I was being very hard on him, but for a long time he gained most of our maple orders.

...and another

For many years we struggled to be permitted to tender for Home Office prison requirements for their woodworking workshops using hardwoods, but we were unable to get an interview. Some time in the spring of 1978, we were contacted by a high ranking official from the procurement executive offering to visit us with a view to carrying out an assessment of Timbmet. A venerable gentleman of the old school turned up. We managed to satisfy his questions, and introduced him to our office and the operating staff who would look after his orders: he could hardly believe me when I said I personally would be responsible. He was impressed by our transport fleet and realised that, as we were making deliveries regularly to all parts of England, we could serve the prison establishments quickly from the very comprehensive inventory we always kept in stock.

We tendered bi-annually. The third time, after six years of being an approved supplier, we succeeded in getting our first contract. With our large stocks of beech and other hardwoods we managed to satisfy all the workshop managers; and we did not call unless personally invited.

It was Adrian's and my responsibility to complete the prison tenders. This was always an anxious time. In later years we individually spent many hours costing their requirements before going through these together. However good one's service, one could lose the contract by a fraction of a percent. On one occasion we were requested to visit head office in Croydon where it was indicated that a few adjustments might be helpful. We asked for use of an office or some space in the canteen; this was refused, so we adjourned to a small local café and recalculated some of the most crucial items, returning with our proposals and offering our reasons for which we were thanked as we left.

We delivered on time and our documents were correct, and payments were made promptly. Margins were tight, but the prison workshop where they were making chairs, occasional furniture and toys did not often need long lengths. We were able to sell these dimensions at a premium for joinery. When occasionally we failed, I phoned personally to apologise and this was appreciated. From 1980 to 1995, we must have been the major suppliers to prisons.

Rumanian visitors

Rumania supplied very substantial quantities annually to the UK hardwood trade, mainly steamed beech, and at this time Timbmet would have been the fourth or fifth largest customer. A government sales delegation came to London each spring to negotiate quantities, specifications and, above all, prices for the year. Price Morgan, their agents, tried to get importers to declare their requirements giving provisional figures of all sizes broken down to lumber, waney edged, steamed and unsteamed. Gliksten hardwoods, the largest importer for Rumanian beech, were present at, or took part in, some of the heated discussions and negotiations. They were not shown the breakdown of individual importers requirements but no doubt saw the total "shopping list" so that they had a good idea of their share in the market.

It became customary from 1978 onwards for up to four sawmill production directors to accompany the marketing team, no doubt as a reward for their achievements. They were not partaking in the negotiations, but importers were asked to entertain them and show them how the trade operated in England. They were to see some yards, kilns and re-sawing mills and possibly visit a furniture factory producing chairs.

The agents thought that Oxford would be a good place. A junior member of Price Morgan was despatched in a large Volvo car with a group of men who spoke very little English and were accompanied by a communist party official acting as a stool pigeon! We showed them our yard stocks; they were particularly interested in our cranes and side-loaders, and wanted to know more about the properties and uses for the tropical hardwoods.

We then took them to Oxford to see the famous sites in the city. At lunchtime we booked into the Randolph Hotel and asked to be shown the á la carte menu. They chose smoked salmon followed by Scottish beef for the main course. When the wine waiter came I asked whether by any chance they had any Rumanian wine. The waiter said "Yes, but I wouldn't recommend it sir!" The whole party stood up in disgust and shouted in unison that Rumanian wine was equal, if not better than, French. We toasted their health, the wine, the timber trade and the president of Rumania.

On one occasion the delegation was delayed until the summer. The managers, however, were brought to Oxford; we did the tour of our yards and because of the holiday season, it was left to my wife to show them our city. The party was dropped off at Christ Church, to be collected from the Randolph Hotel after lunch. The men saw the Cathedral church and then they were shown Oriel and Corpus Christi Colleges. They walked down Merton Street and turned into Magpie Lane, crossed over the High Street into the City Church of St Mary's. This time two of the visitors became obviously overwhelmed by the holiness of the building. One of them, who had pretended he couldn't speak a word of English, began to ask questions and wanted to know the history of the Church, and of the colleges!

At the time it was possible to phone Duke Humfrey's Library, part of the Bodleian, for an appointment to take a small party along to visit, and Rosie showed them around the building. One of the men became absorbed in a book in a side alley. Their escort became very concerned in case he absconded, and it became pretty obvious that he was their "minder." The Rumanians were allowed very little spending money for their journey and were not able to buy any souvenirs to take back to their families.

Development at Bicester

In 1979, we were introduced to Mr Granville Grossman of Chaucer Estates who owned an under-developed estate at Bicester and offered to rent us the land. Our architect was Mr Harry W Smith whose office was at Cumnor Hill. He had industrial experience and drew up plans for our requirements, similar in layout to Oxford, but giving 25% extra kiln capacity as the kiln chambers would be 10 feet high. Chaucer had difficulty in accepting that a building 280 ft long x 190 ft wide would need so many entrances. We had to persuade them that if we ceased to be tenants they would have to fill in the cavities, as well as the traverser well which would also have to be levelled. The kiln building could be turned into nursery units. Eventually they agreed, and planning permission was applied for.

We ordered the "jumbo" sized Cubbage kilns, similar to the ones so well proven at the Cumnor yard. We placed an order with Trepel UK of Sheerness, Kent, for a scissor lift capable of lifting up to six tons, with cantilever bridges at each end. Leslie Boustead and Jim Pitts, the works engineer, with Wise Handling of Bradford, Yorkshire, designed a transfer car to carry the kiln charges with a 60 ton capacity. Leslie was convinced that a pole crane, 20ft high with a 36ft feet jib which could slew 360 degrees over the scissor lift, would speed up the delivery of the bundles to be sticked as well as select the lengths more efficiently than a fork lift truck or side-loader.

Wise Handling ordered a steel tube from Holland, normally used for building oil drilling platforms: this heavy one-metre diameter cylinder needed about sixty tons of concrete to anchor it into the floor of the main building. This idea was only of limited success; it was not often that our ideas failed to achieve our objectives. It hurt Leslie a good deal and we all tried to console him.

This product was partly financed by Barclays Merchant Bank Ltd. The developers appointed Gresham Construction of Henley in Arden to build the extension. We were aware from the start that Chaucer intended to sell the property to a pension fund, and we fixed the rent for the first five years at £1.20 per square foot. The sale was eventually concluded.

Timbmet installed heat recuperators to the kilns to re-use the steam generated in the drying process. When these vent, the hot wet air passes through the heat exchangers and returns hot dry air back into the kilns. The prospective developers wanted to ensure that the excess dampness would not rust the steel or damage the roof of the kiln cover building. We accepted this as a last minute modification. It proved to be more difficult technically than originally envisaged, but in the end our fuel saving was more than adequate to cover the cost.

*****

We spent several holidays in the Channel Islands. The destination was chosen on purpose to call on a few potential customers, and one summer we were in Guernsey. We had a connection, Mr Edwards, an Oxford surveyor, who had gone to live and work at St Peter Port. He introduced us to other companies; it seemed that competition in the building industry was not as rigorous as in England. At first they were keen to keep the work available for themselves.

I wanted to visit two customers in St Peter Port, who were near the harbour and castle. I thought the castle was a museum, and suggested to my wife that she might show the children the exhibits. She agreed rather reluctantly. When I came to collect them, I found the family were soaking wet! The building was without a roof and open to the elements. It took Rosie a long time to forgive me.

By 1979 exchange control regulations were abolished in the UK and, as a result, many banks and financial institutions from Britain were opening up branches in the Channel Islands. The local economy was buoyant, and I felt that giving up a few hours of my holidays was worthwhile. I never thought there would be so much business for Timbmet, and we decided that a company representative should visit the Islands twice a year.

CHAPTER 27

1979: The Far East

The double glazing home improvement industry was now big business in the UK: it was an important market for our firm. We had visits from Philippine and Malaysian shippers with their British agents and regularly placed large orders, mainly for meranti and lauan. We bought the largest volumes through EAC: they had Danish staff based in Singapore, Kuala Lumpur and Manila, with yards and stocks of their own. In addition to buyers and local graders in most producing areas they ensured that wherever possible shipments were made on time. Above all, they made certain that any quality claims were settled within a reasonable period.

On many occasions previously I had refused invitations by producers in the Far East, but in 1979 I felt that in accepting I would gain a lot from personal contact and seeing for myself the producing mills. I chose to travel with Finn Grube with whom I had had a good deal of contact since the opening of the EAC office in England. He helped me to plan a three week journey, including visits to their own export yards and shippers, as well as to other Timbmet suppliers who were represented by various British agency houses, and encompassing the four countries of Malaysia, Singapore, Philippines and Indonesia.

At that time the most regular and reliable air connections to the Far East were from Singapore so we flew there where we spent two weekends and the last Saturday of our visit. We stayed at the small Garden Hotel in Balmoral Road. Coincidentally, this was where my brother had lived with his family and worked as a medical consultant for ten years after he had left the British army.

Singapore

We spent some time in the EAC offices at Kranji, Singapore. Nearby were a number of large sawmills converting locally grown hardwoods, supported by logs brought by road and barge from the state of Johore. As most of the companies we dealt with are no longer in business, I will mention just a few of our suppliers in Singapore at the time: Lim

Manufacturing, Contimex and Kim Timber. I visited the head office at Bormill who had fine concessions of serayah forests in Sabah, and other non EAC suppliers.

EAC prepared 800m³ of dark red kiln dried meranti, supposedly of above average quality, ready for my inspection in the dock area. I looked at it in bulk and was convinced that it was not up to grade: I particularly disliked the texture and grain of the wood. For my sins, and the displeasure of the local EAC management and Finn, I spent two very hot, humid and dusty Saturdays re-grading the worst affected bundles. I did not have much time left for sightseeing or shopping!

Malaysia

We left Singapore by the causeway connecting with Malaysia and on the way we stopped at several sawmills. EAC had a large depot at Kuala Lumpur, managed by two very young men. One was Christian Mengel, the other Ong Kai Kok, with whom I made firm friends; I admired them for being able to manage such a large business on their own. Christian had been through the EAC training course.

In the evening we were taken to dinner at the home of the general manager of EAC Malaysia: a very able person, middle aged, he and with his wife lived in a large house. She was an Englishwoman and a charming hostess. It became obvious that he kept a close eye on the "youngsters." Apart from the food distribution business, EAC also imported Japanese scooters into Malaysia, and had other local interests.

After a ten year stretch in Malaysia, Christian had requested a transfer to London which was eventually granted. Soon after this, he married Benedicta, who came from an aristocratic Norwegian family: I made him an offer to join us, but she preferred to live in a big city. He now works in Greenboro', USA and we are still in touch today.

The new larger cargo ships could not tie up at Kuala Lumpur at that time, and all loading was done from barges by ship's derrick. Commercial trade kilns existed but the overall capacity was much smaller than it is now. The kiln owners used local components as much as possible, but bought burners, control panels and other electrical parts from Germany and Japan.

The suppliers I visited included KTS, Selangor Timber, Malimex and Transworld Lumber. I spent half a day on my own travelling to the outskirts of Kuala Lumpur, looking for a gentleman of Indian origin who

158

had supplied discoloured, poor quality jelutong. The owner, Mr Abdul Rahman, had had to go out urgently, and his manager had all sorts of excuses. In spite of my persuasive powers, and Churchill & Sims' intervention, the claim remains outstanding to this day.

From there we travelled towards the Cameroon Highlands on a newly finished dual carriageway. As soon as we were a few hundred metres above sea level, the climate became more pleasant.

On the way to Kuantan we visited Golden Harvest, Unibest and Penang Timber. We stayed overnight in Kuantan, a picturesque town on the west coast where a new harbour was under construction. Some of our suppliers shipped from here but even now it is not a regular container port. We did visit the principal sawmills in the town on our return journey, and called briefly on Mentiga; we visited the factory manufacturing plywood made from veneer leaves of equal laminations.

From there we went to the Jengka sawmill and plywood factory at Bandar Pusat, near Termeloh, in Pahang. This was a project financed by the World Bank to help the local Malaysian population run their own industries without outside assistance. In order to have adequate raw material supplies in perpetuity, the government allocated 6,000,000 acres of almost virgin forest in the highlands for Jengka, provided proper felling rotas were kept and some enrichment planting undertaken where and when needed. Unfortunately the directors did not manage the project skilfully; they called in European consultants, but ultimately had to sell off round logs regularly to the trade to make ends meet. Today very little of this company is functioning.

I was taken for an extended day trip to see part of the forest and logging operations, and learned to identify the standing trees and many basic ideas about good husbandry; I was accompanied by a Malaysian forester who did his training in Australia. This was also my first visit to a modern plywood plant. They were peeling, but also did some slicing of, thin leaves; their technology was well advanced and their boards were in demand. I managed to purchase a small parcel. A fair amount of their solid production was in nemesu, a hardwood very popular in Belgium. We introduced this species to England: the density was adequate enough not to require fire-proofing, but the silicose content in certain trees made it harder for some companies to use.

We flew back to base in Singapore for the weekend. (Although, as already mentioned, I spent time inspecting timber in the heat and dust at the harbour.) In the evening we were invited to the home of Mr

Mortensen, general manager of EAC Singapore, when we met his wife and petite four year old daughter, and also other Danish staff. On Sunday morning I was taken by car on a short tour of Singapore. It was remarkable how well organised and disciplined the population was. There was no litter; everyone obeyed traffic regulations and was generally law abiding, and the police had powers to act swiftly whatever the offence. The Prime Minister, Mr Lee Kuan Yew, had almost dictatorial power. He was highly respected at home and abroad.

In the afternoon Finn and I flew to Manila to be ready to meet shippers and exporters the next morning. We had been together now for over a week and we got on well. I coped easily with the physical strain of the journey and enjoyed the mental absorption; this was both a pleasure and a great experience.

The Philippines

We were met by Jan Novakowski at the airport. He was in over all charge of the Luzon Mahogany Co. the fully owned EAC subsidiary, who had their head office in town with their own yard and kilns outside the metropolis. He had at least three European assistants as well as a number of well trained local Filipino graders. I spent some time in their yards. Lauan was difficult to kiln unless naturally pre-dried; I tried to iron out problems of badly sawn dimension stock, and I always tried wherever I went to discuss possible problems so as to prevent any future claims. Finn used to say, "Now turn on your gramophone" turning his hand as if winding up the spring.

Industries Development Corporation, known as IDC, was a large group with many interests. They owned a number of sawmills, and were prominent in mouldings and furniture manufacturing: they could provide equally branded volume, but were not able to nominate which of their sawmills would produce the order. The best lauan came from the north of Luzon Island, better in colour, weight, and texture and free of the phloem, which looked ugly on window boards. For many years afterwards I kept in touch with the owner's son, Joselito Ong.

The Blue Star Mahogany Co. was owned by Tropish Hout, which in turn belonged to Dr H Stoll's family in Germany. Their director in charge was Mr Keller. They bought stock from smaller mills and took the timber to their yard for grading and kilning. The bundling, end painting and general protection of their product were exceptional and often commanded a small premium for above average stock. I will not mention the various medium sized suppliers we visited as many of them, if still in business, are unlikely to be engaged on timber export from the Philippines.

We travelled in a black Mercedes with a local driver to the north of Luzon Island. I think the car belonged to the Danish embassy, which offered some immunity as there were anti-government rebels in the area. We had a night stopover at Tuguegarab and stayed in guest rooms at a Danish owned tobacco factory. It was lights out at ten o'clock when the power supply was closed down, but in any case we were glad to be in bed as we got up at 4 a.m. for an early start. There was a primitive bathroom between the two bedrooms. The next morning I heard an awful lot of body movement and some swear words and found Finn trying to find his socks and underwear by the glow of a lighted cigarette! I was able to offer the loan of a torch which ended the crisis.

We travelled all the way to the northern coastal town of Buguey where we visited a number of sawmills. Some belonged to large groups, others were in single ownership; not all used EAC as selling agents. When Finn withdrew tactfully from the negotiations, often sitting in the car having a nap, I was able to speak to shippers personally. Off the north coast ships were being loaded with solid logs, taken out to sea in barges and exported to many countries. Finn said he was not prepared to travel into these forests, many of them almost adjoining the seashore, as it was too dangerous. On this journey I saw large hill areas completely cleared of trees, which seemed very wrong: it was pure greed to get the biggest volume felled and sold with the least expense of road building.

We made our way back to Manila and in the late evening boarded a plane to the southern island of Mindanao.

CHAPTER 28

Far East travels: continued

Mindanao

We visited a number of sawmills. Invariably the lauan was of lighter weight and colour and included some interlocked grain. This kiln dried slightly more easily than the darker stock grown on the north on Luzon and was readily available kiln dried from the bigger firms. Each company had large batteries of drying kilns, more so than elsewhere in the Far East in 1979.

As always in England, "the cheapest is the best" and some of our customers did not want to admit that Mindanao material was slightly inferior until they received a much lighter colour parcel than usual. There was no definition of shades in the grading rules (personally, I would have preferred dark red meranti to lauan grown in Mindanao or the surrounding Islands.) In spite of this, huge quantities were produced and exported to many different countries of the world.

I spent some time with two firms, Cagayan de Oro Timber Co., and shipping mark 'Catimco' who between them must have produced the biggest volumes. They were not represented by EAC. Timbmet had for some years been dealing with Mr Alarico Lim; he and his wife had visited England frequently, and had a most capable young son, Ferdie, who had been educated in America. The company was represented at the time by 'Ralli'. We had many battles over quality, but traded large volumes. They not only had their own forest areas on the island but also bought rough sawn timber produced from many small islands. This was sawn on bush circular mills, loaded into barges collected by tugs and unloaded at Matimco plant, which was not far from the sea. The stock invariably had not only to be re-graded but also regularised to size, the lengths mostly measuring up to 12' only.

The sawmill equipment at Matimco was Japanese and very modern. The first machine that was used to break down the logs was not a full band mill, as used by European or African mills, but was only able to cut a log into four quarters. The flitches were carried by conveyors to two substantial band re-saws who converted them further, then passed them to four smaller re-saws in one line which cut the timber to its final sizes. The sawdust and slabs were carried away by conveyors so as not to congest the main production line.

Catimco had Korean and German kilns and were also manufacturing mouldings for the USA market; the moulders were mainly German Weinigs. There I saw the first Japanese-made jointing machines for splicing solid pieces of timber. Both of these firms may have had a shared venture with American food producers, replanting cleared land with coffee, cocoa, pineapples and other fruit.

From there we flew to the island of Cebu to visit Matimco. In almost all details the business was a duplicate of Catimco. The senior director Mr Lim Liu gave us a warm welcome. We had an early evening meal with his family and this was the only time we saw something of a local family home and were able to observe some Chinese customs. We spent the night in a modern holiday style hotel laid out in very lush surroundings.

I spent a few hours with Finn touring the Valderama Lumber Co. sawmill complex, which has a very large of sawn lumber for export, in addition tt producing components and joinery for the local market on machinery provided immediately after 1945 by USA rehabilitation funds. They also produced joinery for local demand. This company, probably one of the oldest timber firms in the Philippines, whose manager and vice president was Mr R M Borromeo, was represented worldwide by EAC, Ralli and other firms.

Everywhere on our travels we saw a great deal of poverty such as I have never seen before. People were living in shacks along streams of stagnant water which was used for all purposes including drinking. There are occasional uprisings against the government, which the army seems to put down fairly quickly.

On Friday evening we flew back from Cebu to Singapore. On Saturday I went back to the dock area to finish sorting and grading the parcel of meranti, which we finished mid-afternoon. After a change and shower we enjoyed a meal at a Chinese restaurant. The party included Ole Petersen, managing director of Indu-Bois at Sete, a wholly owned subsidiary of EAC in the south of France: they were selling mainly sawn air dried and freshly sawn logs from Africa and the Far East into Western Europe. Ole Petersen became our travel companion for our journey to Indonesia.

Indonesia

The three of us set out the next morning to fly to Jakarta. We stayed for one night in an opulent Hilton Hotel fitted out fully in teak in an eastern décor. Again, we saw the same very poor picture on the way to and from the airport to the city centre.

On Monday morning we went to the EAC Jakarta office which was situated in the Danish embassy building. We had a briefing on the local economic and political situation from a member of the embassy staff, and Finn and Ole met their local colleagues. One of them was Hans Jensen who became manager of the Antwerp branch and who, in later years, sometimes got us out of trouble by making nemesu available to us from his stock in Belgium. Two EAC shippers came to meet us, representatives of Emporium Group and Hutanraya Timber Co.

Very early the next morning we left Jakarta on Java Island for Balikpapan in Kalimantan. On arrival we found we were unable to claim our reserved seats on the local commuter connection to Samarinda as army officers had commandeered our seats. Finn was perturbed as the alternative to the half hour flight meant at least five hours by road; there was a taxi rank but all the cars seemed old and, above all, poorly maintained. Finn cursorily examined the taxis and made a deal with one of the drivers. It was a rough journey; mechanically the vehicle hardly managed to climb the hills. About halfway there was an almighty bang and some sparks flew. The undercarriage had come away! We were very lucky that the car never rolled over or left the road as otherwise we would have fallen down a ravine and somersaulted until possibly halted by trees. We could have been severely injured. I never made much of this episode so as not to unduly worry my wife and make her more anxious then she always was when I was away from home.

We did not have too long to wait on the roadside before a jeep pulled up willing to give us help. It was decided that Finn and I and some of our luggage should be loaded and we made our way to our destination leaving Ole with the rest of our cases by the roadside. We stopped somewhere on the journey and Finn phoned the local office of EAC. They immediately sent out a rescue vehicle, so Ole was back long before dark at the guest house we were staying in at Samarinda. Finn announced quite by surprise that it was his birthday the following day. He had a bottle of cognac with him, and between us we had emptied the contents by morning. The guest house had a dining room, but no lounge or other facilities, so we drank sitting in one of the bedrooms. It was one of the few occasions in my life when I got tipsy.

Samarinda is a small town at the mouth of the River Mahakam. On one side were seven large sawmill complexes sawing mainly dark red meranti and light red serayah for Japanese house building requirements. The sawmill had kilns and some were already manufacturing mouldings. On the other side of the river was a large veneer manufacturing plant owned by the USA giant Weyerhauser. Many of these have now closed. I spent some time inspecting rafts of logs, as I was interested in their growth and size. These were awaiting export, lying in the river in large quantities, partly alongside the sawmills, ready to be lifted out of the water as soon as needed for conversion. Ole imported logs to his yard in the south of France and sold them in Western Europe either in the solid or freshly sawn, or partly air dried.

The second quarter log export quota from East Kalimantan was quickly nearing exhaustion due to good demand in the world and enough ships to lift the cargoes. To make the quota last longer, shippers under-measured by 20% and adjusted the price upwards. When the logs were sold in Europe everyone received greater measure and this created chaos. It was also embarrassing.

England was never a large buyer of Far Eastern solid logs, as they contained a lot of open heart shakes which caused a greater loss in conversion than good African logs. The sawn widths were seldom over 10". In my zest to educate myself I slipped walking on slimy logs and as a result had a few bruises. I also slipped getting out of a motor boat trying to climb ashore and fell into the filthy oily water. As a good swimmer I soon got back to dry land. There is a photo somewhere of yours truly looking rather bedraggled and damp, to say the least!

Hanafy took me by road to several smaller sawmills. They were cutting red and yellow balau constructional sections for the local market, the nearby oil fields at Balikpapan and for general building work. Samarinda and the east coast were developing fast.

EAC's local office was staffed by two Chinese inspectors who remained on station for some years. Hanafy and 'Mighty' Mo were invaluable members of the team; Mo was a special judge of timber and a very fast and accurate measurer. They employed and trained local young men to grade the wood who were badly paid so they were not always impartial! To save themselves money they often slept in the saw shops at the sawmills, but were always on the first floor, where they were less liable to be bitten by snakes and/or ants than at ground level. As most employees were given a staple diet while working, they also enjoyed some free food.

The three of us went to see three large, almost new, plywood mills where the solid logs went in one end and the finished boards were graded and packed at the other end of the line. The machinery in each place was worth a large capital sum, and since most employees had probably never had a regular job before, they needed a lot of training and discipline. The key workers were Japanese and Koreans. The offices were beautifully furnished, but it was obvious when visiting the toilets that the management had never been used to western conveniences.

We said our goodbyes to 'Mighty' Mo and Hanafy and flew back to Singapore. Mo continued to write to me for some years. Due to our delayed arrival at Samarinda, we never visited Tawau, an area where we got supplies of good keruing.

On our return flight, we stopped over at Kota Kinabalu to refuel, not realising how important Sabah would be as a supplying region in a few years' time. The largest plywood factory we visited was Sumberbas Indah Plywood, run by Mr Ava Havarto, and the most important sawmill was Meratus Kalimantan Timber, run by Mr Juhari Wijaya. We arrived in Singapore late on Friday night. Finn and Ole wanted to make a return visit to a Singapore mill on Saturday morning: United Logging also produced good, long teak decks from Burma or Thailand teak logs, and they had a lot of expertise. We did buy some special planks for ships decking from them at a later date.

It was proposed that we had a leisurely afternoon on the Saturday at a European swimming club, with Mr Mortensen and his family, before taking the late plane back to London, as we only flew economy class and the plane was likely to be full.

*****

While away I sent regular telex messages to Adrian informing him of purchases made and local market conditions. In most cases it meant queuing at reception desks in the hotels during the late evening; Adrian in turn sent messages from home advising me of any important events at Timbmet and on the home front.

My main regret always will be that I did not take the opportunity to visit Australia for a few days to see my uncle and cousins and a few school friends who had survived the Holocaust and had settled in Melbourne.

Back in Oxford

I was very tired on my return, and it took a few days to settle into the normal working routine. I found it very gratifying that all departments had worked in harmony during my absence.

I never returned although the Far Eastern business kept increasing. I must have left a favourable impression in most places as we continued to communicate directly with the suppliers, in spite of all purchases being made through accredited agents or international traders such as EAC, Ralli and others. At this stage our auditors felt that we needed a qualified accountant. We accepted their advice, advertised the position and had many applications. From the many applications, Leslie and I selected Geoff Clough to be the person to take us forward towards the Millennium and to introduce more advanced computer systems into the company.

We had a timber building alongside our saw shed nicknamed 'Fred's Café' where we provided hot drinks and light snacks for our manual workers free of charge. The shed was extended several times as our labour force increased, and for a long time it was managed single handedly by Fred Cox who, in the last few years, had a lady to help him during lunchtimes. Fred never stopped working and even found time to tidy the yard as well. He was well liked by everyone.

In 1979 we decided to put up a single storey building to serve as a canteen. It was fitted with modern kitchen facilities and a toilet block with wash rooms. This was, and still is, appreciated by both the manual and the office workers. Timbmet subsidised the main meal provided by the caterers but after a few years we had to increase the price of a three course lunch and asked the staff to contribute. Eventually by mutual consent, we simplified the menu making it less expensive although still nourishing, and to a budget which was acceptable to both staff and the company.

Four years ago, Jill Jarvis who had been previously employed by the caterers, took over the running of the canteen and now provides the breakfasts and lunches. She is doing a very good job and is respected and well liked by everyone.

CHAPTER 29

1980

A confrontation

For the year ending 31st March 1980, Timbmet's turnover was £12,300,000 [equivalent in 2005 to £30,000,000.]

Early in the year we had a visit from a young American based in Belgium who was the selling agent for Montheath, a hardwood company in New York State and based in Belgium. He was very persuasive and we gave him an order for a container of 3" kiln dried FAS white oak. No other company up to that time had wanted to dry this thickness: it was important to offer the whole range of thicknesses in each species. We warned him of the problems and explained to him how we dry the English oak, and the care and time it took. We wondered whether we would ever get delivery of his stock.

In due course the goods arrived. The parcel was not entirely up to expectations. This was not a disaster as no one else had this material to offer. Some of the pieces were surface checked and bowed, but had to be included in orders: we had some complaints and were compelled to make allowances. We advised customers to take care and examine each piece before machining, as with skill the rejection rate could be much lower than at first sight.

The supplier regularly sold this type of oak to Belgium and Holland where it was used for the manufacture of reproduction furniture. The pieces were made from bulky sections and looked heavy and very ornate; dark polished, the surface checks and small faults were desirable features. It was difficult for the mill proprietor to appreciate why we needed such a high standard for the UK market. To keep Montheath interested, to improve the kilning of the thick planks and to encourage him to take greater care, we also placed orders with the company for the thinner sizes. We traded successfully and paid our invoices promptly, and never queried instructions from Montheath to pay some of our bills to his continental agent.

At the beginning of 1992 a lawyer phoned from the United States on behalf of Montheath requesting to see us due to some irregularities. The lawyer (a woman) came to our office and pointed out that we had not paid the shipper for several containers. We were able to prove that, at Montheath's request, we had remitted the money to an account in Belgium in the name of his agent.

The lawyer left, but early in January 1983 Mr Montheath phoned to say that he was coming to England with his attorney and would like to call on us. Strange as it all seemed I accepted the arrangement. On a cold frosty Monday morning, Mr Montheath arrived, accompanied by three men. I had a job to fit them into my small office. He introduced his lawyer, the second advocate, representing his agent, and the third man who spoke with a strong Brooklyn Irish accent. He was enormous and settled on a small stool which he provided himself; then he put on his lap a stenographer's console ready to record every spoken word.

I was asked about non-payment of invoices, and had answers and evidence ready. After about half an hour I halted events and told them that they had no right to hold American court proceedings in the United Kingdom. I requested one of the attorneys to come with me for a short private discussion; this was accepted and Mr Stephen Weinstein, supposedly defending the agent, joined me in our small reception room. He readily answered a few questions. It appeared they intended to visit eight firms in Western Europe to find out where the money had disappeared to.

I suggested that with all respect he was wasting his time and simply increasing costs without much hope of finding the missing cash. If the agent got a prison sentence and an order to repay in instalments, it was likely to be a lifetime before he could settle any significant sums. I suggested that they adjourn to a local motel, discuss the dispute after a good rest, and endeavour to reach a settlement between themselves. He said he would persuade the other lawyer to accept my advice. I also felt that although both attorneys practised in New York State they were more like small town lawyers rather than of any national or international stature. They had never travelled outside America and thought they would have a little trip to Europe at their client's expense. The party left our premises; and we heard nothing for about two weeks, when I received an airmail letter from Mr Weinstein. He thanked me for my wise suggestions and informed me that they had ultimately resolved their problems and returned home.

He ended by comparing me to "Wise King Solomon." I have the original letter on my files. Needless to say we did not trade with Montheath again.

Adrian had been on winter leave, and Leslie visiting a customer, so I faced a most bizarre event all on my own.

An outsize delivery from the Far East

On my visit to the Far East, I had purchased large quantities of dark red meranti and lauan. We had on order some material bought before my trip, some of which was delayed. Most of this was from Tawau on the east side of Kalimantan, which was not a regular port of call for the main shipping lines, and we were all aware that we could not expect early shipments. We anticipated the need to hold larger stocks of air dried timbers and made improvements to our storage area on the western side of the yard. I also decided that, with care and good groundwork, we should be able to stack up to 30 feet in height.

To enable us to implement this, however, we needed cranes with longer jibs than the telescopic machines we were currently using. Leslie looked out for offers of secondhand self-propelled cranes with long lattice jibs. He found two advertised in Scotland by a company that was closing down; he discussed the specification with Jim Pitts, our maintenance manager, who recommended an inspection and they flew to Scotland: This must have been the first journey by air for both of them. They found what was needed and bought the identical pair on the spot at a reasonable price. These old very solidly built machines served us well for many years and one is still in use today.

At the end of 1979, the "Bencruachan" loaded first at Tawau, no doubt not only for Timbmet but also for other importers in the UK. From there the vessel picked up cargo in Samarinda, then in the Philippines and lastly at Kuala Lumpur. Our share on this vessel was about 8000 tons, some 300,000 cubic feet. We coped with just over thirty lorry loads arriving daily at our yard during a two-week period but the volume meant that sometimes lorries had to wait on the roadside. This upset our neighbours opposite the entrance and unfortunately also broke up the pavements. As most of the lauan and meranti was shipping dry, we had to find extra contract labour to handle the goods into stick for air drying.

Opening day at Bicester

The first few months of 1980 kept us exceptionally busy, supervising the completion of the Bicester project, which did not altogether go smoothly as it was a one-off venture for the building contractors and they found it difficult to complete the finishing touches, unlike the two local firms who worked for us regularly.

We engaged a few extra men for Bicester and arranged to transfer several skilled Oxford operatives to work there and teach timber handling techniques to the new staff. We appointed Ian Archibald, known to all of us as 'Archie', as depot manager, and Melvin Curtin as kiln manager, both experienced men. We set the opening day for 1 June, 1980 and invited many customers, architects, a few suppliers, and representatives of our bankers as well as from Trade Indemnity. The latter stood out wearing Victorian morning dress, striped black trousers and black jackets. One of our major customers, Anglian Windows, landed in the yard in their own helicopter adding lustre to the proceedings. Leslie was taken for a short trip to allow him to take aerial photographs of the site.

This was probably the proudest day in the history of our company, achieved by only a few of us. The staff at Bicester settled in to their task and worked well together, but it took almost three months to build up enough stock to keep all twelve kilns in continuous production. We had nineteen bogies ready pre-drying, all in one line opposite the kilns which was an impressive sight. After a few months we achieved an output of approximately 1100m^3 monthly, drying a mixture of species of imported hardwoods in a variety of thicknesses; about 80% was square edged material, the balance log sawn. For a long time all home-grown log sawn timber, which had a slower drying process with a lower capacity per kiln due to shape and waney edges, had been dried at Oxford. From now on we had much more control of our drying schedules so that we could give priority to stock requirements and any urgent gap fillers. We were also able to guarantee larger customers greater quantities ready on the day they needed delivery. We dropped the less reliable firms who were doing contract drying on our behalf, but as we constantly increased our turnover we still had a need for custom kilning, and gave them bulk work for the most popular species, partly as back up stock.

The need for credit insurance

Bexley Timber & Mouldings at Hither Green, in S.E. London, which was owned by a young entrepreneur, Alan Lown, grew very rapidly serving the black economy with cheap hardwoods. It became a big business in a short time. Timbmet was a major supplier but Leslie began to worry as none of our debts were insured; and it was also unlikely that insurance cover could be obtained for this firm. Trade Indemnity in past years had been very inflexible to our suggestions but, realising we were a force to be reckoned with in the trade, made several overtures from head office. Leslie and Geoff Clough used their skills to put up a proposal of our requirements which were not unusual except to grant Timbmet cover for £150,000 for Bexley Timber. Since Trade Indemnity already covered a majority of supplies to Timbmet, it made good commercial sense for them to grant good limits for Timbmet's own customers and they decided to insure the all the Timbmet accounts. This was the start of a love and hate relationship with Trade Indemnity.

Alan Lown sold out after a few years to Malden Timber, retail outlet of the Mallinson Group, and retired early to Spain; Leslie, who knew him well, lost contact. A large company could not easily cope with a business organised on "Steptoe & Son" principles! The business closed and the land was sold.

Brazilian mahogany

In the last few years the awareness in the trade of the quality of Brazilian mahogany gradually spread to all timber using industries in the United Kingdom and to some extent in Europe as well. Our stocks, which we had kept for years, then sold quickly together with many subsequently imported parcels. The old prejudices such as "light in colour and weight, insipid and not a lot of character" were completely forgotten. Unseasoned Swietenia macrophylla could travel long distances out of stick. The local timber merchant started to keep Brazilian mahogany. Most customers who came to their yards wanting a few pieces of hardwood quickly would be served with this timber, which the standard softwood cutters would cope with, whereas African hardwoods, having mostly interlocked grain, would need special tools. I do not think many of us ever considered just how much mahogany was used for this purpose. Timbmet was still

Sticking shorts at Oxford for kilning

increasing its turnover monthly so we continued to import from the Far East or Africa.

We bought from a number of producers, guided by the agents as a few of them had already been out to Brazil and inspected the production of the local sawmills. John Rego of Gulf Stream Traders, a far-sighted Brazilian educated in the United States, helped a great deal in developing export to European countries. He assisted many of the timber companies working in the state of Para with grading, export documentation, letters of credit etc.

CHAPTER 30

1981 and 1982

USA: the early beginnings

Month by month we were purchasing more containers of North American hardwoods, picking up additional quantities from spot offers by many of the agents. We were looking for a more structured approach. We did not yet have many heavy duty concrete roads at Cumnor, so our containers were unloaded opposite the office outside the vehicle workshop, and this allowed Adrian, Leslie and me, without spending a lot of time in the yard, to see the diverse cargoes from different shippers that came from various climate zones in the USA.

Boston: a firm relationship and substantial purchase

Charles Craig put a lot of faith in Holt & Bugbee, a well-run concentration yard near Boston, who had good pre-driers and kilns. They bought their fresh sawn lumber from Pennsylvanian forests, measuring and re-grading the stock after kiln drying and before despatch. I had several invitations to go over, but I did not want to visit them alone, as other suppliers might appear to feel hurt. I was not yet prepared to spend two weeks away from the business, and Charles Craig arranged for the proprietor, Roger Pierce Senior, and his wife to come to Oxford to meet us.

For the first time ever we took the opportunity to socialise with a potentially good shipper and to create a long term partnership. We took Mary and Roger to the usual tourist spots in and around Oxford, leaving them to explore London on their own or with their agents. The highlight of the Oxford visit was a candlelit dinner in the dining hall of Merton College for the annual conference of the Chartered Institute of Secretaries' southern section, and Leslie had managed to get an extra four tickets. Mary and Roger Pierce felt they had revived their English roots in these lovely old surroundings.

In the background serious negotiations were taking place for supplies of American FAS white oak, cherry and ash. At the final session Adrian, who acted as scribe, counted fifty containers to be supplied in the period of three to six months from the date of contract, and which included a small volume of 2½" and 3" white oak for delivery in twelve months' time. We stipulated strict quality conditions and details of specifications. At the time there was an economic downturn in the USA domestic market: but firms with foresight started to export and most of them, looking back ten years later, gained by having both markets for their goods.

We kept repeating these block purchases every few months; we placed orders for most of the popular species which acted as a kind of buffer stock. The relationship worked well until Roger's untimely death at a comparatively young age. After a few difficult years, his two sons and son-in-law have built a flourishing business once more, although they chose to export less to the UK.

North America: more white oak

We traded similarly, although on a smaller scale, with Babcock Lumber Company who had offices in Pittsburgh and the principal sawmill at Champion in the midst of the forest area, some sixty miles south of Pittsburgh. The vice president was Bill Eldridge, an Englishman, who after his war service in the Fleet Air Arm, had emigrated to the USA.

Northland Timber in Kingston, New England, became another reliable supplier. Jameson French was the man in charge of the family business while his father looked after the forest estates. They were very environmentally orientated even in the early days.

The Matson family at Dubois became regular shippers as well as good friends. Very unfortunately they lost their eldest son, which affected the smooth running of the company. Yet again the younger generation are now running a successful business.

Jack Furtado introduced us to J Thomson who had a wholesale business outside Toronto. We found out later that most of his stocks were produced and dried by C J Holmes, of Columbia City, Indiana, who helped to finance the new owners when they bought the business on the retirement of Mr Holmes. This firm was able to supply thicker white oak stocks providing we committed ourselves twelve to eighteen months ahead.

The firms named above were able to supply all our requirements for the present and immediate future. We dealt with the companies direct, but the business was done through their British agents.

Missed acquisition

Timbmet badly needed in-house machining facilities. Our time was so fully occupied with sawn trade that perhaps we did not try hard enough to get the machine side going. Edwin Tauber, owner of Parker Kislingbury near Hereford, had built up a very well organised trade mill. The family had come to England from Danzig just before 1939 and taken over a sawmill in Essex, mainly operating as a trade mill for the conversion of solid English and African logs. Later they bought a neglected home-grown sawmill at Eardisley. They discontinued the trade and gradually built up a machining business, concreted the yard and purchased Nissen huts, which were refurbished and put on a brick base; each building contained a Wadkin moulder. They put up some modern warehouse accommodation, improved the timber office building and modernised the saw shop (one of the tidiest I have ever seen). Obviously, all profits were ploughed back into the business. As soon as they had additional revenue, they built a battery of kilns and developed their own standard profiles. Being rather ambitious they worked with a local agricultural engineer to erect a sticking and de-sticking line which was the size of a football pitch. The timber had to travel long distances and it was a slow-moving operation; it worked most successfully with Far Eastern hardwoods of equal length bundled to widths.

Mr Tauber felt his health fading while still at a young age and, as he did not have a son to succeed him, quietly went about offering his business for sale. He told those timber companies he visited to keep the preliminary discussions confidential: eventually it leaked out, which was resented and considered very un-English. We kept away from most of our competitors, but I met Edwin on several occasions and he said, in front of our accountant, that he would prefer the business to pass into our hands rather than to any other firm as he, his wife and family felt that we would keep the business going and so safeguard most of the jobs. Edwin had married a local wealthy farmer's daughter who obviously seemed to care for the welfare of the local rural community. When he felt unwell, Timbmet started preliminary negotiations but unfortunately as soon as he got better, he would change his mind. We wrongly assumed that Timbmet would be the eventual purchaser, and stopped looking in other directions for about four years. Perhaps we aimed too high; we should have started in a small way. We were assured by Barclays Merchant Bank that finance would not be a problem, and they encouraged us to look for something more substantial which, in their opinion, would be easier to administer.

Changes: MDF and plywood

Our sheet material department grew slowly, mainly at the top quality end of the market place. Adrian enjoyed the challenge. We felt we needed a main supplier for MDF, which was difficult as most manufacturers preferred to trade with the builders merchant groups, who presumably resented our presence. However Mr Rhodes, the managing director of Medite UK, eventually agreed to supply us direct from the factory in Ireland. He accepted my explanation that we would never be selling any substantial volume, but would introduce the product to over 2,000 small users who, for the present, did not seem interested – or were even prejudiced against – MDF.

Israeli plywood began to feel the Far Eastern competition in spite of quality differences. For many applications, the Malaysian and Korean WBP plywood was more than adequate. The central Israeli plywood sales organisation included some factories organised on co-operative lines (kibbutz), one factory partly privately owned and one fully private. As the competition stiffened, they broke loose from the central sales organisation and exported direct. Bert Springall [UK agent for Churchill & Sim] might have whispered this information into my ear, as he represented central sales. I made my approach to Lir, the founder and owner of the only fully privately owned factory, a man of my age who settled with his family in Israel from Russia around 1930. Eytan Kunda became a prosperous lawyer and succeeded in bringing out other more distant members of his family from Russia, giving them employment at his plywood factory.

The war partly waged in North Africa in 1939-45 helped him and other manufacturers to become more than cottage industries. They worked principally as packing case manufacturers for the British army in North Africa and they might have had financial help to equip themselves. Now forty years later, Lir had not modernised but still provided a reasonable product which was allowed to be sold in the famous Tabor brand cartons. The sanding of the thicker boards of 18 and 25 mm were not as smooth or accurate as they should have been but the price difference enabled us to sell large volumes to British Rail who used most of this for hoardings and general repairs.

It leaked out after Bert Springall retired that Mallinson had insisted on and gained a special discount, so it was no wonder that any tenders made by Timbmet to the MOD must have always been substantially higher. The agreement with Lir helped us to compete.

In the period 1967-1972 we introduced a system whereby we chose customers who started work early in the day and phoned them then. We selected owners, managers and estimators who were responsible for the buying and told them we had a part load in their area; and offered them delivery the following day if we got a prompt order. We dropped this practice in 1973, the boom year.

Around 1981, however, daily sales were a little behind so we started phoning again. We had telephone books giving customer details in one area rather than in alphabetical order. Several salesmen shared this task. We got some strange comments such as 'You southerners must still be in bed!' I answered by saying, "In a few years time we shall be able to see each other as we speak!" Unfortunately we never recorded all the cheeky comments we had. One Cockney gentleman said to me, "But I bet you have got *** ***..." and I replied, "You are one of a few sods that work early in the morning!" This created a good relationship.

More growth in computing

In 1980 Leslie and I viewed a demonstration of several computer systems. Geoff Clough, a fully qualified chartered accountant, had just joined us as our chief accountant. I did not play a prominent part in the final implementation and training; but I remember that the two expert NCR personnel, who were supposed to be helping us with our software and eventually with the training of our staff, disappeared halfway through. The company made various excuses. Overall the introduction and instruction of our staff was less problematical than with the first computer system, but on the whole help and service fell far below what was promised. We felt proud of having modernised, and kept improving in line with technological advances in later years. Nevertheless, our old fashioned principles and working methods did not unduly prevent us from increasing our turnover and profit.

A naval connection

For the year ending 31st March, 1982 our turnover was £14,538,000; translated to 2005 values, this is equal to about £26,500,000. We had made approaches to the Ministry of Defence for some years now and we introduced Timbmet at the procurement offices in New Oxford Street, WC1, but we had a warmer reception from the Navy purchasing department at Bath, and managed to talk about timber to the chief inspector, Alan Groves. He was an all round timber expert, especially for naval requirements.

Early in 1982, we landed a wonderful parcel of African mahogany logs. The logs were exceptional in size and of an unusual, very mild texture. I decided to ring Alan and told him that I could show him a parcel of African mahogany logs that had been grown to the MOD specification! I was fully aware that he would be unable to purchase any, but I offered a good timber man a delight to the eye, free of charge! I knew he went to Chatham naval yard at regular intervals, and the logs were stored at Valentine Wood off the A4, so it did not involve an extra long journey for him. Surprisingly he accepted, and we made a date; fortunately the weather was excellent for the time of year.

I went along with photos of our yard and detailed pictures of work produced from our hardwoods for the finest joinery, furniture and boatbuilding. We chatted for half an hour or so, patting and stroking the logs. He said, "I can't refuse any longer to come to see your stocks": Alan Groves came to evaluate the yard at Cumnor, and as a result we received many forms to complete from the New Oxford Street offices. We had a physical inspection by four officials on 28th and 29th September. They wanted to know a great deal about our senior personnel and their private lives; we responded as best we could, and were very open and let them see our records, purchase and sales ledgers. They must have expected that we would come up to their standards, as before leaving we were handed the registration number dated 7th September, 1982, number 17R TO1. The official certificate from MAFF followed in the post. We still have it, framed in the reception area. This meant a great deal to us, as MOD certification was the best reference in our industry.

We also did some good business over the years. Many of the larger tenders were completed by Adrian, but Leslie and I had an input. The margins were tight and, if the goods were up to standard and paper documentation correct, we received very prompt payment. We had a good relationship with several personnel in the Bath purchasing offices and gradually found out that although the standard of requirements were unnecessarily high, one could negotiate a little leeway. From time to time, Adrian tried to persuade the powers that be to amend their own quality regulations to more closely resemble commercial grades, but no one was interested enough to put this request to the higher echelon of the service. If the equipment available to our forces in the Falkland War had not been built to the highest specifications our losses of life would have been much higher.

We had substantial orders for the restoration of the Victory, which is still ongoing over twenty years later. We supplied huge sections in iroko, which the Ghana navy helped to source, and a large volume of genuine teak.

National Hardwood Campaign

The Timber Trade Federation and the British Woodworking Federation, which was then part of the National Federation of Building Trades Employers, joined forces in 1982 and formed the National Hardwood Campaign to promote our products. I was asked to take an interest, which I did willingly. Until now, Timbmet had been loyal members of the TTF but had never accepted higher office. I promised to do my utmost to work with the newly formed committee and to endeavour to help raise funds.

The organisation viewed presentations from three public relations firms and chose the smallest, David Weston. It proved to be the right choice as, unfortunately, we were unable to raise any substantial funds in spite of the rumblings on the horizon against the use of tropical hardwoods, which gathered momentum year by year. We met at the Builders Federation and the secretary of the BWF, Michael Lee, gave us his enthusiastic assistance. David produced many illustrated articles on the beauty and aesthetic value of hardwoods, their lasting properties and many other attributes. He produced an outstanding, eight minute video which received a lot of praise.

We were unable to collect more than £50,000 annually for this most worthy cause; every effort to get assistance from our shippers brought only an occasional paltry contribution. Looking back, I feel I should have forced myself away from the day-to-day conduct of the business and spent time raising the necessary funds needed for a more effective campaign.

David Weston had great success in arranging breakfast meetings with journalists at first-class London West End hotels: these always attracted many young females from the women's magazines, the technical press, DIY and woodworking journals. It was important for the committee to be present with officials of the trade associations and to answer questions raised by the press; and was surprising to find how many good illustrated articles were published. Unfortunately, this campaign lost its momentum after six years due to David Weston experiencing personal problems.

CHAPTER 31

April 1982: Brazil

Growth in importance of Brazilian mahogany

Brazilian mahogany became one of the most important species for Timbmet and the rest of the European trade. We purchased our supplies through accredited timber agents; the bulk of our business at that time was being transacted through Price Morgan, and our personal contact was their young and very capable Douglas Johnston. The main supplier was Madeireira Bannach in Belem, who had sawmills in the state of Para.

I contacted Douglas and he was overjoyed to be invited to accompany me on a trip to South America. He planned a full itinerary lasting about three weeks to include an extensive tour of the north and south as well as one important sawmill in the middle of the country, belonging to the Sebba family. We set out in the middle of April 1982, and flew from Gatwick with British Caledonian Airways to Rio, with one stop at Recife.

Although Douglas and I were in different age groups, Douglas a mere thirty five and myself in my 60th year, we had a great deal in common and got on exceptionally well, both of us being very serious and hard working. Douglas wanted me to have an especially easy day before starting the arduous journey ahead of us. The first night we stayed at a small but very nice and comfortable hotel, the Verde Oro on Copacabana Beach. When we arrived from the airport Douglas told me to go for a swim, and not to take anything with me; when I got to the door the concierge advised me to give him my watch before going out. It was warm and pleasant, and I enjoyed two or three hours swimming and sun bathing. After a light lunch Douglas took me on a short sightseeing tour of the city. We went by taxi to Corcovado, up the mountain where the large statue of Christ stands overlooking the bay, visible from afar in the South Atlantic Ocean and all round the city. The last part of the journey was on foot. It was awe-inspiring, walking up the steps until we reached the base of the statue.

After admiring the magnificent views, we returned to the taxi which then drove us to the Sugar Loaf Mountain. We took the cable car only halfway up to the first station, as the second stage to the top of the mountain was closed due to very strong winds and it was not possible to go any further. We sat down at the café and had cold drinks, looking at the views of Ipanema and Copacabana beaches. The taxi then took us on a short trip around the town. Douglas offered to escort me to a late evening show to see the Samba and Latin American dancing but I declined as I had to be ready early to continue our journey.

Parana pine

Early the next morning we flew to Curitiba, a large modern city in southern Brazil, built in the style of a European city, and is the centre of furniture production for the whole country. Most of the inhabitants were of Italian and German descent. We visited a number of hardwood sawmills in the area and travelled in the direction of the Paraguayan border. This was the area where the Parana pine was plantation grown.

I recollect two mahogany sawmills by name. One was called Batistella. They had particularly large logs and struggled to convert them with existing equipment; most of the boards had to be flat sawn due to the weight restriction on the carriage, producing only medium length but exceptional width. The second was Estil, part of the Casagrande Group, better equipped and more efficient. Both these companies sourced their logs from Mato Grosso.

We visited a number of sawmills who were converting only Parana pine. The sawn timber was air dried in the open, well covered and often under trees. All export sales were through the government agency CCEM, and it was difficult to order from a specific sawmill unless you were a large buyer. At the port, the timber was left in the open before loading so the dryness on arrival in the UK depended on the season, or whether a heavy tropical downfall had drenched it before loading. It was no wonder that claims for dryness and discolouration frequently occurred. When we started to import we bought kiln dried, but no one wanted to pay the extra 80 pence per foot cube (£28.00 per m³). We reached the Paraguayan border at Iguacu where Douglas had a shipper who dealt exclusively in pau-marfim, which at that time was used in England for axe handles and similar tools. Most of these blocks and blanks came from across the border.

We returned two or three days later to Curitiba where Douglas visited the Estil veneer slicing and peeling factory. I was overwhelmed with the sight of the warehouse, full of imbuia cut veneers, a very fine cabinet wood resembling walnut. Douglas wanted to visit one or two furniture manufacturers: one in particular produced oak-like office furniture. The species was cerejeira which was mainly log sawn, available in big widths and lengths with the colour of oak but not the grain. Many importers tried to introduce this species to the UK but the American white oak was always cheaper than the Brazilian substitute, although it had a character of its own. As there was time, we called on the plywood and door factory of Zugman. We were well received by Chaimi Zugman, the managing director. I kept in personal touch with him, but unfortunately the price of the products did not suit our door department.

For good measure we visited the port of Paranagua. The road was cluttered with lorries full of soya beans for export; at a time like this no one loaded any timber. We returned by car to Curitiba, and took a plane to Sao Paulo. We stayed the night at the airport hotel before continuing our journey to Vilhenia.

Douglas wanted to visit Rondonia, a very under populated part of Brazil where the government had tried to rehabilitate the very poor from the big city slums (favellas). The settlers were given some tools and materials to build themselves a simple hut home as a start; most importantly they were allocated a piece of land which was given to them in perpetuity. It was very hard work; some succeeded, others did not. Sometimes a few people in adjoining plots decided to return home, and they managed to sell the land gaining a little cash in the process. In order to clear the land, the government, or the settlers, had to fell the standing timber or burn the area, in some cases both. This attracted a number of timber contractors to relocate their sawmills.

Inland Brazil: Mato Grosso

The next morning we flew from Sao Paulo to Vilhenia by the one and only daily flight. On the way a very heavy thunderstorm developed and the pilot decided to land at Cuiaba airport. This left us stranded for the day and we booked into a small hotel. An hour or two later the storm subsided and Douglas, ever enterprising, came up with an idea. If we could find a small plane to take us to Caceres we could visit Carl Veit Sawmill, about 120 miles south-west. Did I mind taking the risk and sharing the cost? I agreed with the plan, and he found a telephone number for Carl Veit who said he would be pleased to see us. It wasn't far to the airport and Douglas, with his basic Portuguese, managed to persuade a pilot of a small plane to fly us there after lunch, provided the weather improved. We stayed at the airport ready to take off; the weather settled so the pilot agreed. We landed on a small airstrip near the village and close to the sawmill, which was by the river. The village was built in Portuguese style: three hundred years ago Portuguese invaders managed to travel along the rivers and settle in the middle of the country, far away from the sea.

Carl Veit, his wife, two sons and daughter were Jewish refugees from Germany, a family of timber merchants who had settled in Mato Grosso in the 1930s. After a time they started a sawmill catering for local demand and gradually built up a flourishing business. They invested in modern machinery, and after 1950 started to export. There was a good supply of quality mahogany logs available quite close. They were represented in England by Charles Boss Timber Agency. The stock was first-class, well produced and always slightly more expensive than others, ideally suited for high quality cabinet making; the majority was also colour matched. Twenty five to thirty years later the quality of their timber gradually dropped, although they denied this was the case, as they were using the best logs for veneers. It was due to our unexpected visit that we discovered the reason.

The timber building which was originally the family home was the office at that time. (They now have comfortable flats in Sao Paulo.) We were fortunate that Carl Veit Senior was at the mill the day we visited. He told us about the family background, and how they built the business, often working hard manually to lead and train the unskilled labour. We were amazed to see two large almost new veneer peelers and a slicer: this immediately explained the reason for the drop in quality of the sawn material in the last year or two. It didn't really matter to Timbmet, as Carl Veit were never principal suppliers. These high class veneers were exported to many parts of the globe.

Next door was the sawmill where we saw the input of logs which were of much lower quality. Mr Veit took us by car a short distance to the young teak plantations, which had replaced the mahogany jungle. He was exceptionally proud to return something to the local community who had allowed him to settle and thrive there. We had tea on the veranda and met his wife and son, Carl, who was interested to learn something of my background, and how we came to settle in England. It was late afternoon when we boarded our small plane back to Cuiaba. During our return journey, not long after we took off, another tropical storm blew up. It was a very turbulent journey! As darkness fell we enjoyed the lightning display illuminating the sky.

Rondonia

We landed at Cuiaba safely and after a night's rest we managed to catch the next flight to Vilhenia. Price Morgan's main connection in Rondonia was Mareamex. They were very ambitious, aiming to grow fast and become very profitable without too much financial investment. We had already had received supplies from them. The timber packs were well presented, carefully bundled, with flush ends and waxed with an impressive logo of two palm trees; but on inspection of the individual boards they were never quite of the quality we expected. Mr Alexander had visited on their behalf and argued that theirs was the best quality available.

Douglas wanted to find out more about them while on the spot, and I was only too willing to accompany him. Mareamex owned a very fine house in Vilhenia where we were accommodated; there were not many European style guest houses in the area at that time. I felt that they were always talking in exaggerated terms. (This was not a strange custom for Brazilians and they excelled in it.) I do not think Mareamex owned any mills, and may have done some pre-financing. They wanted us to visit their primary supply sawmill which was deep into the Collerado district, and we boarded a single engine plane at first light, and one and a half hours later landed on the bush strip at Pimento Bueno.

We were accompanied by the owner, Alfonso and his financial partner, Osmar. We were met on arrival by a convoy of two small trucks and a VW Beetle. It's surprising how well this little air-cooled car coped with the road conditions, although I believe the Brazilian version had stronger springs fitted and oversized tyres! We had crossed a large river by a primitive ferry and travelled about 50 kilometres when, coming round a bend, we were confronted by a loaded timber truck which had slewed off the "road" into a ditch and blocked our path.

The Brazilians wanted to turn back. I asked how far to the mill and they said 10 to 12 kilometres; I insisted that we should walk. Everyone was much younger than me, and they had no alternative other than to accept my proposal. Close by we saw some saplings and I asked if one of the

Brazilians, who had a machete, could make one into a walking stick. I took my kibbutz hat out of my satchel and started to walk, ignoring the protests of the others. Douglas walked beside me, and when we looked back the party of Brazilians was following behind us.

It was hot and humid, but we saw the forest better than from the car or plane. We admired the flora and the fauna and could not keep our eyes off the many different types of butterflies. We walked partly through forests and partly through areas that had been cleared, and then burnt, eventually to grow crops. Douglas had very light skin and I noticed he was burning, so I insisted that he should wear my cap and we kept alternating with it to keep ourselves protected. On some of the crossroads we met smallholders pushing a sack of produce on the bars of their bicycles to the market, and on one occasion we saw a man with a pony and trap.

Finally we arrived, tired and hot. The mill manager and staff were expecting very important visitors and were astonished to see us walking bedraggled into their yard. After a very short greeting, I slipped off my shoes, took my wallet out of my pocket and stood fully clothed in the shower to cool off. We then sat in the garden of the mill house and were provided with food and drink. They had tame monkeys, which were roaming around freely.

The mill was only cutting the poor remnants from the previous season as the saw doctor they had hired had not shown up and no one knew when he would come. At the end of the log carriage, I noticed that the widths selection lever was broken near the wheel. This could have been repaired with a 6mm nail and a little soldering, but the sawmill manager would not accept this. I watched them cutting low grade material and they used the thumb to determine the 1" thickness, so I asked how they would cut 2½". The answer given was "duo milo polegaros" (two and a half thumbs)!

We had discussions with Alfonso and Osmar about our requirements and listened to their future plans for the coming season. We eventually retired for the night at the bunk house on a solid wooden bed base with a thin mattress. All the windows were fully shut because of the insects and the monkeys (who made me feel rather nervous.) It was also very hot and humid, but we were so tired we slept. In the morning we washed under the tap and hoped nobody noticed our nudity. Presumably our hosts knew that the road had now been cleared, and we made our way back by the route we had come.

We stayed another three nights in Vilhenia and enjoyed hospitality with Mareamex. On Friday we visited Vaz, a few kilometres outside the town

Philippine lauan air-drying at Oxford, 1982

who had a reasonably equipped sawmill and produced a fair quantity of lumber daily. The owners, Mr Rhohun de Moura and Mr Helis Moreiro, spoke very little English and called on a nearby English Methodist minister to interpret. The next call was to Estil sawmills where they wasted a lot of time trying to show off, attempting to load a long and extra large log onto the band mill, and then being unable to cut it!

They took us by logging truck to a forest operation next to a dry bed in the river. I had to sit on Douglas's knee and we were wedged into the corner of the truck against the door to save us from being thrown through the windscreen at every turn. It was interesting to see how they saved the crowns of the trees for the production of curly veneers; and although they were a well-to-do company and had expensive veneer slicing machines at Curitiba, investment in this sawmill was not nearly adequate.

CHAPTER 32

April 1982: Brazil (continued)

On Saturday we had a conference with the owners of Mareamex. They had grandiose plans and dreams of becoming the largest producers and exporters of mahogany in Brazil, creating a monopoly. They told us that the road from Vilenhia to Cuiaba was now tarmacked so there existed an all weather road to the southern ports. Shipments from Santos and Rio Grande would be despatched at very regular intervals in the future; and there was also a railway link part of the way to Paranagua. Alternatively, timber could be transported by barge from Porto Velho to Belem by various rivers, and if the water was high the journey would take less than six weeks.

Douglas and I stressed over and over again that the requirements in Western Europe were very exacting and that timber must be accurately sawn, properly graded, not stained, but light in colour, and adequately shipping dry, or, better still in the long term, kiln dried. Swietenia kept exceptionally well out of stick for up to six months depending on weather conditions. Unfortunately, Alfonso declared himself bankrupt not many years later; according to Douglas, he lost everything and took a lowly clerical post in a government office.

I had to learn how to be patient in dealing with the Brazilians. Everything had to be repeated over and over again; mealtimes seemed to go on for ever, and I had the disadvantage of not being able to eat the rich meats cooked in delightful sauces. I was content with the plain fish, rice and dairy products available, and as a result I kept in good health. Poor Douglas sometimes complained of stomach-ache, due to the local pork, but it never prevented him from being fully active.

The Sunday programme was for us to go to their yard in Vilhenia where they had accumulated a very large quantity of shorts, offcuts and second quality mahogany which they were hoping to finger joint. They were very proud of this, and wanted us to see the finger jointing plant and kilns. Then they arranged for us to fly back to Cuiaba in a small plane which, as there was no weekend jet service, meant we had to fly at precisely 10.30am.

We got up very early on Sunday morning, had breakfast and thanked the domestic staff for looking after us so well. Alfonzo and Osmar took us by car to their yard and found they hadn't brought the keys. One of the neighbours had a homemade ladder and I climbed up the ladder on to a fence and jumped into the yard, and the owners had to follow. The ladder was not made to British standards but from timbers of doubtful origin and strength!

Yet again they were over optimistic: the small jointing plant and kilns could never have coped with the volume of timber already in stock. In addition to this, we had to tell them that the trade in Europe was not ready to accept finger jointed joinery while there was so much solid timber available in the world.

They took us to the airport where we met the pilot. The weather was kind and sunny all the way. We flew over a lot of jungle and scrubland, and wondered how many days it would take to find us if the pilot were forced to land in an emergency. The pilot told us he aimed to land at precisely three o'clock. As we approached Cuiaba Airport, he was looking in all directions, ahead and also to the left and right. Finally he made a perfect landing. He was relieved to be on the ground safely with his passengers, and confessed that his radio and his instruments were not working properly but would be fixed the next morning! The airport control gave him permission to land at that time as the traffic was very light.

Sao Paulo

Early on Monday morning we flew to Sao Paulo, a very large, bustling city with over 10,000,000 inhabitants: with its surroundings, it is one of the major industrial areas of Brazil. In some wide avenues and subways cars moved freely; elsewhere there was great congestion.

I visited two timber yards unconnected with Price Morgan. We booked into a sizeable hotel, and I was collected by a representative of Herman Binder who drove me to an industrial area well outside the town where they had a large concentration yard with limited kilning. On the journey we passed factory gates where the employer was trying to force the employees to leave. The men refused and managed to shut the gates; and there was a great deal of hustling and booing. When I asked the driver what this was all about he said the men wanted to keep their jobs but that the firm was going bankrupt. By staging a sit-in they were trying to force the management, or the liquidator, to pay them six months' worth of health stamps (health insurance), otherwise they could not get any medical help for themselves or their families.

I met Mr Binder at the yard, a capable young man, son of very rich parents, who owned and rented out much of the industrial property in the area. In addition to this, some of the wider family were employed in timber extraction and sawmills in the upper Mato Grosso area. He hardly ever went there. I imagined it was a low cost operation and that the timber was delivered to the yard virtually ungraded. I assumed that in such a big city as Sao Paulo there was a ready market for every quality.

It was very quickly evident that they liked to produce for export an 80/20 grade rather than full FAS. This gave them a better overall yield. One of the major faults that I disliked was the volume of mis-cut timber included, apart from sap, wormhole and rough grain. While walking round the yard I was introduced to two German graders, one working for a large European importer and the other freelance. They spent at least five or six months of the year living in Brazil. There must have been a good volume of timber coming through in the drier season from sawmills to Binder's yard, but I realised this was not what the English market wanted and I was taken back by car to the centre of town to the headquarters of the Banco Real.

On arrival at the bank I was met by the eldest son of the main shareholder who was normally in charge of the British branch in the city of London. He explained to me that his family were the largest private bankers in Brazil. The building was very impressive and ultra modern. It was the first office block I had seen with a large atrium on the ground floor where there were lovely plants, flowers and trees. They suggested I might phone home free of charge; this would be by satellite link and I should expect a lot of echoing. This was all new to me.

I was taken by an official to the other side of town where, among other interests, the family had a timber business. It was almost a replica of what I had seen at Binders but there were some exceptional long and wide planks available 18–21'. The grading was again 80/20, but in very long lengths. It was a great temptation as customers who don't want to joint are generally willing to accept one or two small faults. They would have liked me to buy large quantities of their products and offered very extended credit terms. Relying on experience, and from Douglas's descriptions of the type of timber available in the northern state of Para, I politely declined. However, I did manage to buy several parcels of very long lengths without a premium, which was shipped as available over a period of time.

193

To confuse those importers who habitually visited the docks to see timber cargoes arriving, I had these consignments marked with Arab first names and without the producer's logo. I did keep my social contact with the young banker in London. The London branch of Banco Real is now part of ABN Amro. I was unable to get any information from them recently on the whereabouts of my former connection.

Goiania

From Sao Paulo we went to Goiania which is a large town in the prosperous state of Goias. Douglas had a good connection with the Sebba family, who were probably of Middle Eastern origin. They had a very large well organised builders' merchants and an agricultural implements business. We were received by the oldest brother, Gilberto, in an office that you would normally see in films! We had an early lunch and were then taken to the nearby sawmill. The equipment was average and, as one would expect, in good working order.

They had a species called cambara available in very large logs, which was cheaper than mahogany but a little more brittle. The main problem was a very distinct light brown sapwood with a darker brown heartwood and this contrast was difficult to blend in when staining. We had sample parcels sent which were not well received by the trade in the UK. I doubt if adequate quantities would have been available in the long term. The species disappeared from the market for a time but more recently smaller quantities were offered from a Belgian source which did not include such a large volume of sapwood. The thicknesses on offer were 25mm, 32mm and 38mm only; no one attempted to kiln dry anything thicker.

In the early evening Gilberto took us out of town to show us five magnificent homes being built, four very large mansions for the brothers and one smaller house in the centre for their mother: they were also constructing a leisure complex including a swimming pool. The high wall surrounding these buildings was already in place. Afterwards we were taken out to dinner. The dish of the day was the rich man's version of a black bean soup. Everyone was surprised that I did not want to eat it. We said our goodbyes to Gilberto, and although Douglas and I found what we had seen most interesting, we wanted to get to Para to visit the major shippers serving the UK market.

Belem

There were no direct flights from Goiania to Belem. We had to fly to Brasilia, the new capital city of Brazil, and change planes to fly to Belem. We had a four hour wait which gave us the opportunity to hire a taxi which took us on a short sightseeing trip of this modern city with wide avenues and new government buildings. We paid a brief visit to the national parliament which was in session and admired the splendid interior. The most interesting building was the new Roman Catholic cathedral; the interior was built to resemble the Basilica of St. Peter's in Rome. The outside was ultra-modern, an outstanding piece of architecture designed by the world famous architect Oscar Niemeyer.

CHAPTER 33

May 1982: North Brazil

It was my first visit and I was looking forward to meeting our main suppliers for Brazilian mahogany in the state of Para. I was given to believe that the timber was of better quality with hardly any defects and of good mild texture. The lengths we were receiving were better than that from the southern region we had just visited and also of a more even colour. The producers had been established a little longer and with the help of John Rego, an export merchant of Gulf Stream Traders, they had guidance as to the foreign market's requirements as well as shipping procedures.

I had met a few of our suppliers when they visited us in England and was looking forward to seeing their mills. By 1982 the annual export of this timber reached about 100,000m^3 to the UK. It peaked three to four years later to 135,000m^3 and then gradually started to decrease due to price and environmentalist pressures.

The English market also purchased a cheap hardwood by the name of virola which grew mainly in the swamplands on the low lying islands in the River Amazon. The timber was subject to heavy blue stain if not properly handled as soon as it was cut. It was mainly stood up in 'A' racks to let the sap run out quickly to avoid staining. Much of the stock was dried in merchants yards in Belem harbour before despatch. The timber was relatively cheap and used in furniture manufacturing in England. The availability was seasonal. In the state of Para there was an abundance of heavy and durable hardwood for which, at the time, there was only a very limited interest, with the main usage being for railway sleepers. Some of the species now are in demand as they are available FSC certified.

The north-west of the country towards Manaus also produced lighter hardwoods which had properties similar to the Far Eastern shorea, which we did not buy in the UK as the dark red meranti from the Far East was more economical.

*****

I'm going to describe my journey and record on paper some of my interesting experiences and mention the names of our principal suppliers.

These are by no means all of the firms visited; many of both the small and large companies were engaged solely in mahogany production.

The Bannach family and sawmills

Douglas and I had an uneventful flight from Brasilia to Belem and were met by Rubens Bannach, eldest son of Mr Alquarinho Bannach, who was founder of the business. We were taken to our hotel where we deposited our luggage and then went to their offices and warehouse in Belem. After all-round introductions, we were ushered into Mr Bannach senior's office where we started negotiations. Douglas had sent our requirements ahead of our arrival. We wished to purchase 3,000m³ of Swietenia, best FAS quality, to be shipped over seven to eight months during 1982. The specification was important, as was the breakdown of monthly requirements.

The day went by very quickly but no agreement was in sight. This was the way most business was conducted. It was very frustrating and very different from Western European practice. We had an early evening meal in a modern air conditioned restaurant. They asked us to visit their main sawmill in Rio Maria and we were eager to go; and they explained that the haze in the atmosphere caused by farmers burning crops was a danger to small aircraft operating in the jungle. We said that we also wished to call on other suppliers with mills in and around Belem, and would be able to get the airport at very short notice, as soon as they felt the conditions became suitable to make the trip.

I spent the following morning visiting Danielo Remor, the owner of Majinco Sawmills in Belem. He was of Italian origin and had a flair for machinery and design. He had the best equipped sawmill I visited in Brazil and kept the plant well maintained. One of the few who was waste conscious and had a little environmental awareness, he also manufactured some value added products for the local market. I came to like and respect him, but for some unexplained reason he was never a large supplier to Timbmet.

There was a phone call from Rubens asking me to be ready to come to the mill in the morning as the weather conditions were improving and the haze would not be such a hazard. We also had an invitation to have an evening meal with Fatima and John Rego, and I was looking forward to meeting them socially. Douglas and I were driven to the outskirts of the town to a very select housing estate on the banks of a lake; we were told that most of the inhabitants were employees of an American oil company. We had a wonderful evening together. They lived in the lap of luxury and laid on a very sumptuous meal, most of which I was able to eat. I was so sad as on the way out of town to their home we passed a large slum area where we saw people living in shacks in great poverty. They probably had an adequate amount of basic food which nature provided, but very little else; I felt like sharing some of the delicacies with them.

I asked John whether he was not afraid to leave his young and very beautiful wife and two boys in the house during his many trips abroad. He assured me that the two guards and their dogs were adequate protection for his family. A few years later the Regos, Bannachs and a number of wealthy local timber producers, joined together and built modern blocks of flats in the town centre where they felt more protected and secure.

It was late evening when we were taken back to the hotel and, after a few hours' rest, Douglas and I took a taxi to the airport where Rubens and another member of staff greeted us. We boarded the company aircraft and after a two hour flight landed at Rio Maria, where a station wagon was waiting to drive to the Bannach Sawmill complex, a few miles away, near Araguaia.

On arrival we were introduced to various members of the Bannach family, all of whom were responsible for different departments. Most of them lived locally, some on the sawmill site. Douglas and I were shown to our rooms, and after a light lunch, we had a tour of the site. The log stock was still low, mainly of the second quality logs left behind from the previous season. The ground was still too wet to transport the newly felled logs to the mill.

The main mill was on a raised timber platform to ensure the safety of some of the drive belts which were positioned to be safe under the floor. The principal band mill was equal to those used in England twenty five years earlier, with no electronic attachments. Above all it was simple to operate and maintain. I was not satisfied with the way the machine performed or with the evenness of cutting. I took my time before I spoke because I did not want to make a wrong statement and cause offence unless I was convinced that I was right in my criticism. In the end I lay on the floor and watched the carriage travel on the rails as the cut proceeded. There was definitely wear on the wheels. It was not long before they called out to me, "Which god are you praying to?"

This gave me the opportunity to express my thoughts. I was very surprised that at the beginning of the new season the main conversion machine was not in good condition. The carriage was not running fully true along the rails and, above all, the two large wheels on which the saw was revolving were out of alignment and this would soon cause major problems. I also felt that the wheels would need to be reground.

As expected the management were very upset. The foreman said he would prove me wrong. He personally would sharpen a band saw that night, and asked if I would care to be at the mill at six o'clock in the morning when the first shift started work. As I did not have far to come, I promised to be present provided some one would wake me. The management and I had a meal after work on the premises before going home, no doubt discussing the next day's work programme. I was persuaded to taste the local alcohol, "Caipirinha" which was made from sugar cane! I spoke only a few sentences of Portuguese. They didn't speak any English, but by sketches and sign language I managed to convey some of my thoughts to them and Rubens translated the rest. I was not the most popular guest at the mill bungalow that evening!

Later on, Douglas and I were left in the company of Rubens, one of his bothers and an uncle. I praised them for their enterprise and the effort it must have taken to establish in the wilderness not only a sawmill but also a plywood manufacturing plant. The machinery must have been dismantled to allow the transport over the last sixty kilometres to the mill on a laterite road with primitive bridges, and full of ruts and potholes.

Early days of the Bannach family

This improved the atmosphere and Rubens told us how it all started. The government of Brazil encouraged farmers in the south to leave their unprofitable coffee and cocoa plantations in the areas where there were risks of winter frosts. They offered them vast timber lands to exploit the forest and gradually establish cattle ranches. Mr Bannach senior promised his sons a better future and above all a car for each of them if they accepted the challenge!

They described how the three of them lived in tents and walked and surveyed part of the 70,000 acres allocated to them. They decided where to establish the mill and slowly, with the aid of very favourable government loans, built their enterprise. They gradually invited other members of their family and acquaintances in the south to join them, and recruited and trained local labour as the business progressed. The

Bannachs were never in full control of the total area as outsiders and squatters moved in to start subsistence farming when the roads were improved. In the process they burnt valuable forest. I am sure this is how the sawmill industry in the state of Para developed. Many other families have similar stories.

Electricity was provided by oil burning generators. The lorries were built for a dual purpose with a square fuel storage tank, above a sturdy floor with drop sides. Due to the road conditions the lorries carried only half their normal capacity in either direction. Diesel fuel was taken to the mill and sawn products back to the port, no more than 10 - 12 tons of payload each way. The sawn timber was packed by hand so as to keep the height of the vehicle as low as possible. All final grading and packaging had to be done at the port.

I was up in time in the morning to see the mill start up. Slightly smaller logs were prepared and the cooler temperature and a new band saw, well-honed, all helped to make it more efficient with less vibration but it did not change my mind. I forecast that they would be compelled to shut down for a major overhaul in the midst of the busy dry season.

I thanked the mill manager and foreman for their efforts and hoped we would meet again. Many months later Rubens wrote to Douglas that I was right. They had had to renovate the band mill as I feared at a most inconvenient time. Rubens wanted me to know that as the Brazilian band mill manufacturers, Schiefer, were well known for creating large bills by recommending the replacement of parts which were not worn to increase their profit, companies were always reluctant to call on their services until absolutely necessary.

Other sawmills

Douglas arranged with Rubens for a driver to take us to visit other sawmills in the vicinity. We returned to base in the evening. I want to mention Serraria Marajoara, best known as Semasa at Radencao, owned by Honorato Babinski, a gentleman of Polish parentage, who only spoke Portuguese and a smattering of English. He was not at the mill but I had the pleasure of meeting him and Mr Kaminski later in Belem, two heavyweights with knives in their boots! The mill was of similar layout to Bannach. They also cut veneers which were, believe it or not, dried naturally in racks. A person was in charge of turning the leaves from one face to another to keep them as flat as possible. In later years they produced a lot of thicker planks in "padron" export grade ("padron" meaning an expert) which was good value.

In the evening we continued our discussions back at the mill with Rubens trying to agree to all details of the contract but with all the efforts of Douglas, we did not come to a final agreement. In order to have a cheaper product available, Rubens offered us exclusive rights to sell andiroba in the UK. Somehow they never got round to cutting it as the extraction from their forest was more difficult. We may not have been successful then, but now we are selling it FSC certified.

On a later visit Rubens tried to take me to the forest which was about 300 feet above sea level but we could not make it, even in a powerful four wheel drive vehicle, and after a few hours we had to turn back.

The next day we spent time in the area visiting other producers and in the evening we flew back to Belem. Douglas and I went to see a number of shippers and exporters in the area of the port. We went to some of the mills together and I visited other companies by myself. East Asiatic and Nordisk each had their own concentration yard and bought from smaller mills, graded and sorted at their yard in Belem for export. They and other companies used the only kilns in Belem, run by the firm of Sao Bernardo which was owned by Mr De Souza. I looked at their kiln schedules; they were very basic, but fortunately Brazilian mahogany could take a lot of punishment and did not easily case harden even with harsh treatment. Some of the timber these firms handled came by river from Rondonia and was close piled in barges for a long time while in transit.

When I visited Brazil a second time in 1994 there was an economic recession. The lower grade did not sell and huge quantities of timber were close piled in the local yards and in the port area. I tried to persuade the owners to put the timber into stick as eventually the boards would discolour and become doaty, but they would not listen. When trade recovered, they started to bundle and sort for export and then suffered big losses.

Other producers

Musa and Impar were regular suppliers. We valued their ability to provide wide material 18" and up for table tops and similar work. Pau d'Arco often supplied extra ordinary specialist grained timber, which we put aside for the production of fine cabinets and musical instruments. We bought from a number of different firms as, for a time, we had difficulties in meeting the demand for mahogany. Some companies are no longer trading; others are milling secondary species.

On all his journeys Douglas paid a visit to the agencies of the shipping companies. Until 1992, Booth Line was the only regular operator shipping from Belem to the UK discharging at Heysham.

Final business with the Bannachs

On the last Saturday of our trip we had a final meeting with the Bannach family at their offices. John Rego was present, acting as mediator, and we came to an arrangement and concluded a substantial order.

On Saturday afternoon Douglas and I had a long walk in the port area to get a feeling of what other markets were buying. We saw timber being prepared for loading to the USA and various European destinations. Sometimes we trespassed and in one instance we got a very frosty, hostile reception from Mr Idamar Perachi, owner of Expordatora Perachi. He was a late starter and, as a result of our unscheduled meeting, became a supplier to Timbmet and at the same time appointed Price Morgan to be his selling agent. His business grew faster than some of the older firms, and in 1985 he established a second plant in Rondonia which he closed five years later. He offered all his stock very reasonably towards the end of 1990 for early clearance.

Freight affairs

We found out that one of the two shipping companies operating a regular freight service from Santos to England had no cargo booked on their last vessel before the end of the year due to the Christmas holidays. We offered them the parcel of timber which they were pleased to accept and we negotiated a very favourable freight rate with their agents. This stock unbalanced our inventory of mahogany. It took us two years to sell but was a very profitable business for Timbmet.

Journey's end in sight

It was a hot afternoon and Douglas and I were both very tired as we walked back from the port towards the town centre. There was no taxi in sight but we were fortunate when a car pulled up offering us a lift. It was no other than Ned St Rose, an officer of the Booth Line and an Englishman. We bought him a drink and invited him for a light early evening meal at the hotel, which he was pleased to accept. As expected, on our own, we discussed freight rates and volume discounts but he had a cast iron excuse. As a port manager for Booth Line, his main task would be to ensure the vessels' quick turn round in port and also assist with the ship sailing schedules. The freight rates were to be decided at the Liverpool head office.

A sightseeing visit

On Sunday we had a rest day. Douglas went with some members of the Bannach family to the beach, quite a long distance from town. I was invited to see Belem by Christian Mengel of EAC, whom I had got to know well since my visit to the Far East, and Christian Mathiesen of Nordisk. They took me to the old town and port which was partly fortified with guns facing out to sea to deter the Portuguese invaders and pirates.

I was shown the Catholic Cathedral, University area and business centre. They took me to the old synagogue established by Jewish Portuguese settlers who came several centuries ago. Many have now inter-married and been completely assimilated. Some of the pews are still marked with the Sephardi family names, and others with Germanic names indicating the last immigrants from Central Europe fifty to sixty years ago. We returned to the hotel and I expressed my hope of seeing them in England soon and said jokingly, "Never thought I would see the day when one Jew was squeezed by two Christians!"

As shippers were complaining year by year of rising costs I attempted to ascertain the approximate costs, the price paid for the standing timber, cost of extraction, milling and all incidentals including delivery to port. Very little information was provided and one often wondered whether they knew themselves. The government provided the producers with very cheap, almost interest free, loans to encourage exports.

We had an uneventful trip back to Gatwick where Pietra and David, Douglas's one year old son, were there to meet us. David stretched his arms towards me thinking I was his daddy, but I stepped back very quickly so as not to disappoint him.

Douglas and I made two return trips, in spring 1984 and 1986. On these occasions we did not return to Rondonia but mostly visited our northern suppliers and Curitiba. It was easier to arrange one's requirements on the spot. Douglas went twice yearly on his own, probably accompanied by other British importers.

HM Customs: a short anecdote

When we began to import during the immediate postwar period, procedures were much longer and more complicated. Customs forms had to be completed and all deletions had to be initialled at either end of the line. If one initial was missing the forms would be invalidated, and if they were returned, it would cause delays at the forwarding agent making the customs entry late at the port. Fortunately this is now all behind us and procedures are simpler. Fax duplicates are accepted providing original documentation follows as soon as available.

We were beginners and foreigners so HM Customs Oxford branch took a fatherly interest in Timbmet, sometimes giving good advice. One youngish official came more regularly than others so we got to know him quite well. Although we moved offices in March 1963 and came under Abingdon, and then later Milton office, we still saw the Oxford friend passing the yard occasionally.

In the middle of 1982 he phoned Leslie and said he would visit us to say goodbye. He was retiring and moving away from the area. I knew of his interest in fishing and thought a book would be an appropriate parting gift to express our gratitude.

He turned up as arranged. We offered a cup of coffee and he began to recollect the day in 1948 when a large crate similar in size to a 20-foot container was unloaded in the front drive of our home and offices at 110 Banbury Road, Oxford. The crate was sealed and could only be opened in the presence of a customs officer. He wanted me to know that he felt sorry for my father and the misfortune that had befallen our family and wanted to help.

However he did not believe father's declaration that all the contents were second-hand. He described the very fine reproduction bedroom furniture in the 'Biedemeier' style in cherry, and sycamore lined wardrobes and the painted country scenes on each piece with a young girl wearing local costume. The walnut dining room suite was much heavier in style and the beautiful cabinet had glass doors for the storage of silver and porcelain. There was only one original chair with cabriole legs, the others just a cheap modern version. He did believe that this belonged to the family and that my father found this with an antique dealer who bought this from a Nazi officer when he fled home after the allied troops drove the German army out of Slovakia.

But he knew the kitchen cabinets were new as he saw the sawdust in the drawers. The fine china dinner and tea service did not have a chipped plate and was all in perfect condition as was an executive desk in oak with a bentwood chair. Soon after he finished his story he took his leave and we wished one another well. We never heard from him again as he left no forwarding address. Unfortunately I do not remember his name. It did show that HM Customs could sometimes have a human touch.

CHAPTER 34

1983 and 1984

Sales organisation

Our turnover for the year ending March 1983 was £18,900,000 which equates to £28,000,000 in 2005.

How did the sales department manage without email, mobile phones and blackberries? My story would not be complete without mentioning our sales philosophy. We went to extraordinary lengths to satisfy our customers, meet their wishes and put up with their idiosyncrasies. We made time to go and inspect the timber whenever there was a large claim; we watched for those customers complaining regularly about quality and were very precise before we issued credit notes. I studied the international timber markets and always kept myself up to date with economic and political events worldwide. I exploited all weaknesses in the trade to make advantageous purchases.

It was our policy to buy whenever possible from first-class shippers. The price difference was insignificant against Timbmet's lower overheads. We could easily afford to supply premier brands while our competitors would only deliver average grades; the larger furniture manufacturers nearly always bought on price alone and could not be persuaded to compare the difference in waste factors of the quality produced by different shippers.

Early in our trading days, we also bought and air dried dimension stock, e.g. strips, shorts and squares, provided that the material was well produced and graded. We always kept a great variety of species in stock in the main thicknesses used in the UK [⅝" to 4" KD], and in some we also had a small quantity of timber air drying up to 8" thick.

We gave a speedy delivery service. The aim was to supply 70% to 80% of orders by our own transport and the remainder by haulage contractor. If kept properly sticked and protected in the open, most hardwoods, particularly African redwoods, remained in good condition; in fact, they improved by drying gradually. When these parcels were put into the kilns they could be finished off to 10% to 12% moisture content very quickly and with hardly any distortion or degrade.

With six outside salesmen, we covered nearly all England and Wales. In recollection, circa 1980–1983 the sales team was:

In the office	On the road
Mike Mowforth (Office Sales Manager)	George Clarkson
Ian Hipkin	Tom Bunting
Martin West	Peter Pearce
Sean O'Sullivan	Vic Webb
Noel Learoyd	John Hawley
Tom Eley	Ken Stokes
Steve O'Donoghue	
Nigel Warmington	

Steve O'Donoghue and Nigel Warmington looked after the larger consumer customers and regional, family owned timber merchant businesses, but not the large national importers.

By the end of 1987 we had split the north of England into two sales territories. John Hawley did the north east of England only, and Noel Learoyd, who was happy to relocate himself and family to north Cheshire, covered the north west of England. This proved a very successful arrangment.

Six men covering most of the country meant high mileage and a lot of time travelling by car, and to provide maximum efficiency we encouraged the salesmen to stay away overnight. The cost of modest hotel accommodation was more than repaid by the ability to make additional customer calls. We aimed at six weekly cycles during which George Clarkson had four consecutive nights out in the Leicester area, four consecutive nights out in the Portsmouth area and four in Norwich. John Hawley spent nine nights out in each period in the north; Tom Bunting and Peter Pearce managed to get home every night.

Of this team three have passed away, one has retired, four have left to work for competitors, and one joined an evangelist society. The rest are still with our group of companies.

Each representative was expected to post daily details of his customer visits on forms provided by the company, and these would be altered from time to time. They were encouraged to use post boxes which had a late collection which ensured, in those days and in most instances, that the letters arrived overnight. They were instructed to make on the spot decisions during their calls, and if a larger quantity were involved, the salesmen were required to ring the seniors in the office, DK, LB, or MM, or at least talk it over with their colleagues for the area. For speed of decision we used the following guide:

• Do we wait for the customer to come back of his own accord?
• Do we follow up the same day?
• Do we reduce the price?
• If decide to follow up, who makes the phone call?

    i. Senior management
    ii. Inside salesman, or
    iii. Outside salesman

Once the decision was made there was to be no recrimination. We didn't win all the orders but we aimed to obtain a sizeable proportion without sacrificing too much on the price.

I spoke to each of the representatives personally every evening, which gave me a feeling for the market. I took details for urgent written quotations which I dictated on tape at home, ready for typing up the following morning, and which left me free to deal with other matters during normal working hours. When I felt it necessary I would contact the inside salesperson early the next day, and brief Mike Mowforth on major items of interest. In later years Sean O'Sullivan was our sales manager, and from about 1995 onwards the more experienced inside salesmen talked to the outside salesmen direct.

The written reports were scrutinised in great detail and we had lists of good customers, "sleeping beauties" and "hard nuts": the two latter were phoned regularly and contacted in writing. Over a period of time one learned to distinguish between genuine calls and smaller customers who had spare time to chat: in many cases they were working while they talked.

For a number of years I met George Clarkson and Tom Bunting monthly, often on a Sunday morning, and occasionally they came home for lunch. I met the other salesmen once a month on a weekday. Eventually the business became too large for me to spare the time for this, and Sean helped me. During the summer holiday period we found it hard to cope which meant that these visits were not as productive as intended.

I had two long-serving secretaries, Marion and then Anne, who created a magnificent alphabetical contact address card system, contained on six drums. Unfortunately it was never transferred onto a database. This year, Chris Cox and the IT department have created a similar programme called "customer first" providing many more details, and they are in the process of adding potential customers.

The bid for PK

Edwin Tauber of Parker Kislingbury Co. Ltd., the leading moulding producers, never sold his business. He had good, loyal staff and gradually allowed them to take charge, although unfortunately he did not enjoy partial retirement for very long, as in March 1983 it appears he had a heart attack while driving his car, struck a tree and died almost instantly.

The business was put up for sale. Soon afterwards, the vendors were instructed to give preference to Timbmet, although presumably only if the price was close to the best offer. His wife's family were anxious for the jobs of all the workers, some of whom were related to those they employed on their farms. We already had our contact at BMB (Barclays Merchant Bank) and I made an appointment for LB, our accountant Mr Greenbury, and myself to visit 56 Gracechurch Street, London, EC3, when we met several senior executives of the bank. Our main contact was Mr John Standen, a slight, forty five year old north country man; he was capable, and shrewd with a very quick grasp of any situation, the best Yorkshire could provide. BMB was anxious to build up a reputation in capital markets. The bank knew our strength, but was only willing to lend what they considered Timbmet could afford to repay within seven years.

We had a number of meetings with the executors of the estate. We were able to view the premises and they willingly answered any questions; and they allowed us to see a total list of their accounts without revealing individual turnover. We were not surprised to see that we were already trading with many of them, though in mid Wales there was a number of small to medium sized firms which were not Timbmet's customers. Eventually we got the feeling that they were looking for a higher price although the PK accountants denied wanting to create a Dutch auction. They pretended that the widow wanted us to make the purchase as this would be the safest way to protect the interest of the employees.

I went back to BMB and asked the following hypothetical question: If I wanted to purchase this business to add additional stability to enable us to serve our customers further prepared products, should I add some of my personal savings and increase the offer to ensure that Timbmet became the owners of this well-run business of profile and moulding manufacturers and timber importers?

This brought a very harsh reprimand from John Standen, which I shall never forget, "Every transaction or purchase must wash its own face!"

By late July 1983 there was an offer made for PK for £4,750,000. Our offer, backed by BMB, was £3,500,000 which BMB were prepared to increase by an extra £250,000. We were all very disappointed at the outcome, and so were many employees of both firms. Our search for a business with moulding facilities continued, in our preferred locations of Lancashire or Yorkshire. The business had been purchased by Wm Mallinson who did not want it to fall into the hands of very successful, though much smaller, competitors.

Generally business in the UK at that time was below normal and interest rates high, with the bank lending rate at 10% to 15%. In the autumn of 1983, VAT was introduced on house improvements which hit the double glazing industry hard. The severe winter and the prolonged miners' strike hindered the recovery, and business did not return to normal for another eighteen months. We would have had a difficult time depending on how many customers of PK had had to cut back on their orders. Mallinsons were in a stronger position as they were building up their Malden branches which were a ready market for mouldings and other prepared timber items for the DIY market, and for smaller builders.

1984

The year started with severe weather conditions lasting six weeks and affecting the whole country. Nationally there has not been a winter since with similar conditions.

The government was in conflict with the trade unions and Mrs Thatcher battled with the miners, who went on a prolonged strike. The country was in poor shape and unemployment increased. Britain had an unfavourable trading balance with the rest of the world, and interest rates were very high.

ITTA

The International Tropical Timber Organisation (ITTO) originates back to the mid-1970s. The ITTA (International Tropical Timber Association) was

210

HMS Victory at Portsmouth: delivery of long iroko baulks for restoration, 1985

formed in 1983 at the fourth session of the United Nations Conference on Trade and Development (UNCTAD).

The object was to promote conservation, combined with management of trade, of tropical forest resources. Fifty nine countries became members. A council was formed with offices in Yokohama, Japan and members met bi-annually, once at head office and once in South America. The organisation consisted of a small team of staff working under the executive director.

Friends of the Earth in England and in other countries started a national campaign against the use of tropical hardwoods. As time went by, they became more active.

CHAPTER 35

1984

At the end of March 1984 our turnover reached just over £28,500,000; in 2005, the equivalent of just over £51,000,000.

A second trip to Brazil

In April 1984 I visited Brazil, again with Douglas Johnston. It was very important to buy Brazilian mahogany at advantageous prices as the demand in Europe receded and it was difficult to conclude favourable purchases other than by personal negotiations. We called only on principal suppliers in the state of Para, and three or four companies in the south.

We were fortunate to have many smaller and medium sized customers so the recession in trade did not affect us as badly as it did other timber importers. These smaller firms had lower overheads and survived better than the larger companies, many of whom were domestic furniture manufacturers.

Trading with Africa

There was a lot of political instability in Ghana which affected the production of timber. In the republic of the Ivory Coast some of the more popular species became harder to obtain so we gradually started looking to other areas of supply.

We approached Interholco, owned by the well known Danzer family in Reutlingen, producers of fine veneers worldwide, in the hope that the two companies would work closer together. They had established a tropical hardwood business in Zaire, now the Democratic Republic of Congo, with a sales office in Switzerland. We started trading, establishing good relations which grew quickly; our main contact was their international sales manager, Peter Czerny.

The mill was situated at Maluku, and the main timber concessions were further northeast in Bumba. No roads existed, so all the logs had to be floated from the forest to the mill and the heavy logs barged over long distances. The mill was well equipped and had adequate kilning facilities: they kept spare parts at the sites to ensure continuous production. The main species were mild sapele, utile and good mahogany, the anthoteca variety. From time to time large quantities of agba became available as well as afrormosia which was of a darker colour, not so popular in England.

Interholco exported logs and sawn lumber transported in barges on the River Sangha which joined the River Congo. The timber had to be landed in Kinshasa due to the rapids and then taken by road or rail to the port of Matadi. The roads were in poor condition and the railway engines were always breaking down. When trading with the company, we always had to think of large quantities and long-term, uncertain arrival dates. Timing depended on weather conditions; the rainy seasons happened at irregular intervals and, when it was too dry, the barges would get stuck in the mud for weeks on end. We traded amicably and successfully from 1984 until 1997, working to the mutual advantage of both companies. If undue delivery problems arose because of delays in shipments, Danzer would compensate us financially mainly by allowing longer term credit.

Ethnic strife and civil war had interrupted production for some months in late 1973 and early 1974. In spite of difficult conditions shipments resumed from April 1974 through to the middle of 1977. In May of that year Colonel Joseph Mobutu, the self appointed president, was toppled by a rebellion led by Laurent Kabila. Fighting continued for two years during which time the mill was cut off from the timber concession and no production was possible; the sawmill was occupied by government supporters and the forest was in the hands of the rebels. When production eventually resumed it never regained its full potential.

Switzerland and Peter Czerny

Our office contact over the years in Bar, Switzerland, was either Mr Graevert or Mr Herger. All purchases were arranged with Peter Czerny whom I have come to know well over the years; he would come to Oxford once or, at most, twice annually and on occasions was accompanied by the current production sawmill manager. Staff changes were frequent at Maluku. The accommodation available was first-class, but life was still harsh with very few facilities outside the sawmill compound, and at times it was much more dangerous than in other parts of Africa.

Despite the European personnel staying for only short periods, there must have been a small and devoted nucleus of expatriates as the timber produced and delivered was nearly always of consistent quality, well produced and presented. We very seldom had any quality problems. I never visited the mill in Africa, but used part of two summer holidays to visit the offices in Switzerland. On one occasion my wife and I stayed in Lucerne where we attended concerts at the music festival; and another year we stayed at Lake Como in Italy, not too far away. On both occasions we met Renate and Peter Czerny several times.

Peter was quite a reserved person as far as his private life was concerned, but eventually after a very good meal and a few drinks in a restaurant on Lake Lucerne, he told me his family background and history. His family originated from northern Bohemia (Sudeten Land), part of the Czechoslovak Republic that was annexed by Germany at the time of the Munich agreement in September 1938.

Hitler threatened to invade the whole of Czechoslovakia and the agreement was to allow him to occupy the German speaking parts of Bohemia. This was a compromise reached in Munich by the prime ministers of Great Britain and France, Neville Chamberlain and Edouard Daladier. They guaranteed revised borders for Czechoslovakia. At the same time the Germans occupied the Sudeten Land, while the Poles claimed parts of Northern Moravia (Silesia) and the Hungarians got a slice of Southern Slovakia. The Germans treated the Czechs very badly and deprived numbers of people of their properties and livelihoods. When the allies were victorious in 1945, the Czechoslovak Republic regained its freedom in their former borders.

The Czechs took revenge on the German minority, but for a long time this was unknown to us in the West. The Czerny family suffered immensely. Peter's father was unjustly imprisoned on some "invented" charges. His young wife and two children found shelter with distant relatives in Germany. His father was released after spending eight years in a Czech prison, a broken man; Peter had had a hard upbringing and always aimed to improve his position by self-education and diligence. I learnt from him how 3,000,000 Germans living on the borders were badly treated by the Czechs after the Second World War. Claims for compensation remain unsettled to this day. Overall the German atrocities and homicide are incomparably greater, but the suffering of the Sudeten Germans by the Czechs still remains largely unrecorded and unknown.

1984 (continued)

About this time Nick Goodwin started his agency company, NHG Timber Ltd, after gaining experience working in the Republic of Cameroon. He spoke fluent French and understood the business mentality of the French and Italian timber traders in Africa. He had good connections with Lebanese traders. Timbmet gave NHG a lot of support from the start. As communications were more primitive than in other parts of Africa, it was harder to travel in Cameroon, the Central African Republic, and the countries of the Congo basin, but for Nick it was home territory. He was respected in the industry as well as in high places.

We traded with Tropish Hout in Holland as they produced and exported good quality lauan from the Philippines: the managing director at the time was Jan Van Haastrecht whom I managed to work with closely. Unfortunately, due to his exceptionally bad eyesight, he was forced to retire early. To the best of my knowledge, the family were practising Lutherans who, I think, helped Jews in Holland hiding from the Gestapo during the German occupation.

The owner, Dr Hinrich Feldmayer, also had substantial concessions and sawmills in the Republic of the Congo. The CIB brand was well known for reliability, producing most of the African species used in the UK. I established a good business relationship with Dr Feldmayer, via telex and phone, some years before I met him in person, and we bought CIB products regularly.

We also received supplies from Liberia; but ovangkol, a heavy hardwood which dried well and was very reasonably priced, did not stir up a great deal of interest in the UK. This species is not to be confused with the beautiful decorative wood from Ghana marketed correctly as hyedua (Daniellia ogea).

Niangon was a comparatively small diameter tree and shippers were prepared to produce scantlings to door and window sections. We were unable to market the volume in this country, although it was very popular in France. Supplies ceased after only a few years due to civil unrest. Much of the infrastructure was destroyed through fighting between government troops and rebels. The additional African supplies from these sources were necessary for us, partly to offset the smaller volumes available from traditional sources in Ghana and the Republic of the Ivory Coast but, above all, because of the continuous expansion of our business.

216

Fire!

As a company, we have always been security conscious and guarded against fires. We worked a lot of overtime including weekends so that there was always staff at the yards for about sixty hours every week. In addition we arranged for mobile patrols by security companies to visit several times during the night and on Saturdays, Sundays and holidays.

By 1984 we had a caretaker living with his family in a modern bungalow at the Oxford yard. One damp and misty night early in November 1984, as I locked the office just before seven o'clock in the evening, I smelt burning. I investigated but could not trace the source, whether from the direction of the houses opposite or from our premises. I was not satisfied, so I called on Charlie Norgate to make a thorough investigation by walking around the site. He had just changed to go out for the evening, so he was not exactly pleased, but he put on his Wellingtons and we went to investigate. At that time we were still burning the waste in a dug out pit which we always stopped by midday, so that there was no glow by the time every one went home in the evening. Unfortunately, we did not find the seat of the fire.

I left for home after two hours and was greeted by a disgruntled wife who said my supper was spoiled. I was too tired to go back and it would have upset Rosie. The caretaker went out, leaving his wife and baby at home. It must have been about 11.00 pm when a passerby noticed flames rising from Shed 4, and notified the fire brigade. At the same time Charlie returned and did likewise. He also phoned Leslie Boustead, who rushed to the yard on one of his super fast motorcycles and phoned about ten of our most skilled yard foremen and machine operators. They all responded to the call. By the time I got to the yard the shed was well ablaze. There were at least six fire engines in attendance, with a mobile command centre and refreshment caravan.

Timbmet owes a debt to Jim Pitts, our works engineer, and two loyal and skilled employees, John Scarsbrook and Charlie Norgate, who helped and guided the firemen into the building. The brigade would have been content to let it burn out and concentrate on saving the rest of the site. Jim was convinced that by quickly demolishing a wall, the firemen could reach the seat of the flames; Leslie and I consented to his scheme, and the fire officer in charge reluctantly agreed. The plan worked and they managed to save the surrounding buildings and gradually got the fire under control. Howard Rogers, the works manager and I, along with the other Timbmet staff who were called out, moved bundles of beech out of the shed which was on fire with mobile cranes and side-loaders. I acted as a slinger. The combined smoke and stench was most unpleasant but we carried on regardless, and saved a good deal of the timber.

We held a large quantity of steamed and unsteamed Yugoslav and Rumanian beech, principally lumber, but also waney edged. At the time we had contracts for government departments, mainly for supplying to all the prison workshops. The stocks were kept in No 4 shed and were mostly sold in complete bundles by volume rather than specification. The building had a gantry straddling the whole length and width enabling us to store very large quantities; this left just two alleyways for the operator to walk, moving the packs by remote control to the loading area. The shipping season lasted barely six months of the year, from late spring to early autumn, so at the time of the fire our stock was at its highest to take us through the following six months.

By early morning the fire was under control. We had moved several hundred tons of beech out of the building; we left the fire brigade to finish their task and went home covered in soot and filth. Without exception, we all returned after a shower, change of clothing, and breakfast.

After midday it was possible to examine the extent of the damage, and Geoff Clough called the insurance company who came the following day to make an assessment. We had lost about 200m³ of stock, nearly all beech. Ash and soot was the big task in clearing up the debris. Much of the stock had to be sorted board by board, so as to remove the partly charred ends. The building was declared structurally sound: only a few purlins and part of the roof section had to be renewed, and some of the stock re-dried. It was some weeks before all was tidy and shipshape again, but it could have been so much worse. The fire brigade investigator concluded that the fire was caused by an electrical fault.

We decided to substitute mobile patrols with static guards who were based on the premises at all times during non-working hours. It gave us all peace of mind and I am sure that Charlie Norgate slept more soundly at nights!

We quickly got planning permission to build two sheds, each open on one side. The local authority asked us to reduce the height to 6.5 metres and specified the type of roof panels to be used; and the backs of the sheds were to be clad with fireproof timber.

CHAPTER 36

1985

Import of hardwoods from the Far East

We had an enormous demand for Far Eastern hardwoods, which would sell quickly upon arrival. The orders were in varying specifications and in mixed thicknesses but not large enough to be delivered direct ex-ship. The new sheds were ideal for short time storage and quick handling, relieving the pressure on the fully covered storage accommodation.

At the end of the financial year 31st March 1985, turnover was £30,900,000, (2005 value, £56,000,000.) Over £7,000,000 worth of business at the time was sold north of the M62. To the west of the Pennines we were represented by Noel Learoyd, who relocated with his family from Oxford to the Wirral, and to the east, John Hawley. It became more and more obvious that we ought to open a branch in the north of England, preferably one with machining facilities. We intensified our search, but Leslie would not relent on the purchase of a business in the Liverpool area, and we missed out on several opportunities.

Supply and quality: an ultimatum

The quality of supplies available from most parts of the world was diminishing and the service deteriorating; and at the same time we had many claims with shippers for poor quality merchandise. Dealing with them took up a lot of our time and full compensation was seldom received. At Easter, on 3 April 1985, I decided on a bold move and sent a telex to all the shippers' agents. I blamed them for their complacency and inadequate attention to their customers' requirements, insisting that if they wished to trade with us in the future, the shippers and the agents would have to agree to the following:

- To provide good quality stocks well up to grade of the contract;
- ensure shipments were made on time;
- insist on fair measure by all suppliers;
- keep prices competitive.

Should an occasional claim arise in the future -

(a) Agents would have the authority from their principals to settle promptly
(b) If the sum were large, a representative would come to England quickly to ascertain the damage
(c) In future Timbmet would be prepared only to pay for all purchases after satisfactory receipt and inspection of goods in the UK (and not on receipt of shipping documents as at present.)

Not surprisingly, the agents were shocked and angry. We received threatening letters saying that their shippers would cancel all our orders and we would remain without suppliers. In reality, after a few weeks things calmed down and we achieved our objective with the exception of purchases from countries where the sales were made only through government agencies, mainly the eastern European block and Burma. For a few years we were saved from paying a lot of interest.

I had the audacity to take the steps set out above as we had the support of Barclays Merchant Bank, which was providing "acceptance credit facilities." This enabled us to have credit at lower rates of interest, and for a time we were almost free from any indebtedness to our bankers.

Leslie in N America

In November 1984, the Tennessee Electricity & Water Authority took a stand at the Inter-Build Exhibition in Birmingham. The gentleman in charge was Eric Lacey. Timbmet management never took the time to attend these shows, so we asked our Midlands representative, Martin West, to look around and report on anything of interest. He was attracted to the American stand and undoubtedly talked to Mr Lacey, who sent me a letter in January 1985 asking me to visit him and briefly outlining the opportunities for hardwoods grown on the lower slopes of the Appalachian Mountains. Large mature hardwood trees were available in Tennessee, as President Franklin Roosevelt had ordered the planting of woodlands during the depression in the 1930s in order to relieve unemployment in the area.

As so often Leslie, Adrian and I had a brief council of war, and we decided that Leslie, who had never been on a business journey abroad, should make the trip. He went in April and spent two weeks in the USA, visiting the major shippers in the area. He learned a great deal and found it most interesting: although Leslie was a chartered secretary by profession, he had a good understanding of timber, and was able to teach the Yanks a thing or two. He knew the importance of how to look after timber once it was sawn and while air drying and kilning.

Leslie established a few useful connections with the shippers in the area who had a good domestic market but had never exported. They were accustomed to selling their timber to the local furniture industry and to concentration yards (wholesalers) in the northeast of America. These companies had the expertise of shipping the products once dry to various countries in the world; and some of these firms remain our suppliers to the present day. To mention just a few: G F Hardwoods of Moss, Spann Brothers of White Bluff; Edgar Grey of Stewart Lumber in Morristown, and the legendary Brenda Sandusky of C'wood Lumber of Collinwood. Leslie used the experience he gained to give illustrated lectures to our own staff, groups of joinery managers and to local schools and colleges. He was a very gifted and witty speaker.

Around 1985 Mike Mowforth, our office sales manager, left our employment. Leslie and I knew immediately that the ideal replacement would be Sean O'Sullivan, who had been with Timbmet for ten years. Still a very valuable member of the team, Sean is now sales director for Timbmet Oxford. As the business expanded, we had to increase our yard and office personnel. The NCR computer system needed to be expanded by adding hardware and purchasing more software, which involved Geoff Clough.

Due to the size of our business, Adrian was able to arrange for Timbmet small but meaningful freight rebates from shipping companies carrying our cargoes from the hardwood producing countries. He was also skilful with the decorative panel purchases, and we were able to offer boards with slightly better quality veneers than most other firms, which helped in the growth of sheet sales.

We gradually changed our fleet of lorries from Bedford trucks to Leyland "Clydesdale," and later again to "Cruisers" with fifth wheel tractor units. Jim, our works engineer, often had good ideas for modifications, some of these being accepted by the manufacturers and incorporated in later models. We also purchased second hand trailers and refurbished them in our own workshop. Jim managed some financial saving by buying in a sale good secondhand side-loaders, as well as two swing lift fork trucks which proved to be invaluable at our Bicester site, as we were able to block stack and save a lot of space.

CHAPTER 37

1986/87 Rochdale: Timbmet goes north

An interesting speculation

In March 1986 I had a phone call from Ed Burns (the owner of Lawton & Brierley, customers of ours in Rochdale). He told me that Ken Meyrick, the owner of Fletcher Bolton, wanted to retire and was selling this old established family timber merchants' business. I had visited them occasionally, and we traded on a very small scale. Before the larger, multiple groups had opened branches in every town in the land, George Hill at Oldham was the lively and go-ahead, family run merchants' business in the area.

I described to Leslie what I knew about the place and we decided to make contact and arrange a visit to see the premises. The main building was a very high, stone built, substantial former railway maintenance shed, with railway lines running through it. The floor was cobbled stones; on each side along the length of the shed was a ramp, which was usual in all goods station sidings to facilitate loading and unloading. Alongside they or the previous owners had built a small, two storey modern block, which was on three floors and provided six reasonably sized rooms for office accommodation.

The total site area was about three and a half acres. The main railway shed was about 40,000 sq.ft. itself adjoining a light structured timber shed providing undercover softwood storage. Opposite the main yard there was an old, low building of approx 14,000 sq.ft., which was the retail department.

The machinery was ancient: two old Robinson moulders, with square blocks and very old-fashioned tooling, and built in Rochdale in a factory across the road from Fletcher Bolton; several circular saws, one band re-saw, an antiquated panel planer, and numerous other items of dubious value. As a useful sideline the firm was still box making, producing crates for individual requirements, but apart from ultilising pneumatic clamps, only hammers, nails and stapes had been used.

We were convinced that Ken Meyrick had had enough and would not refuse a reasonable and fair offer. He warned us, however, that any development would not only require the consent of the local authority, but also of the British Rail property and maintenance office. He was prepared to allow us to contact both British Rail and the local council before we made a firm offer to purchase.

We approached a local architectural practice, Cooper & Jackson, and their partner, Peter Dawson. With their help we drew up plans for a 10,000 sq. ft. extension to the existing main building to provide additional storage. This was a sensitive issue as it was close to the railway lines of the main trunk route from Manchester to Leeds. On the other side of the premises we wanted to build a small storage shed six metres in height which would allow us to erect modern racking for side load operation.

Planning permission

A few weeks later, Peter Dawson, Leslie and I visited the Rochdale city planning department. We found the officials very understanding and helpful. They felt the development was to our mutual advantage as it was our intention to provide extra employment in the area.

When Leslie went to the railway property department in Manchester, they put forward a number of objections, but an unofficial arrangement was agreed to by sacrificing some storage space, and the new owners being willing to erect a very substantial security fence. Leslie was also reminded that any covenants and obligations agreed to by the present occupiers would be binding on any perspective purchaser: for one, the cul-de-sac at Wood Street was an important emergency access and had to be kept clear of parked vehicles, etc., at all times.

We arranged a meeting with our accountants and solicitors. They listened to our plans and felt we should go ahead as the vendors were not asking an excessive price, and especially as we could buy the business without borrowing. We made no secret of the fact that development of the site would cost several times the initial outlay. Our solicitors were instructed to draw up heads of agreement and our accountants to take due diligence. Everything went smoothly, until we discovered that Fletcher Bolton had a number of small family shareholders. Some of them lived in far flung parts of the world, including Patagonia, and Ken had lost touch completely. Tracing them was a time-consuming process, as no one had received any dividends for decades; but they returned the share certificates without any demands. I understood that once over 90% gave their consent, it was enough for the lawyer to recommend that the deal could be completed.

Timbmet moves north

On Friday 9 July 1986, Bruce Potter, partner in Cole & Cole (Timbmet's solicitors, now known as Morgan Cole), my wife, Leslie and I travelled to Birmingham to the offices of Ken Meyrick's solicitors where we completed the transaction by handing over a banker's draft of just under £300,000. It was a sad day for him. He explained that his wife, a distant relative of the original founding family, was the last link. For us our dream of owning a timber merchant business in the north of England, complete with machining facilities, was fulfilled. Looking back twenty years I have just realised that at the time I was only nine months short of normal retirement age!

Four of the old staff, Peter Holowackyj, Sue Devine, Bob Macdonald and Teresa Jackson are still with Timbmet today. In Rochdale recently, I exchanged reminiscences with Bob MacDonald. I knew that he had a great respect for the old family firm and had collected memorabilia. He has photographs of some of the most venerable former directors, in the dress of their period, and has old documents and ledgers which he treasures greatly.

The Bolton family history

Bob had researched the family history and found they originated from Warrington. The Boltons were a Quaker family and potters by trade, and they had built up a flourishing export business to America. During the War of Independence in 1809, the Americans passed a law forbidding trade with England and France, and as a result the Bolton family became impoverished. One young enterprising member, named Fletcher Bolton, "emigrated" to nearby Rochdale, then a thriving wool and textile manufacturing town, to start a new life and trade. In 1830 he first established a business as a clog maker, and later as a timber merchant also providing pit props for the local coal mines. Until we bought out Fletcher Bolton, it had been one of the oldest businesses in town, remaining in the ownership of one family for over one hundred and fifty years. Originally the firm had traded on the Oldham Road and relocated to Wood Street in 1952; the last Fletcher Bolton passed away in 1954. The account was the oldest at the NatWest bank in Rochdale.

Summer 1986. Introducing Timbmet as the new owners

Leslie, Geoffrey and I went to Rochdale on Monday 12 July to introduce ourselves to the workforce. We made a superficial check of the stock and other assets, and Geoffrey looked over the records with the company secretary, Linda Buxton. We invited Ken to remain with the firm for three months, but he wanted to leave as soon as practicable to live on the Wirral, where he had bought a bungalow. I was convinced that he was a real gentleman and would want to hand over to the new owners everything belonging to his company.

We were fortunate to find very quickly an overall manager in John McCreath. He had just lost his post due probably to his age and was pleased to join us; he was an active individual of about sixty years of age, who had worked all his life in the timber trade in northwest England. He had many useful connections. Some months later we approached Brian Black to join us as sales manager: Brian was of a similar age and background to John; and Peter Holowackyj was promoted to yard foreman, later to yard manager.

Disappointment with machinery

To achieve our main aim we needed a modern moulder. We had already made enquiries with our customers who favoured Weinig, the German manufacturers but, for personal reasons, I preferred to buy British goods whenever possible. We had had discussions with Wadkin two months earlier, and they had recommended their XJ220 model, a powerful six cutter with a universal head. They promised to adjust the spindle head speeds to suit the machining of tropical and other hardwoods. We had a demonstration of a very similar machine in their showrooms, and as soon as we took over Fletcher Bolton, we purchased the machine recommended, which was delivered as agreed in November 1986. Among the first jobs produced were pitch pine gutters for replacement on terraced houses in the area. These were sold consistently, and there is still a small demand today.

The moulder proved to be a great disappointment. The spindle feeds were too fast for our requirements and the main drive belt kept slipping. We had regular assistance from their maintenance section in Leicester, and help from the Robinson engineers across the road where they were

1986/87 Rochdale: Timbmet goes north

Aerial picture of Oxford yard 1987

still repairing and refurbishing their secondhand machines for export. Production of Robinson moulders had ceased and most employees had been made redundant a few months earlier. Wadkin owned Robinson, but in spite of all efforts we had constant delays, and got a bad name for late deliveries and an often poor finish.

A reluctant change of mind

Early in 1987 Geoff Leigh joined us to help build up and modernise the machine shop. He and every one else urged me to purchase a Weinig moulder. We went to Abingdon where they demonstrated a Unimat 22E, new on the market: I was persuaded to make the purchase, but did so reluctantly. The following morning I went to Rochdale and found the Wadkin machine broken down yet again. Their fitters were in attendance with a new main drive belt. In these circumstances, I would have been considered most irresponsible to refuse to buy a foreign made machine. At the same time we also purchased a Rondomat 931 grinder with a quickset OMA setting stand. This enabled us to minimise the idle time on the moulder between jobs. We are now, almost exclusively, producing all our profiles and mouldings on Weinig equipment.

Not long afterwards we were granted the planning permission for the two extensions described earlier, and engaged a local contractor to build them for us.

Expansion gets under way

We continued to supply our northern customers from Oxford, as before, but at the same time started to stock more hardwoods in Rochdale. We began with as many of the popular species as storage space permitted.

The two northern salesmen continued to report to me and came to the Oxford yard every six weeks where Sean and I had discussions with them. Some time later Noel Learoyd moved from Buxton to Halifax, and became the Rochdale office sales manager. He was replaced on the road by a promising young man, David Johnson, who was recruited in 1986. After learning the business and gaining experience fora few years he replaced Noel as sales manager.

CHAPTER 38

1988: an important contract

An invitation

In May 1986 I was approached on behalf of TRADA by C R Carr of Sandell Perkins (now Travis Perkins) to become vice chairman and to take over as chairman in 1988.

After careful consideration of what the duties involved and bearing in mind my other commitments to Timbmet and the imminent purchase of Fletcher Bolton, I reluctantly and sadly declined.

Timbmet, from its early beginnings, had always supported TRADA and received good advice from its technical and scientific officers, and this relationship continues to the present day. Now thirty years later, Simon Fineman our CEO was invited to join the board of TRADA, and he was pleased to accept.

Our simple research had anticipated that customers would be able to give us machined orders in addition to sawn. Not many months after having purchased our first Unimat 22E moulder with seven cutters and a universal head, we bought another almost identical machine and very quickly found work for both of them.

We gained a large order to machine solid maple panels, 32mm, for the new London underground trains on the Bakerloo line. The work was to be of an unnecessarily high standard: for example, the grooves made to facilitate the cleaning of the floor were measured right through all stages of manufacture by a resident inspector using micrometer gauges. I am certain that the dirt and dust from the passengers' feet soon altered the shape without any risk to the travelling public.

Another MoD contract

We won a contract from the MoD to provide machined decking for the Antarctic survey ship "Discovery" which was then being built. We accepted a very tight schedule; the supplier let us down badly and we had to take shortcuts with the kilning. The planks were 3" thick and 16' long, white serayah. We were a little late, but fortunately did not have to pay a penalty. The ship was constructed at Swan Hunters' yard on the Tyne. This yard closed for the second time a few weeks ago causing us to believe that it was unlikely to open again.

Anglian Windows, our good customers for sawn lauan and meranti, decided to discontinue the milling of timber for the window surrounds and boards. We tendered for this service instead of for sawn timber, and our quotation was accepted which gave us a regular, monthly workload. The machined sections were difficult and expensive to distribute in smaller quantities to their many depots all across England.

"Britannia" – a prestigious order

We were already highly regarded by the historic ship division of the MoD. When the royal yacht "Britannia" had a complete refit at Portsmouth naval dockyard, we had the opportunity to tender for the machined woodwork, mainly in genuine teak, for the joinery, all flooring, margins and the observation deck. We were delighted to win the contract but were full of trepidation in case Timbmet would be unable to achieve the high standard expected of us.

The yacht was built by the John Brown Shipyard in Clydebank and launched by Queen Elizabeth II in April 1953, and had two Foster Wheeler geared steam turbines developing a total of 12,000 horse power. During the refit, alterations were made to enable the ship to be used for international trade fair and conferences. Fortunately, when the job was completed, we had very few complaints, only a few niggles.

Our machining experience was still limited, so after much thought and approached the firm of J J Dean of Leytonstone to undertake this work. They knew what was demanded of them and were fully up to the task, having previously done work for royal palaces and ministries.

A personal tour

The director general of the Timber Trade Federation was a retired rear admiral, Austin A Lockyer, who had served on the royal yacht. It was a great pleasure when he invited Leslie and me to see the ship after it was fully fitted out just before she sailed for sea trials. Leslie did his national service as a midshipman stoker so you can imagine his pride in being piped aboard as an honoured guest! We had an extensive tour of the ship including the boiler room and the laundry room both of which, as one would expect, were in pristine condition.

The lunch was excellent, the wine superb and the conversation interesting and amusing. We thanked the officer in command for the wonderful opportunity and a memorable occasion.

CHAPTER 39

1987-1988

For the year ending 31 March 1987 our turnover was £25,300,000, equating in 2005 to £38,000,000.

Planning permission for another shed

Our panel product sales kept growing, and in 1986 we applied for planning permission to build a shed in the southeast corner of the site, adjoining the main Cumnor Hill. The planners did not present too many difficulties but insisted that the building had to be well-insulated, with a double skin roof, as they wanted to protect the nearby residents from as much noise and pollution as possible.

Bicester site

Chaucer Estates had developed the Bicester site to our specification as far as practicable. After we became tenants they sold the site to Vickers' Pension Fund. Six years later, as we negotiated our second three year lease, Vickers had their pension review, and in their wisdom decided to put the site up for sale. They felt this property did not meet the institutional industrial property investments standards.

One day in April, quite unexpectedly, their agents phoned, asked to speak to Timbmet's MD and, making a genuine effort to sound reasonable, demanded £1,000,000 for the freehold of the premises. To their surprise I offered an extra £25,000, all subject to contract. I assured them that I could get the finance. I provided them with the name of our solicitors and bankers. The deal went through smoothly and my colleagues were delighted with the purchase.

Friends of the Earth and the Green movement

Friends of the Earth, whose followers were mainly young intellectuals with strong left-wing views, established a more formal organisation and opened an office in Camden Town, London, NW1. Francis Sullivan became director and they employed a small staff. Their objectives are well-known and our involvement gradually became more obvious. I tried to attend as many meetings of their supporters as possible in the small towns around Oxford: Bicester and Didcot formed groups very early and had good local support. I do not think many members of the trade at that time did likewise in their own part of the country.

The professional staff of the TTF attended the main, national gatherings. Our trade association did not have enough resources to go to the various evening meetings in the provinces. At Oxford the FOE was particularly strong, and quite a number of academic staff and students were loyal supporters. Jonathon Porritt was an eloquent and polished speaker, a highly educated, capable man who could influence any audience. George Monbiot was a writer, journalist and an exceptionally skilled radio broadcaster. He could captivate an audience with his ability to mimic the birds and animals of the forest using only a record for the background sounds of nature.

I attended a number of meetings where George was the main speaker on behalf of FOE. I was sixty-five years of age and still working full-time. I would have a short lunch break in the canteen and take with me two rolls for a late tea which I ate at my desk before leaving to go straight to an evening meeting. I felt I should have some support and Geoff Clough was the only one from our company who volunteered. Jeffrey Thomas of UCM, Michael Sharpe of Churchill & Sim and, occasionally, Douglas Johnston of Price Morgan would act as my "bodyguards": they agreed to come with the proviso that they would not be expected to argue our cause.

On one occasion, the meeting was supposed to start at seven o'clock but was deliberately delayed. Stalls were laid out in the hall selling native crafts made by African and Indian tribes, as well as literature. Before the main speaker took the platform, others described the plight and deprivation of some of the primitive people. It was gone eight before George "invited the audience to accompany him into the rain forest"; when he finished, an hour and a half later, his audience was spellbound and believed everything he had said.

I tried to attract his attention and, when given the opportunity to speak, pointed out where he had exaggerated. For instance, that not all forestry was bad and in many instances it improved the life of the local people. Quite obviously he didn't accept my views, although the audience applauded after I managed to shout one or two more observations. George exclaimed, "Who is this man? Evict him!" so we decided to leave.

On the way home we debated with one another how we might persuade the trade to put in more financial resources to defend our interests. The Friends of the Earth and other like concerns were given plenty of finance by their supporters.

I knew Arthur Morrell of Parker Kislingbury quite well and was well aware that he had acquired a good deal of knowledge in environmental matters. As soon as he retired, I approached him and asked him if he would become my unofficial adviser, to which he readily agreed. Gradually we received more letters and enquiries from customers and, if the questions were difficult, I called on Arthur to answer them: these occasional enquiries increased to include private individuals and local authorities, and the responses became quite time consuming.

*****

By 1987 our imports of American hardwoods amounted to just under 500 containers annually; our regular shippers visited us frequently and we came to know and trust them. I decided it was high time that I visited the United States and saw for myself the forest and production facilities, as well as meeting some of the management of the sawmills. As I had never taken Rosie on a business trip, we decided we would travel together and at the end of the tour spend our annual holiday in Miami.

Boston

We flew to Boston. The airport was enormous; we thought we would never come to the end but at the edge of the airport we found directions to the plane to take us to Dubois. To our great consternation it was a small 'otter' commuter plane. We boarded for the short flight; hardly anyone had any luggage but the plane was still cramped. The journey was very bumpy, and for Rosie it was a frightening experience.

Matsons

When we landed we were met by Bob and Joan Matson, owners of the Matson Lumber Company. It was Sunday midday and they drove us to a pleasant lakeside restaurant for a meal; the place was full of little black bears, which we were not used to! Afterwards, they took us to some of their own forests, mainly of red oak. It was a hot afternoon and the air was full of insects. The ladies stayed in the car while Bob took me for a walk and explained the make-up of the forest. Later they put us up at the motel close to the sawmill.

The next morning, at the office, we were introduced to Jean English who was the office manager, an important part of the team. Joan Matson collected Rosie and took her to her home for the day. The house was in the forest, and Rosie was uncomfortable as the bears roamed around freely in the garden.

For the first time I saw an American sawmill and, at the eldest son's request, spent a considerable amount of time at the kiln plant which was a few miles away from the mill. On the way he took me to a modern medical centre where he seemed to be under constant observation with an eye problem: in time this became much more serious. He died later from an unrelated illness.

Babcocks, Pittsburgh

The following morning, Bob drove us to a meeting point and handed us over to Bill Eldridge of Babcock Lumber. The journey to Pittsburgh took two days as on the way he wanted to show us life in rural America. We visited a large number of sawmills which were supplying Babcock, producing small quantities of timber on large circular saws; the power was provided by coal-fired steam engines. We also saw disused coal and iron mines and abandoned villages, and observed small scale farming similar to that in England.

We arrived at Pittsburgh the next night. In the morning we were collected and taken to Babcocks' head office where we met senior staff, including the group company secretary, Carl Stillitano; Babcocks was also a sizeable builders' merchants. We spent a leisurely day and had a short river trip on a traditional paddle steamer.

We went to bed early so that I would be ready for a long day. Rosie was taken care of by Bill's wife Norma, and Bill drove me to Champion, the principal Babcock sawmill in the heart of Pennsylvania, where Carl's brother was in charge.

They themselves converted a lot of timber in a modern sawmill, and this was supplemented by sawn green supplies from the smaller mills, some of which we had visited on the way. They had a large kiln plant and grading facilities, and I spent a few hours on the grading line. I was also able to inspect dry timber in their warehouses before despatch and we discussed some of the weaknesses of the grading rules required for the British market.

Babcock had a simply equipped mill on the site where they produced profiles and mouldings from tulipwood and red oak for Wal-Mart. We arranged to have samples delivered to Oxford, but when we gave these to a number of inland merchant customers, found we were ahead of our time. To maintain an economical price, only these two species were offered, as white oak would have been considerably more expensive. Eventually the Far Eastern shorea species filled this gap in the English market.

Nearby there was a hunting lodge surrounded by a deer park belonging to Mr Babcock Senior, where I was able to stay on a later visit.

Back to Boston

We returned late evening, travelling through cherry forests; we took our leave the following day and flew to Boston. We were met at the airport by the eldest son of Roger Pierce of Holt & Bugbee, who took us to the Ritz-Carlton in the centre of Boston where he left us saying the family would meet us for dinner at the hotel. At reception, we were amazed to find that they had booked us into an expensive suite: we asked them to cancel the booking and find us a cheaper room as we were only "poor Brits" and the pound was weak against the dollar! They obliged and I settled the cost with my American Express card. Surprisingly, in the evening Roger and Mary turned up together with their European agent, John and Mary Goodwin of Charles Craig. We spent a very pleasant few hours in good company.

The next morning Roger Junior collected us from the hotel and took us to the sawmill and mill works at Tewkesbury. The premises and the production were similar to Champion, but on a larger scale and better organised, some of it computer controlled. Roger Senior had great plans to create a modern machine shop in perpetuity for the two sons, Roger and Philip, and was considering purchasing German moulders and ancillary plant, as automated as possible. It was all very interesting and I learnt a great deal; and possibly also I was instrumental in teaching them something as well.

Both parties were keen to discuss the position of current contracts and to negotiate future business in the presence of their agents. At this time Holt & Bugbee were Timbmet's principal suppliers.

We took our leave in the full knowledge that the shippers would come to England in six months' time. We thanked them for their hospitality, and were taken back to our hotel in Boston.

Troy, Vermont

The following day we were collected by Jameson French of Northland Forest Products at Troy, Vermont. I was delivered to the mill, and later Rosie was taken by his mother, Shirley to see the sights of Boston: highly educated and knowledgeable about local history, she was on the board of the Boston Museum of Fine Arts. Northland was a small producer who aimed to grade fractionally better than most and, together with good marketing, gained a lot. The day went by quickly as Jameson told me the family history, and was most interested in my own background. We traded through their agents, Alan Thomas, and this was the first time that we had the opportunity to have a heart to heart talk on our own. He was also deeply and genuinely interested in environmental problems and took the time to explain to me how America was fortunate in that many of the forests regenerated themselves naturally. I was also able to meet his father for a short time. Jameson took me back to Boston and drove off course a little to show me his home in Portsmouth, New Hampshire. We had a light meal together and then said our goodbyes.

Buffalo, and a visit to Niagara Falls

The following morning Rosie and I booked out of the hotel and took a flight to Buffalo. At the airport we were met by Ron Mercer, manager and director of the old established family business, Fitzpatrick & Weller, at Ellicottville. It was late morning and he insisted on driving us to Niagara Falls nearby. We actually crossed the Canadian border where we had a light lunch. Afterwards we proceeded to the mill and on to a comfortable motel. Ellicottville is a beautiful mountainous area and a very popular skiing resort.

Laminating

The next morning we met the senior director, Dana Fitzpatrick, who took us round the mill. We spent a lot of time in their laminating factory; theirs was one of the most advanced and modern equipped plants in the United States. We concluded a limited amount of sawn business and purchased three pallets of laminated sections, for samples, mainly large squares in maple and cherry. Snooker was a popular game at the time and most quality tables were produced in England, but when the squares arrived and we tried to introduce them to the manufacturers we had very little success. Only solid material was wanted, if possible, and this was difficult to procure in thick sizes fully dry. Many squares were given away as free samples while others remained under my desk and Sean's for a long time! In Fitzpatrick & Weller's office there were several portraits of Ronald Reagan and, in the place of honour, was a framed photograph of the President with Dana and his brother, Jesse.

We were taken to dinner that night by Dana and his wife. We had a day to spare and Dana lent us a car assuring both of us that the roads were good, the traffic light and that we were unlikely to come to any harm. We spent the time touring, and visited the Salamanca Lumber Company. At the time this was a small concentration yard with a good battery of kilns, belonging to the Taapken family in Holland. Although we were not expected, we received a very good reception from their manager, Barry Yohas.

We returned the car in the evening, and the following morning flew from Buffalo via Boston to Miami, looking forward to having an enjoyable holiday in new surroundings.

Dan's observations on the US market

To summarise, I gained a great deal from this visit and felt better able to understand the American timbers and the production and drying methods. The four main extensive visits were to companies who up until now had supplied the majority of our requirements for North American hardwoods. As our sales grew, we found additional sources of supply.

I pointed out to everyone how inadequate the NHLA [National Hardwood Lumber Association] grading rules were for our market requirements in joinery. In the USA the lumber is used mainly for furniture, which needs shorter lengths. I was promised a special Timbmet grade containing less wane and sap. This was differently interpreted according to how good or bad sales were at the time the orders were despatched.

As a general observation the firms who, at the time of the economic recession in 1978/79, started to look for export markets fared much better than those who preferred to serve the home market only. In most instances they used their profits to invest in more plant and equipment,particularly kilns, to enable them to serve the domestic demand which had improved by this time. Thus they kept their new markets in various parts of the globe.

Leslie in N America

In the autumn of 1987, Leslie travelled to the United States for a second time and took Adrian with him. They visited the shippers, introduced to Timbmet by Eric Lacey of the TVA [Tennessee Valley Authority.] The sawmills were mainly in Tennessee. Leslie impressed most of them with his profound knowledge of all aspects of the trade; he had taken with him a good many slides illustrating our operations, and the care we took in looking after our stocks while air drying and kilning. Unexpectedly he was invited to a local meeting of the NHLA, and gave them an impromptu lecture which was very well received. To Adrian the trip was a great experience and no doubt of great help, as he gradually took over purchasing USA produced hardwoods.

Adrian and grading rules

Adrian also started to take an interest in clear softwoods grown on the west coast of North America, and we felt that Timbmet could sell the top grades alongside yellow pine from the southern states. All the producers sold through their UK agents, but Adrian felt that the agents' executives selling these stocks had very little knowledge of what they were marketing: for example, they were unable to explain the grading rules, which were different from those applying to hardwoods, and varied from species to species.

Eventually Adrian contacted John Groves of Patrick Timber, who represented the Canadian Export House, specialising exclusively in the west coast softwoods: we set aside one Friday afternoon and John brought a map of the producing areas on which the main production sawmills were marked. This provided us with meaningful samples labelled with the grade, and taught us the most important of the grading rules. We were both spellbound and listened intently, making copious notes; this was time well-spent, giving us confidence in the products. Patrick Timber gained a lot of business and, as a result, for some time afterwards we purchased almost exclusively from his company, who represented the best shippers for Douglas fir, hemlock and western red cedar. Adrian took sole charge of the buying and kept me updated.

We both did some homework on the grading rules, and as goods started to arrive we passed on the knowledge to the yard and sales staff. Douglas fir is a most wonderful timber, fit for decorative use with many of its properties close to a lightweight hardwood.

CHAPTER 40

1988-1989

Expansion at Rochdale

We realised that, in order to cope with the increasing business, we needed larger premises at Rochdale. Ideally we wanted to rent or buy close to Wood Street, but there seemed to be very little available to suit our purposes as we needed a level site, if possible.

Morris & Dean, a local estate agent, eventually put us in touch with a wheeler-dealer called Mike Fenton who owned land at Chichester Street: this covered about ten acres, partially flat, on which stood offices and a sizeable, solidly built warehouse that was used for a metal smelting process. The building was known locally as "The Klondike."

The site gradually dropped to a lower level, leading to the River Roach; Mr Fenton seemed to have bought the land from a number of people and we do not know to this day what trade or business was carried on. The vendor asked for an excessive sum but someone had the audacity to ask whether he was in possession of all the deeds for the total site.

It took Mike Fenton a considerable time to gather the deeds to all the small parcels of land. It was obvious that in the meantime he tried to sell the property to others, but at his asking price he didn't succeed. Some months later, he approached us again offering to sell at a more reasonable figure which we accepted.

The Rochdale planning department was only too happy for us to use this neglected industrial site without first obtaining full planning permission. We started to use the new facilities, and gradually repaired and improved the offices then began to store timber: this gave us a larger local stock holding for an even better delivery service in the north of England. By shipping direct from overseas to Rochdale, we saved a little on the costs of transport.

Environmental issues and the Government

The Friends of the Earth [FOE] published their "Good Wood Guide" recommending just a few species, some of which were available only in small quantities, mostly very heavy in weight and density, and suitable exclusively for exterior construction. The rest of the timber species were known merely to foresters who travelled to the most distant places where there was no infrastructure available to produce or ship.

They made a few small investments by providing bush sawmills and some training to small villages in Papua New Guinea and elsewhere. The results were pathetic: the few parcels of timber that arrived, after long delays, were of almost no commercial value. The stock was badly cut, discoloured and full of shakes.

At this time the environment was the responsibility of the DTI (Department of Trade and Industry) with huge offices in Queen Victoria Street, London. TTF representatives were in regular contact with ministry officials. The government may well have expressed concern over the rise in tropical hardwood imports and in the activities of the Green movement. On some occasions members of the timber trade were invited to participate in the discussions and conferences. Terence Mallinson had a deep knowledge of all aspects of the trade worldwide: a good speaker with a strong personality, he was invaluable at public meetings, and gave his time willingly to our cause.

The TTF encouraged the government representatives of the supplying companies to the UK to meet with our civil servants. At this period, the World Bank still allocated sizeable loans to various parts of the world to aid timber production and help relieve poverty in some of the poorest countries: but little was achieved, largely due to corruption.

Many of us in the trade hoped that the ITTO [International Tropical Timber Organisation] would find a solution acceptable to everyone: most timber producing and importing nations were members. By May 1990, the ITTO announced that its goal was to achieve sustainable forest management by the year 2000; the British government representative regularly attended meetings, and was accompanied and advised by Arthur Morrell, on behalf of the TTF.

Meetings with the Minister

Mr Austin Lockyer, director of TTF, asked me to attend a number of private meetings with Alan Clark, Minister of State for the Environment. On one occasion I was invited to continue discussions with two medium ranking officials who indicated that they hoped I would assist them to understand the practical working of the trade and all that was involved. I agreed readily, and we had several meetings over a period of time; they twice visited our yard and spent time looking at the stocks and comparing the different values and uses of tropical versus temperate hardwoods. I lost contact with these gentlemen when environmental issues were transferred to the ODA [Overseas Development Administration] which was part of the Foreign Office.

A royal invitation

It was a great surprise when in February 1990 I had a phone call from one of them asking me for a few personal details, and enquiring whether my wife and I would like to attend the royal Garden Party in July as a "thank you." I graciously accepted. Eventually the invitation arrived and Rosie and I set off to Buckingham Palace in our "finery."

After a light tea with traditional cucumber sandwiches, the courtiers asked the visitors to stand in rows and we lined up out of interest. At four o'clock, as the national anthem was playing, Her Majesty and other members of the royal family descended the steps into the garden. I was the proudest man in England and had never stood so erect before in the whole of my life! Unknown to most of the guests, people who would be introduced to the Queen on her walkabout had been placed in various selected spots by the courtiers: luckily, standing near us was a Member of Parliament and his wife, chosen to meet the Queen. We were able to hear their conversation clearly and appreciated that Her Majesty was well aware of everyday life and the problems of the ordinary man in the street.

Rochdale affairs

We engaged Chris Moran to be the accountant at Rochdale, and in late 1987 we decided to look for a younger, more energetic person to become the MD. Leslie engaged a headhunter familiar with our industry and he provided several candidates whom we interviewed with great thoroughness. We chose Tony James, with several years of experience in the softwood and builders merchants' trade: he had many good ideas and inspired the workforce. Tony joined Timbmet Rochdale in September 1987, replacing John McCreath whose appointment was only an interim one pending his future retirement.

The young sales team was led by Noel Learoyd, who had been trained in Oxford and represented us for some years in northwest England. He now accepted the office manager's role, and was ably assisted by David Johnson and Shaun Griffiths; what they lacked in experience they made up for with their enormous enthusiasm. David is currently sales manager at Rochdale, and Shaun is estimating manager at Oxford.

Tony James explored builders' merchants businesses to research the profiles they used and which varied from one part of the country to the other. By trial and error Tony selected the best patterns, sometimes modifying existing sizes; and eventually framed the standard "Timbmet range." As our price was competitive, customers accepted our sizes even when they varied a little from their own. This was a useful machining order for the mill and would be produced during slack periods.

We also engaged Geoff Lee to be our mill manager; and, at about the same time, Graham Clarke joined us as a sales representative for the northeast. He had had a sound training with his previous employer, a small importer in the north of England. He was able to put his experience to good use with us as we stocked such a great variety of species.

TTF versus TRADA

A continuous rift developed between the TTF and TRADA [Timber Research and Development Association.]. The Federation criticized TRADA's emphasis on pure research and wanted to increase promotion and advice to timber users. At the same time, the government reduced its annual grant to TRADA and the Federation had to provide the largest part of its income for them.

As many timber companies wanted to have the choice of belonging and contributing to one or the other, it was decided that the links between the two organisations should be broken. The Federation would concentrate on timber promotion, legal, shipping and trade advice, international and industrial relations and related matters; the Association would provide the results of its scientific research and investigations, and organise training facilities. The Federation provided a sum of money for three years for TRADA to find funding for more private research projects. The government, instead of providing an annual grant, channelled individual research projects that were fee earning.

Had I accepted the chairmanship of TRADA, this turn of events would have given me additional anxieties. Fortunately, due to the great ability of the director, Dr Chris Gill, and a handful of his colleagues, TRADA is stronger today than ever, enjoying full independence and an excellent international reputation.

Hardwood promotion campaign comes to an end

The hardwood promotion campaign came to a gradual end mainly due to lack of funds. The president of the Federation, Neil Donaldson, appealed to all sections of the industry to improve the image of the trade by increasing timber consumption. With great difficulty Neil raised £250,000, including some overseas contributions, and asked the advertising agency Travis Dale & Partners to achieve the best possible publicity nationwide with the comparatively small sum available. They came up with the "Think Wood" campaign which featured the model of a wooden human head made from layers of many different species of timber. Each layer was named by species along with its main uses. Through the use of this model head it was possible to indicate how humans needed timber at every stage from the cradle to the grave. The picture was printed in the national and trade press and magazines creating a great deal of interest everywhere, and the firm won an award of excellence. Other advertisers from different industries copied the idea. This campaign also came to a premature end due to lack of money, but one feels it was well worth the effort to promote a better image to the timber trade.

"Forests Forever" campaign

In 1989 the TTF, together with the British Woodworking Federation and the Furniture Manufacturers Association, combined to start the "Forests Forever" campaign. The object was to inform the British public of the importance and role of forest and wood products, and to stress to importers and consumers that all timber should be sourced from legal and environmentally friendly sources. A large sum was collected in the first year, partly by contributions from overseas suppliers, but it was still not adequate to cover the cost of the extensive advertising needed to defend the industry in the national press and on television.

Terence Mallinson was appointed head of the campaign, and Michael James, a former diplomat, became the co-ordinator and administrator. A committee was formed to organise fundraising, meetings with architects (who are always very influential in the matter of materials to be used,) consumers and environmental organisations, as well as government departments of the producing countries. I joined the committee and became a very active member, giving support wherever necessary and devoting a fair amount of time to the cause. Timbmet was the largest individual contributor among the companies.

One of the committee's first tasks was to appoint a public relations firm. From a short list we chose Stephen Key of Edson Evers, who gave us a great deal of support and advice.

Dan Kemp 1987

Mill at Rochdale 1993, following acquisition six years earlier

1988-1989

A view of timber yard and storage sheds at Chichester Street, Rochdale 1993

The first tool room at Rochdale, 1991

CHAPTER 41

1989-1990

Further expansion at Cumnor

During 1988/1989 we applied to construct another 36,000 square feet of shed space on the western side of the Oxford yard above Shed 8. The area between the buildings was left open on purpose to facilitate the unloading of large vehicles with incoming goods, and although the site was slightly uphill it was the most suitable place. Its construction was very similar to the existing buildings; and, on this occasion, planning was readily granted with a few provisos to ensure that the building merged with the landscape once the timber cladding weathered. A third of the space was quickly filled with clear softwoods, and another third with English oak, which up to now had been stored in a homemade wooden shed which had seen better days. To ensure we had an adequate power supply for the future, we also arranged for an electrical sub-station to be put up on the site.

At the time the banks were in a lending mood, so we successfully applied for an additional sum to concrete a large area between the old and new buildings, which would make loading and unloading of goods much safer. We call the area "Barclay Square." We continued our investment programme by purchasing three large Bollman gas-fired kilns, with a total capacity of 270m³. These were erected at Bicester and proved slightly more economical than the existing oil-fired kilns.

Staffing levels increased

Once more, the continued expansion of the business required additional staff in all departments of the office and yard, which necessarily involved the provision of specialised training. The instruction of measurers and team leaders in particular played an important part in our success. In order to cope with the additional handling in the yard, John Langston had to employ more sub-contract labour to boost our own permanent staff of operatives. We also kept adding hardware and software for our computer system, although at the time Leslie and I did not appreciate how much computers could facilitate the development of our business.

Native hardwood sawmills became fewer as less raw material came on to the market. In order to conserve and allow the forest to regenerate the Forestry Commission reduced the amount of felling quotas, and at the same time provided grants to encourage replanting. Gradually it became the custom of the home-grown trade to sell their best quality cuts in the round to veneer and timber merchants. Timbmet were compelled to purchase their logs in the solid to have them stored and cut in what remained of the sawmills, which were mainly small units. More and more sawn lumber came from the tropical producing companies whereas before they supplied mainly logs. As a result the larger trade sawmills in the UK gradually closed.

Peter Manion

This required more travel and supervision on our part than before as we used to obtain fresh sawn native timber ready cut and delivered to the yard. We felt that Peter Manion would be the most suitable person to assist John Blizzard: he was a firm but fair negotiator. Peter Manion began his career with Timbmet thirty years ago and has gradually moved from measurer, foreman and now timber buyer. Later he started buying temperate hardwoods in Europe, and aquired an adequate knowledge of French.

Leslie's lectures

We made time to attend meetings and conferences, and got to know some of the managers from leading companies who were members of the Joinery Managers' Association. They had a number of branches in London and the southeast of England and met regularly. We began to be invited to their meetings and eventually persuaded them to visit out yard at Oxford and see our stocks and operations; the visit was well attended and everyone was most surprised at the size and quality of our stockholding. Significantly, many of these managers were in charge of factories where the highest quality joinery was produced, especially for Whitehall, royal palaces and the city of London.

This gave us a greater opportunity to trade with these companies at the top end of the market, and from then onwards we were invited to many of their evening meetings where Leslie lectured to them on the subject, "Why dry wood?" He enlivened proceedings with a bucket of water and a small piece of beech: he measured the beech, placed it in the water and after the talk, he remeasured and demonstrated to the audience how much the beech had expanded. Leslie disliked the smoky, beery atmosphere of the public houses where these meetings were held. He also had an aversion to golf and although I was not a player, I attended the tournaments, which were held twice a year. I walked the course with some of the players and watched them playing, and remembered to talk during the game only if spoken to. The end of the game was always followed by a very pleasant dinner, and gave me an opportunity to meet more members of the trade.

Leslie was very patient and had a great ability to spot talent in the most unusual places, and one was a young lady, Miss Janet Munt who joined us in 1988, and progressed rapidly up the promotion ladder. Janet learned quickly and became a good leader and in only one year, she passed the Institute of Wood Science examinations with distinction. At the same time, Gordon Cook started playing an important part in helping Howard Rogers to run the yard. Gordon joined us as a young man. He was very reliable and would help out in any situation, and right from the start one could see that he was determined to become part of the management team.

More transportation

Gradually we added more lorries, side-loaders and fork lift trucks. The Leyland cruisers proved to be excellent and reliable workhorses; Jim added two ERF lorries to the fleet for the longest journeys and night trunking.

Continuous drying processes

Dick Clapham managed the kilns well. He undertook the maintenance and small repairs and was also in charge of the labour; he lived nearby and if anything caused him concern he would return in late evening or even the middle of the night to investigate. The staff had a weekend rota so the plant was never unattended for long. Dick ensured that the company got the maximum throughput from the kilns without taking undue risks.

Each charge is given conditioning treatment before the end of the run to equalise the moisture content. The only technical progress in kilning over the last fifty years or so has been the introduction of vacuum kilning, and this process accelerates drying and reduces degrade.

Dick asked the directors to buy secondhand two early designs of vacuum kilns, from a company that did not understand how to make the best use of the plant. With Jim Pitts's help, he modified them to our requirements, and for a small outlay, they gave us satisfactory service for many years. He was loyally assisted in Bicester and Oxford by Ian Archibald, "Archie", who is the present kiln manager and has been with the company for over forty years.

About twenty years ago we received 3" white oak from a source in New York State which was radio-frequency dried: the first shipments were satisfactory, but subsequent supplies were a disaster. I think it probable that we never received full compensation as the proprietor became ill and did not recover, and to the best of my knowledge no one continued with the claim.

On my last trip to the USA, five years ago, I visited the sawmills at Salamanca, NY. The manager suggested that I make time to look in next door where I would see a new and interesting timber drying process. This firm was successfully drying small sections, such as squares, by radio-frequency. As far as I am aware, this process is not yet used extensively anywhere else in the world.

Shed expansion at Rochdale

We needed to increase covered accommodation in Rochdale, at the bottom of yard, and erected c.60,000 sq.ft of shed similar to that in Oxford. It was on reclaimed ground which was full of methane gas, which meant that special foundations and air ventilation had to be provided. We also undertook major modernisation in the Chichester Street office.

Resumé

Looking back over the previous decade, we felt justified in being very proud of our achievements. We had established an excellent name for our products and reliability of service, now covering virtually the whole of the country. Due to our overall efficiency, and without charging high prices, we returned good annual profits. Nevertheless, it became very obvious that if we were to expand we should employ someone to cover Scotland where already we had a few larger customers among leading builders and coffin manufacturers. We appointed Jim Alexander as sales manager in Scotland: diligent and capable, today he is director and general manager for the Timbmet Glasgow branch.

CHAPTER 42

Trading with Africa and the US

Equatorial Africa

French and Italian companies started to invest further south in Africa, enabling us to buy additional primary species for our trade.

SMGL in the Cameroons became one of our main suppliers, and at the time was owned by Philippe le-Flanchec who, in spite of many different business interests, took personal charge of his sawmills. Another supplier in the republic of Congo was CIB, owned by Dr Hinrich Stoll. He had a worldwide timber empire and was always approachable. We purchased through his Dutch company, Tropish Hout, whose executive in charge was Jan Van Haastrecht.

The biggest volume came from the Danzer group in Zaire (formerly the Belgian Congo, now the Democratic Republic of Congo), whose sales director is Peter Czerny. All communications were through their Swiss sales office, but no one from Timbmet had visited the sawmills before the year 2000.

In the Far East, Philippine lauan became scarce and expensive whereas in Sabah, dark red seraya was very plentiful. The interests of North Borneo Timber were acquired by the Pacific Timber Company, owned by Innoprise, a Malaysian group. (They had a sales office in Staines managed by Egon Nielsen, an ex EAC-trained employee.) We bought quantities of shipping dry material for air drying, often at favourable prices, although direct shipments were infrequent; in some cases the sea journey could last almost three months. To their credit, they always made sure the timber was adequately dried before despatch. Adrian visited Sabah for the first time many years later, but we had delegations of management visit Oxford every two years, and on one occasion the regional Prime Minister and his entourage came. We hosted lunch for them at the Randolph Hotel.

USA

We continuously needed additional volumes of USA hardwoods. Peter Thomson had a concentration yard in Alliston, Ontario, and he also financed a number of sawmills, and kept stocks at both these locations which they despatched from there, direct to customers. He could often provide a gap filler quickly, especially from Ontario, and sometimes goods would arrive in Felixstowe, ten days after leaving his yard. He employed a young Lebanese named Elie Ghanem, in whom he put a lot of trust. Through travelling extensively to many of the producing mills, together they became a formidable purchasing team in the US timber trade, and in addition they developed a domestic brokerage service.

After a few years, Elie left Thomson Lumber and started to trade for himself from Nashville. He had a strong personality, charm and exceptionally good manners and persuaded a number of producers to put their trust in him. As he had little capital of his own, he offered to sell for the producing companies and put the overseas buyer in touch with the seller, and afterwards collect his commission from them. This enabled us to be in personal contact with the shipper. It took me some months to forgive Elie as I knew that Peter Thomson had taken him under his wing from an early age and trained him fully. Adrian spoke up on Elie's behalf; I gave way and we started to trade. Some of the timber was from our existing suppliers but the majority came from new sources. He persuaded some firms to start exporting; and often these companies were sizeable but satisfied to deal only with the home market. It was not long before we started to rely on him more and more, and it was useful to be able to send special enquiries to him. He would search for the stock and, with the time factor in our favour, his replies would arrive the next morning as we started work.

As he spoke fluent French he very soon gained customers in Belgium, France and Italy; his personality suited the Latin temperament. Timbmet needed the highest quality: Elie was able to place the lower grades with firms elsewhere, which helped him to please the suppliers.

Promotion of USA hardwoods (AHEC)

The US Department of Agriculture opened an office in London to promote hardwood sales in Europe. Its first director was Michael Buckley. They did not support any individual American producer, but set out to help the UK and European countries to understand the properties of the various hardwoods as well as their shortcomings under the NHLA grading rules. They produced useful promotional literature which we passed on to our customers; the sample photos were of too good a quality for a natural product. On the whole the AHEC [American Hardwood Export Council] performed a useful task for the sellers and buyers.

1990

In the year ending March 1990 our turnover was £48,800,000, which at 2005 value would be £67,000,000. This figure was not equalled for a number of years. We had made good profits, and gave us the courage to continue investing in plant and buildings.

Mrs Thatcher was prepared to see our industries decline rather than give in to the demands of the trade unions. Wages increased and we gradually lost our export markets: so ended an earlier boom of 1988-1989. Unemployment continued to rise and our balance of payments turned into a large deficit. At the same time, the government found it difficult to cut public spending in the midst of recession and as a result borrowing requirements escalated. The Bank of England was forced to raise the bank rate, and in October 1990 it reached 13.88%.

Timbmet by now had grown much larger and could no longer, as in past recessions, remain unaffected. The turnover decreased and our profitability dropped dramatically. From October 1990 to the end of January 1991 many of our customers became bankrupt; I dreaded opening the mail in the morning, and if by chance there was no bad news I breathed a sigh of relief.

Barry Tooth joined us in Rochdale as sales director to assist Tony. We invited Frank Gallagher to become Timbmet's door sales manager as we wanted to increase that aspect of business. Based in Rochdale, he used our existing customer base very successfully to introduce internal veneered fire-check doors marketed under the Aristocrat brand. A year or so later he recruited Martyn Webb, who was based in Oxford, to assist him.

A delegation to Ghana

In March 1990 I was asked by the TTF to visit Ghana. The three man delegation comprised Ian Menzies of Menzies Hyslop, Chris Holmes Smith, secretary of the TTF, and myself. Our brief was to stress to the government departments concerned the importance of introducing and maintaining a strictly controlled felling policy. With the help of the World Bank, a complete new forest enumeration was available: this was achieved by using the maps and plans that the colonial government administration had created in the early years of the twentieth century.

Wherever we called, we were well received in the friendly manner which seemed a natural characteristic of the Ghanaian people. Our first and most important visit was to the head office of the Ghana forestry commission, where we had meetings with the chairman and top level officials. The next day we were taken to a largely extracted area on the Atlantic coast (Cape Coast), where we were shown the replanting undertaken, mainly in quick growing species, such as rubberwood, gmelina and others.

The next day we spent in Takoradi visiting officials of the Ghana marketing board whose managing director was Dr Peter Pepra. They wished to see the small local native sawmills improve their production, and we suggested that the marketing board give them simple specifications to produce, such as iroko cills, in fixed width and thickness, allowing for a variation in lengths. We pointed out that in the long term the board ought to consider establishing a sizeable kiln plant at the port to maximise income. We met an old friend, Mr Peter Boetang, now back in office, and several middle ranking employees who had spent time training at our Timbmet depots.

After this we had three days free before our return. At my suggestion we invited ourselves to the Mim Timber Company, who were by now producing veneers and mouldings, although the sawing of primary species of lumber was much reduced. The new production manager was an old friend, Hans Kronborg.

They took us to their concessions and showed us the nurseries, mainly planting makore and mansonia. In their experience, these species, had the best chance of reaching maturity in under 100 years. We went trekking into the jungle and saw enrichment planting on a fair scale; we stayed overnight, and met the other directors. Provided with a reliable four-wheel drive vehicle to visit the Gliksten sawmill at Sefwi Wiawso, we found everything very neglected and in poor shape, merely a shadow of its former glory. There was little activity in the sawmill and the small amount of plywood produced was very inferior, only fit for the domestic market.

The Range Rover provided proved to be incapable of climbing any of the hills except at a snail's pace. We were fortunate to be given help at Glikstens, and continued our journey to Sambreboi, arriving in the late evening.

The United Africa Sawmill was partially modernised and re-equipped, producing kiln dried lumber for export. The next day we toured the extensive plant and went into the forest concessions, where we saw logs prepared for delivery to the port. Peter Spence was in charge of production at the time. The following day, on our return to the airport, we passed the Ashanti gold mines which, following modernisation, were back in limited production. Old waste slag heaps were being sifted again, yielding some small nuggets.

We drove back to Accra and flew home to England.

*****

My mother, Margaret, died in 1990 having been widowed for over thirty years. When she first came to England in 1939, she found it hard to live in a more modest way: she had been accustomed to a very high standard of living, and now she had to do everything for herself. Mother was a good cook and succeeded in feeding us well on the rations available. When war broke out, and the horrors of life under the Nazi regime were revealed, she realised how fortunate she was to be in England.

After the war hostilities ended in 1945, my parents and I lived very comfortably in a large flat that was part of a big house on the Banbury Road which my father had purchased. Although she never felt really settled in Oxford, she gave a good deal of help to refugees in the area who were much less well off than she was. In later years, my wife and I thought often that my mother might possibly have integrated sooner and more quickly in the north of England, where she found people friendlier and easier to approach, just as she particularly enjoyed the winters she spent in the Canaries. Once she was unable to make the journey, Rosie sacrificed much of her own personal life to look after her.

My mother was a director of Timbmet almost to the end of her life and always wanted to be kept informed about the financial side of the business.

CHAPTER 43

1991-1992
Difficult times persist

The Green Movement gathers momentum

We continued to suffer from lack of business due to the prevailing economic conditions in the UK. The activities from the environmental movement did not help. Friends of the Earth and WWF (now known as WWF UK FTN) started to canvas large stores to persuade them not to sell products made from tropical hardwoods, especially Brazilian mahogany. They also visited furniture manufacturers exhorting them to change the species; they stood outside the large department stores in big cities (without obstructing the entrances) with placards, handing out leaflets to the public. They exaggerated the true facts. As they gathered more support from the public, their language and propaganda became stronger and more virulent.

In a few instances some of their fanatics deliberately stole small wooden items from the shops, which they concealed then took to the nearest police station in order to create a scene, and thereby attract the press and gain publicity. In the Far East, Greenpeace tried to obstruct ships loading logs and sawn timber destined for Western Europe and Japan.

I personally received several hundred postcards made of recycled paper, green in colour, from each branch of the Friends of the Earth in the United Kingdom. They were signed by members and made out that I was the principal culprit and responsible for the destruction of the tropical rainforest. The TTF asked me to pass them on so that they could reply on my behalf. If all the cards had been put together they would have covered the walls of a large room.

The FOE and WWF collected large sums from wellwishers to facilitate a sizeable press and, later, television advertising campaign. Because of the intervention of the advertising standards authority, a number of their claims and visual support had to be withdrawn. After the first year contributions to the the Forests Forever campaign decreased, and all the committee's efforts to raise funds from importers and shippers brought in only a small amount. Forests Forever could not even consider advertising in the national press. At times it was soul-destroying. Instead we decided to produce factual pamphlets, illustrated leaflets and a video, copies of which were available to members of the timber trade. We used this as a tool to support lectures and talks to trade gatherings and groups of customers.

Our defence was that

- Up to 98% of logs felled in the tropical forest countries is used for fuel as the population did not have or could not afford an alternative
- The CO_2 in old trees is just about in equilibrium, whereas young trees absorb carbon dioxide
- The production of steel, aluminium and concrete requires a much greater fuel consumption than timber
- We had facts from the ITTO at our disposal explaining the process of natural regeneration and we were assured that their global forest plans would be ready for the year 2000.

The British government was being urged by the TTF to request the governments of the producing companies to provide meaningful figures of their forest reserves and annual production. The trade in general also lobbied their MPs to do likewise.

The Forests Forever director Michael James, and our PR, Stephen Key, made themselves available to visit the provinces to talk and debate on local radio. Terence Mallinson was the ideal person to visit architectural practices to put our case forward: the profession was very biased towards the Green cause.

Unfortunately this considerable concerted effort was not enough to convince the public and counterbalance the exaggerated propaganda machine created by the so-called Green movement.

Timbmet and other hardwood distributors received letters from customers who asked for assurance on the origin of our products. I wrote several hundred letters, all in the same vein, but dealt also with the individual needs and concerns of customers. One principal undertaking given was that trade in the majority of tropical hardwoods was not prohibited by the EEC. Arthur Morrell, our environmental adviser, helped me to answer highly sensitive enquiries from public authorities.

I often ended my replies with the words, "The well-meaning British public has been misinformed and misguided."

The timber trade was never exceptionally profitable and was often dependent on the building industry and the vagaries of government decisions. Nevertheless we should have been able to find enough money to put forward our case adequately and to defend our rightful business.

An unnecessary and false claim

When customers are less busy, complaints about quality always increase. People forget that we are trading in a product of nature and even the best grades allow for a little defect, sap and variation in grain and colour. Colour matching has become more difficult as most of what we sell, and what they want, is now served to them as square edged lumber, and not in log sawn form.

In several instances customers buying the same species from three suppliers put the lowest quality of each purchase on one side and claim allowances. Stock sometimes originates from the same overseas shipper or the shipping marks fade, making them difficult to trace. This allows them to make the claims from all three merchants.

The worst scenario was a case of 4" iroko: two importers delivered the same stock to one customer. The complaint was directed against Timbmet. Our salesman viewed the stock and reported that we had supplied poor quality goods. On his recommendation, for the sake of the account, we collected the goods; but when the stock arrived in the yard, we immediately realised that the timber was not ours.

We explained to the customer but he was unrepentant, and took us to court. Armed with shipping documents for our stock and photographs of what we had received back from the customer, Leslie went to court, accompanied by our solicitor. An hour before proceedings, the opposing lawyer requested an out of court arrangement. Our customer admitted what he had done, and obviously had to face up to the consequences.

Leslie must have been planning at this time to write about the pitfalls involved in the sale and utilisation of hardwoods. This last event upset us all and he was deeply hurt. Within weeks he had produced his "Hardwood Problem Solver's Booklet." It was full of factual information with photographs, diagrams and drawings; it was exceptionally well received by our customers and by specifiers and architects. We had many requests for copies from schools, technical colleges and overseas. A second edition was printed after Leslie died and a third, revised edition, is being prepared.

By mid 1991, the recession was still continuing. We all worked together trying to increase sales of both sawn and machined products but without a great deal of success. Everyone knew we had to take the next inevitable step although we hated the thought, and the decision was delayed over the summer, in the hope of a miracle: but in the early autumn we had to make a number of people redundant. ACAS demanded that the reduction of staff had to be spread equally over all departments.

1992

Difficulties compounded

Leslie died suddenly and most unexpectedly at Cadwell Park, Lincolnshire, on Easter Day, 19th April 1992. He loved amateur motorcycle racing and suffered a massive heart attack at the starting line just before he was due to take part in a race. Paramedics and a doctor were on the spot but were unable to revive him.

Rosie and I were at home, and at teatime Leslie's brother Melvin and his son Alex came to see us and told us this most tragic news. We could not believe it as we thought he was in such excellent health, having recently passed a medical test for life insurance, and leading a clean, balanced life. Leslie did not smoke and only had an occasional drink outside work. He enjoyed restoring classic motorbikes. He had been concerned at the time about his wife Janet, who had just had a kidney transplant.

Timbmet staff were in shock and mourned his loss as Leslie was well-liked and always fair-minded. The sad news spread far and wide, and we received phone calls and letters of condolence from suppliers, customers, competitors and members of the timber trade. His funeral was attended by a large gathering wishing to pay their last respects. At the time John Cole, the family and company solicitor, said of Leslie and myself, "Never in my experience have I met two people so different yet so united in their working relationship." John delights in telling the story of the long discussions Leslie and I had as to whether or not the main drive of the yard should be concreted. I did not want it done, but Leslie did. Nothing happened until I went on holiday and, as soon as I had gone away, Leslie had the work done! When I got back I did not mention the subject and nor did Leslie – we just got on with running the company.

The loss of Leslie had a huge impact on the future conduct and direction of Timbmet. To bridge the immediate gap, we asked Tony James to become managing director of Timbmet Oxford, and appointed Barry Tooth to take over the management of Rochdale.

Leslie Boustead, Director and Secretary 1958 - 1992

Rose and Dan Kemp on their way to the Royal Garden Party, July 1990

CHAPTER 44

A thoroughly unwelcome invasion

We had hardly had time to recover from Leslie's death when we were unofficially informed that our premises might be invaded by various Green movements organising a day of action sometime in May. We contacted the Oxford police, who made their own enquiries. Not knowing their plans we obviously felt anxious, and were eventually told by the police that a Tropical Timber Day of action was planned for Monday 11th May. The police would post officers at the yard, and others on standby in case of need; and they gave us advice on how to act on the day.

Tony James and Jim Pitts took the leading roles, both to prepare precautions and coordinate plans. One of the major decisions taken at the meeting we held on 8th May was to load all the lorries over the weekend and send them off the premises. Some would start the journey on Sunday so as to be out of the Oxford area on the day of protest. In order to assemble everyone to be at the yard by 6.00am on Monday morning and to minimise the number of cars, we made arrangements for employees to be picked up at various assembly points by coaches and key personnel to travel together.

I was to collect the mail as usual from the sorting office with Geoff Clough and one other person, but not to use my car. We cancelled all incoming goods deliveries. Yard vehicles and trailers were to gather together in one area. The fuel tanks were to be protected and any inflammable materials put under lock and key. Roger Scarsbrook, the workshop foreman, was to remain off site in his vehicle stocked with heavy bolt cutters and equipment. All staff were briefed on how to behave and react to provocation. Over the weekend extra guards were provided by the security company to keep a special eye on the kilns.

The organisers must have contacted students from different university societies with left-wing and anarchist leanings together with others, not necessarily politically motivated, who were only too willing to join in the fun. A party with plenty of food and drink was organised the night before in a field near our site.

In the early morning, soon after daybreak, the mob invaded our premises from the rear. They climbed the roofs and spread out placards and slogans. Some chained themselves to machinery to ensure that we could not go about our work; others skilfully managed to put glue into our main gate locks.

By mid morning we had several hundred strangers at our yard, roaming around chanting and singing, generally making a nuisance of themselves.

Kate Geary of 'Oxford Earth First' and Angie Zelter of 'Reforest the Earth' were the main organisers. Angie was a solicitor and knew how to exploit every situation, allowing protests to go to the brink without actually breaking the law.

We eventually persuaded them to come into my office to try to clarify their demands. The police were anxious for the situation to remain peaceful, for both parties to come to an arrangement and the protesters to depart so that Timbmet could return to their daily lawful business.

An announcement was made to the crowd that negotiations were about to begin and requesting the protesters not to do anything provocative in the interim. Tony James decided he could leave his field command post. We sat together for some time arguing and discussing the obvious problems. Both parties knew their positions. We had similar aims: for example, to provide a better living for the poorest sections of the world population.

After some length of time we were no further forward; we were not prepared to give them the undertaking they requested: that is, in brief, not to import any tropical hardwoods. We repeated assurances previously given to the FOE, WWF and other organisations as well as the media. We adjourned to allow Kate and Angie to hold a meeting with activists and various organisations in the yard. Surprisingly, when they returned, they demanded that I appear with Angie and Jim Lockheed, an international environmentalist, on independent television. Reluctantly, I agreed despite having had no previous experience.

We undertook not to resume work for the rest of the day and to pay full wages to all our employees. No one was to be penalised, which we accepted. They promised to depart after the arrival of a group of student protesters at our yard who were on the way from Balliol College, carrying a coffin and placards with "Mahogany is Murder" written on them. They were marching from town via the Botley Road up Cumnor Hill. We accepted this, knowing very well that on their arrival they would receive a rousing reception from their fellow protesters. To allow them to enter, Roger Scarsbrook was permitted to use his bolt cutters and oxyacetylene equipment to open the various gates. The appreciative voices must have been heard far and wide.

By two o'clock most of the unwelcome visitors had departed. We allowed our staff to go home with the exception of a few who prepared for an orderly return the following day.

Before we debated on television we had time to talk to Angie and realised that she was highly intelligent, and I felt sorry that all her knowledge was used to perfect the art of protesting and looking for opportunities to create disorder within the framework of the law. A few months later, she broke into an aircraft factory and damaged a trainer aircraft ordered for the Indonesian government.

We discovered that the hardcore of activists came from a long sit-in at Twyford Down where they were protesting at the route of the new M3 motorway into Hampshire. They were travelling from Oxford to the Isle of Skye for a "summer break" to protest against a bridge being built to connect the island to the Scottish mainland.

We were joined in the TV debate by Geoffrey Pleydell (editor of a monthly timber statistical journal) who came to give us moral support on behalf of the TTF. Personally, I felt that appearing on television was a greater ordeal than dealing with the protesters!

*****

I thanked all our staff, and particularly Tony and Jim, for their support and help, above all by staying composed and influencing our yard labour and office staff to remain calm and well behaved. I opened the post then waited until most of the lorries returned to base and, somewhat exhausted, I returned home. I thought it could have been worse. This event cost us tens of thousands of pounds.

We distributed prepared press releases and paid for statements to appear in the Oxford Times stating we were trading honourably and legally. Newspapers always prefer sensational statements rather than true facts.

A few more invasions of timber yards were planned but most were not of any size. Police officers prevented protesters from entering any of the premises. Others visited offices of the large timber companies, uninvited, and then refused to leave. In most cases they left quietly after being received by some of the directors, who listened to their grievances.

On 22 June 1992 the north-western Greens of various shades came in fair numbers to our premises at Wood Street, Rochdale. The event was well advertised in advance in order to attract the crowds. Our premises were next to the main railway line from Manchester to Leeds and Hull, and the local police alerted the railway police and the Special Branch in Manchester both of whom turned up in riot gear. One end of Wood Street is an evacuation area in case of a railway accident which was specially guarded. Although the police looked quite frightening the crowd would not disperse as requested. The demonstrators were not given long before the police started to take action; some of the protesters were hurt and it was not very long before the site was cleared.

*****

Timbmet Oxford was the only timber trade site which Earth First, with their followers, decided to visit a second time, exactly a year later. The event was organised in a similar way to the previous one. We employed extra security staff and more police were in attendance, sitting in vehicles close by.

The protesters arrived with an enormous inflatable chain-saw which looked quite menacing. They were supported by members from different radical organisations including the animal rights movement. (One group was making breakfast on an open fire and a toddler was scalded by hot water!) The police were filming the activists, but were reluctant to make any arrests stating that if they did the magistrates would only order their release.

At times the protesters became violent. A few put up a long plank to the first floor of the office and one climbed up and nearly got in through the window before falling down. Our women staff were really frightened.

It was hard to restrain our fit and strong yard workers who wanted to take matters into their own hand. Most of them were standing outside the canteen and Tony James and I had a difficult job to pacify them and stop them coming down the main road where the crowds were gathered.

The senior police officer on the spot appealed for calm and spoke to the organisers including Angie Zelter, who seemed highly respected. We sat down together and worked out a way for the protesters to withdraw without losing some of their "dignity". It took time. We were compelled to debate on TV and by early afternoon there was an orderly departure. Unfortunately, this time there was some deliberate damage to machinery. Some of the more energetic "visitors" mixed up a lot of the stock randomly, and it took a few hours' work to straighten out the sheds.

We thought long and hard as to why Timbmet, Oxford was so honoured. I think it was partly because I was one of the few senior members of the trade who took seriously the threats to disrupt our industry whilst others ignored these, and hoped the problem would go away. Another reason we were attacked was because radical and extremist movements always seem to find a ready following in Oxford. Examinations for many university students are held in June, and May is the ideal time to break off from intensive studies for a day with ample food and drink thrown in free! This makes it easy for the organisers to supplement the numbers of "professional" protesters.

It was particularly good to have Arthur Morrell as our environmental consultant. His views and opinions were highly respected in the trade and by our overseas suppliers, and he would rise to our defence whenever a bad word about our company was uttered.

I made absolutely sure that the staff, above all sales personnel, understood the issues involved and could answer the questions our customers raised. After a few weeks, when the storm had subsided and the issues dwindled into the background, we regained the lost turnover. Arthur was also adviser to the UK government delegate at the ITTO meetings. He kept in regular contact with the leading European hardwood companies who had business interests in tropical timbers, among whom were C Wijma & Zonen Bv, at Kampen, Netherlands and Hinrich Feldmeyer GMBH, of Bremen.

In November 1995, Arthur, together with Mr Andrews, the government ODA representative, attended the ITTO meeting at Kyoto. At that time, the ODA was part of the Foreign Office, and environmental matters are now run by DEFRA (Department of Environment, Food and Rural Affairs.) This conference was most demanding and unofficial heated arguments between delegates regularly went on late into the night.

A tragedy

On the third evening Arthur felt very unwell and retired to his hotel room. His colleague called a doctor but, unfortunately, he died within a few hours. When I received the news from Paul Harris, then director general of the TTF, I believed that someone must have harmed him. Talking to Mr Andrews on his return he assured me that Arthur had died from a massive heart attack. In spite of many misunderstandings at meetings, he had no enemies and was highly respected even by those who strongly disagreed with his views.

Paul Harris arranged for his body to be returned to England. Arthur was a staunch member of the Catholic faith and had a very dignified funeral Mass at Belmont Abbey, the Benedictine monastery near Hereford. Several hundred people attended, including those representing all parts of our trade, and many of his personal friends. Rosie and I have kept in regular contact with Kathleen, his widow.

I took the advice of Professor Jeffrey Burley, of the Oxford Forestry Institute, a mutual friend, on how best to commemorate Arthur's achievements in the trade. I thought of a scholarship, but he suggested a scientific book dedicated to Arthur. I accepted his suggestion, and a few weeks later he introduced me to Andrew Grieser Johns, at the time a research associate at the Forestry Institute. He was keen to publish his work on "Timber Production and Biodiversity Conservation in Tropical Rain Forests". I agreed to pay for the publication. When Andrew finished his book, he readily found a publisher in the Cambridge University Press. The first edition came out in 1997 as a dedication volume to Arthur Morrell.

CHAPTER 45

1993

Elie Ghanem

By the second half of 1992 our requirements for American hardwoods were increasing month by month. In spite of this, our turnover was in decline and at best static: the lighter colour oak, maple and ash parcels partly replaced the red and brown hardwoods from West Africa. Elie Ghanem's supplies provided the majority of the extra volume. He travelled regularly to make purchases, visited sawmills, and graded and inspected lumber for export; he was experienced and always tried to obtain the best quality at competitive prices. Although his personality and charm could be at overwhelming at times, but at still he managed to use these to his advantage. Elie felt that a personal visit from Adrian and me would be appreciated by all our suppliers, some of whom had already visited Timbmet at Oxford on several occasions. It would be useful to travel together as it was intended that the purchase of our hardwoods would be gradually handed over to Adrian, starting with the American supplies.

To Tennessee with Adrian

We left on 5 March and flew via Washington to Nashville, Tennessee (TN). Elie met us at the airport and took us to a hotel in the city centre. Like it or not, he insisted on a full dinner in the gourmet restaurant. He showed us the proposed itinerary of our two week journey; and we gladly accepted his plan to take us to his suppliers in TN and then gradually north to the New York State borders, including some to our older shippers from the early days. On these occasions, Elie would stay in the car unless invited in by the owner of the plant. I will describe below only a selection of our visits, mainly those where we gained most experience.

The first call was on the following morning, Saturday. We were collected by Mark Taylor, export sales manger of Steel City Concentration Yard at Burns. Fortunately, as it had snowed heavily during the night making driving conditions hazardous, he came in a four-wheel drive vehicle. The cold spell was totally unexpected and we were not prepared for it.

Once we arrived, the weather improved and we were able to tour the premises. Adrian was most impressed with the investment and modernisation made since his previous visit a few years earlier, although it was difficult to judge quality as the piles were covered in snow. Mark introduced us to one of the owners, Bill Joyce, and to the general manager. I never failed to use every opportunity to stress our requirement for quality, giving details of the undesirable defects to be excluded, and our need to secure a product which is better than NHLA grading rules.

Our hosts suggested that we went for a hot meal. On the way we passed several of their suppliers, small country sawmills, but were unable to approach nearer because of the snow. You could just see piles of round oak logs, mainly small in diameter: there were buffalos roaming in the fields.

We stopped at an American diner, an overheated wooden cafeteria, where all the guests could eat were large rib-eye steaks. The only vegetarian meal they could provide was a kind of gruel, which was not very appetising even though it was topped with two poached eggs. On the way back we went to a shopping mall where Adrian was able to buy a few items of warm clothing. Strangely there was nothing in my size, but in any case I was better off, having travelled in my usual footwear, good leather waterproof boots, and a warm anorak. Our hosts insisted on an early dinner, and then went off to an evening of country dancing, for which Nashville is so famous. I chose to retire early.

The next morning Elie came to collect us, very punctual as always. He drove us around the Nashville area, pointing out the sights, and took us to the outskirts for a brief walk around an undercover complex called 'Opryland' which had a Caribbean theme: it all seemed too big and unnatural to me. Apparently, many unknown musicians and singers performed there, unpaid, in the hope that they would be talent spotted. The large courtyard was full of palm trees and tropical plants: on Sundays it was laid out with trestle tables topped with every type of food, all self-service. This was cordoned off to ensure guests paid their bills before entry, but I was convinced one could have eaten there without paying!

Alabama

We decided to try something a little simpler on the journey to Collinwood to visit Brenda Sandusky; we arrived mid afternoon and met her and her brother, who owned a very small kiln plant, and most of the timber was bought sawn and kilned by C Wood. As a woman, she put great emphasis on the cosmetic presentation, good bundling and clear markings on pastel coloured base paints. Elie then drove us to Sheffield, Alabama where strict Sunday rules still apply. No liquor was sold and all the shops were closed.

After an early start on Monday morning we spent a long time with Bill Hughes of Hassell & Hughes. It was our first visit and we were not impressed. The sawmill was small and we did not agree with the layout of the drying sheds owing to the humidity and climate in the south of the USA. We were certainly satisfied with his dimension plant. Elie secured substantial orders for oak for them from French and Italian furniture manufacturers.

Bill and Elie talked openly about the quantities, costs and prices that their European customers were prepared to pay for dimension stock. By listening carefully, and with a few calculations, we became aware that Elie was working on modest margins.

We left in the early afternoon to visit Graham Hardison at Linden TN where we met the owner, Bill Hardison. He had well controlled pre-dryers and good drying sheds to cope with the climate. Most supplies of sawn was bought from small sawmills nearby, and from his partner, Graham. Everything was kiln dried on the premises before sale. They specialised in strips produced in most species, both pulled and also ripped, after kiln drying.

In both places, Adrian made some purchases on the spot. It was a most interesting and educational day. We talked about what we had seen for many hours into the night and in the following days in the car. I was convinced that with suitable machinery in the UK, one could produce dimension stock ex good, No 1 C&S quality to the customer's requirements in England. This avoids the risk of clients cancelling orders due to late shipment and last minute changes in design.

On Tuesday we started the long distance journeys. Elie never admitted he found it tiring although occasionally, however reluctantly, he let Adrian take the wheel on some easy stretches of highway.

He was always very generous, and knowing I liked Kitkats, bought me a box of fifty when filling up his vehicle with gasoline! He always wanted to pay for hotel accommodation, meals etc. His main topic of conversation was good food and fine wine, which he considered cultural necessities. I argued with him that music, literature, and alleviation of poverty in the world were just as important. The arguments helped to pass the time spent travelling in the car!

In my address book he wrote six suggested young red wines to put down to mature for future drinking as well as for investment. On checking three years later, five of the burgundy reds he chose became very sought after and had increased considerably in value. At the time, I was not interested.

Tennessee

The next appointment was Spann Bros Lumber Inc, White Bluff, TN, run by a very wealthy family of timber merchants and farmers. The production was on fully automated circular saws. They produced most of the species, except maple, using modern machinery, kilns and de-humidifiers. Different members of the family were engaged in different operations in the business. Danny, ("Snooky"), is the grader; his sister does the tallying. We had upset them because we had a measurement claim on previous supplies, but we managed to compromise and asked them to cut the timber slightly wider from green to allow for shrinkage. We parted on good terms.

The following call was at Averitt Lumber Co at Clarksville TN, and here we were received by Larry Averitt and Eric Lacey. Everything was tidy and well laid out with three sawmills on one site. The veneer logs were sold first, but the average quality and size for the sawmill was better than elsewhere: it is likely that the low grade logs were sold in the round. After inspection we had a sandwich and coke for lunch and then discussed trade matters of mutual interest. The firm enjoyed phenomenal growth, and we saw the beginnings of a component plant, 150,000 sq.ft. Some machinery which had been delivered was still in its wrappings, ready for installation. It was too difficult to ask who was providing the finance.

Next we went to Stewart Lumber at Morristown, TN, where we met Edgar Grey. He had a state of the art sawmill which Leslie had photographed and used for his lectures. Unfortunately, due to a fire, there was only temporary machinery on site. Edgar was an expert in pre-drying and kilning white oak. He looked after this himself and, by using his experience, knew how long the timber had to be in the pre-drier and kiln according to the initial moisture content and the texture of the timber. Adrian formed a good friendship with Edgar and we had a constant flow of 2" and thicker white oak of larger than normal sizes from this source for many years. He also produced dimension stock for the domestic market.

We had an eight hour drive ahead of us so could not accept the lunch offered by the president of the company, who came to meet us and would have liked to discuss the ecological problems in England. The weather was still very cold but raining, with snow in the mountains. We paid a brief visit to Mike Knight, manager of Mullican Timber, a flooring plant, with whom we had dinner that night.

The next day, we spent time at Taylor Lumber at McDermott, well-known the world over for rift and quarter sawn white oak lumber. They used specialised machinery to resaw very quickly and efficiently the quarter sawn flitches. Everything is air dried naturally before kilning. David Graff promised to produce 10/4 (2½") and 12/4 (3") lumber for Timbmet.

We spent the weekend at Waverley, staying at a brand new motel, which we thought adequate. In the evening we met a friend of Elie's, Bill Weil, who was a specialised producer of white oak staves used for barrel making. Lynn Downey, of Sherwood products, also joined us for dinner. We visited both sites on Saturday.

We found Bill very inflexible, only willing to produce what suited him, but on Saturday night over a few beers we managed to place some business with him, and since then we have been trading on a small scale. Sherwood produced ¾" from small lumber which many other sawmills did not want to manufacture.

In the afternoon we joined Bill Weil and saw his production of barrel staves using first grade white oak all of which had to be quartered and half quartered. Some of the operations are still done manually. Mrs Weil had a restaurant in a modernised old hunting lodge where we dined that night. The food was exceptionally good.

On Sunday we travelled to the outskirts of Columbus in Ohio where we met up with Gene Almondinger who spends the weekends at home on his farm. With Adrian and Elie following, I travelled in his car to Fort Wayne where they owned Holmes & Co, and met the other partner, Herb Kamemeyer. On arrival at the yard we found the Union Jack flying, which made us feel welcome and proud. It was all very impressive, not modern, but good enough. They described their future plans but were restricted by lack of capital. In the past, this was the mill that sold most of its production to Thomson in Canada, who had pre-financed.

On Monday morning when we returned for business discussions, there was again a lot of snow on the ground. We watched the sawmill at work. They had access to supplies of good white oak and ash logs and the ability to kiln them properly. We placed substantial business with Holmes up to two years ahead and promised to pay very promptly on shipment of goods. They had two extremely efficient lady administrators in the office who regularly sent us schedules of production and kilning for our goods. This relationship continued for many years.

March/April 1993

Second part of the journey with Adrian and Elie in America

We were taken to Wayne airport by Gene Almondinger. In the car we promised him again that we would help him develop his business, and offered our loyal support, providing Holmes could deliver contracted lumber shipped on time and up to grade.

We flew to Pittsburgh and changed planes for the short flight to Cranton in northern Pennsylvania. We were met by Ordie and Aline Price and driven to South Gibson, a distance of about thirty miles. We were accommodated in their modern farmhouse, built into the mountainside to save fuel and heated by indirect solar heating. As honoured guests we were provided with electric fires in our bedrooms, which the children gave up for us.

We toured the premises and the mill twice, both in the afternoon on arrival, and again in the morning before departure. All the equipment was modern and up to date except the large circular log mill. Ordie firmly believed this was the best way to convert a solid log into four quarters. The rest of the plant is fully automated; all the re-saws are new and connect to the grading lines. Conveyors transport the lumber to kilns, straight line edgers or bundling equipment.

Ordie Price has about 200,000 board feet of kilning capacity. His sawmills do not produce enough to fill them to capacity as he prefers to employ only a few trusted local men. Ordie is his own mill manager and his wife does all the administrative and clerical duties, as well as dealing with the shipping documents. He hopes that his sons, when older, will join him in the business. Now, after university forest training, Ordie junior has become his father's right hand man. The sawmill is in an area of rich forest, full of cherry and maple. Timbmet had traded with them previously; Aline and Ordie appreciate the family connection as well as the business relationship. My wife and Aline exchange faxes of family news on a regular basis.

Elie always managed to rustle up a few surprises for us in the evening and on this occasion he "found" some bottles of fine wine in the boot of his car! He also helped Aline to prepare a gourmet meal, which we all enjoyed very much as he is an exceptionally good cook. It was a very warm parting; they wanted us to stay longer but in the end we had to leave to keep other appointments.

We travelled north and made a short stop at Pattison Lumber Co at Wellsborough, where we found a very efficient, modern sawmill. Next door, Larrimer & Norton produce and dry squares in a big way, principally in ash. We continued our journey to Ulysses where there is a small sawmill from which we had received poor quality supplies. They had never acknowledged our claim. It was raining very heavily and we could not find the place. I saw a farmhouse near the road and suggested I would call and enquire. Elie grabbed hold of me bodily and shouted, "Dan, you are not getting out of the car!" I asked "Why not?" and he replied, 'If you approach the driveway you are likely to be shot before you utter a word. This is the way of life in rural America." I was rather shocked.

Our next call was to the Ram Forest Corporation in Shinglehouse, again in Pennsylvania. As Elie explained on our journey, it is now the most modern, efficient and automated hardwood sawmill in the USA. The best mills in Africa would have similar breakdown capacity but not resawing facilities as efficient. Bob Mullery junior had a special flair for sawmill machinery design and built the mill himself to his own plans. The plant was housed in a brand new steel building whereas most of the older mills were of timber construction. At the in-feed is a very modern de-barker capable of high speed and accurate work, dealing with logs up to 40" diameter. This connects to a large fast band mill which produces four flitches from each log, and is then automatically transferred to modern resaws, each one working on a turntable. The second sawyer is the more skilled of the two.

The pieces then proceed to a computerised optimiser, with overhead lasers, and the computer decides how each piece is to be trimmed, whether it is worthwhile taking a foot off to yield a piece of No 1 common rather than No 2 common. From there the lumber proceeds to a moving line where the boards are taken off and sorted according to thickness, grade and species. The whole building is served by a large gantry, which lifts the cradles holding the sorted timber onto the sticking area.

Shinglehouse is situated high in the mountains and has a dry climate. Ram air dry all lumber, including maple, prior to kilning, in the open, with no sheds or pre-dryers. Their kilning capacity is not equal to their sawmill output. A good part of green lumber is sold to furniture manufacturers, domestically, and other exporters in the USA. We have always found their production well up to grade. On this occasion Adrian placed orders with them for nineteen boxes in various species. We looked at the quality of the round logs in the yard as well as kiln dried timber being de-sticked, and were pleased with the quality. Here, as elsewhere on the journey, much of the best round timber is lying prepared for export for veneer production. This is regrettable, particularly as all the logs available are winter felled.

The sales manager is Mike Tarbell and until recently they sold mainly on the home market in large volumes. The office staff is small, giving the impression of general efficiency. Bob Mullery's office is modest; he told us he spends most of his time in the sawmill and visiting the family forests. The office was decked in balloons as he had recently celebrated his birthday. They may have known that it was also Adrian's and arranged a celebration, an evening dinner at the Old Library restaurant. It was a wonderful place, built in New England style, constructed and fitted out as a law library for the county courts. The food was excellent. Elie never fails to exploit such a situation and spares no expense so, in addition, he arranged for a birthday cake to be sent to the table after dinner and chose some extra fine dessert wine from the restaurant's extensive cellars. We had a tour after dinner. Mr Mullery suggested we visit a gambling den to play blackjack; I excused myself and arranged for a taxi so that I could have an early night.

The next morning, as Mike drove us to the airport, we had enough time to visit Ulysses. At the sawmill we met one of the brothers, Dennis Watson. We were high in the mountains and, although it was already April, a lot of snow had fallen overnight. The highway authority cleared the road very quickly. We had another few hours left before flying back from Buffalo to Chicago so Mike took us to Niagara Falls. We arrived in good time in Buffalo and booked our luggage through to London. We were surprised at the lack of security. Our flight from Chicago to London was delayed by more snow. We always flew economy class in those days but, as the flight was not full, we were able to spread ourselves and get some sleep.

Since then I have visited the American shippers only once more, in 1996, when I attended the NHLA annual convention in Boston. I found it very interesting but do not think it is a venue for conducting serious business.

The American Pulp and Timber Association held a brief environmental conference there, chaired by their president, a former senator, who was not very convincing. I attempted to point out the errors I saw in his opinions, but I was quickly shouted down with, "If you don't shut your mouth, we shall do with you what we did to the other Brits in Boston harbour!"

Adrian, until his recent retirement, visited our USA suppliers regularly as American light timber had become an even larger portion of the hardwood sales in the UK. He cemented new relationships and maintained many of the original shippers. His personality and love of golf made him very popular, and his conduct was always unbiased, strict and fair.

CHAPTER 46

Timbmet moves over the border

Purchase of Woyka

In May 1993 the bank appointed a receiver for Woyka, and Mr Blair Nimmo of KPMG was entrusted to find a buyer. They were large importers of Scandinavian softwood and clears, as well as Far Eastern and temperate hardwoods, and had milling facilities. Many different companies from England, Scotland and overseas showed an interest but no one made a serious offer. Timbmet visited the site on several occasions but felt the price was more than we wished to pay, in spite of the fact that Woyka had a debenture entitling them to five football tickets at the Rangers ground for all home games!

Many months of negotiation followed. Tony James, Barry Tooth and I looked around for the third time and decided that if we did not want to continue with a large retail department we could manage with part of the premises only. We made this proposal to Mr Nimmo, who consulted with the major creditors and they agreed to sell the company to us providing they could dispose of a three acre site to another party. Once this proposal was accepted we started serious negotiations with the help of George Hecht of Hacker Young, our accountants, and Mr S Silver of Leonard Wolfson & Co, local solicitors. Towards the end of October our offer was accepted and contracts were exchanged, subject to the valuation of stock and machinery. The Strathclyde Council purchased the surplus land for a modern waste disposal station and eventually all creditors were fully paid, and the shareholders received a worthwhile sum also.

I went up to Glasgow on 5th November when the stocktake had already started. We were assisted by Peter Holowackyj and four men from the Rochdale branch. It was a very cold November, but we did the job conscientiously and with good heart and spirit. On Friday night, when it was all over, we were joined by Jim Alexander and had a jolly evening at the Glynhill Hotel. Geoff Clough narrated the Monty Python "Four Yorkshiremen" sketch.

Immediately on completing the purchase we started discussions and detailed planning with the management team in Glasgow. Jim Alexander

Timbmet moves over the border

American white oak supplied by Timbmet for The British Library (officially opened in November 1997)

took the position as sales director, working very closely with David Slater as managing director. Frank Conboy and Jim O'Donnell, IT and operations managers respectively, were part of the team. Jim Alexander very quickly recruited Cameron Frame, from Garland & Rogers, as sales manager.

Our intention was to re-introduce a larger variety of hardwoods into the Scottish market. An additional attraction to Timbmet was that Woyka at that time was already producing fully finished factory door sets in Scotland for the domestic market.

Following the acquisition, Timbmet soon gained leading position in Scotland, thanks to the wider range of stock and the enthusiasm of the staff.

CHAPTER 47

The FSC

The FSC [Forest Stewardship Council] was formally inaugurated at its founding conference in late 1993 although the seeds of its creation were sown in 1990. Calls for third party certification mechanisms to prove the worth of sustainability claims in the marketplace were being debated in various forums on both sides of the Atlantic. Existing companies offering third party verification, such as Smartwood and SCS in the USA, and Soil Association in the UK, were involved in discussions which also included representatives from WWF, retail groups such as B&Q, timber importers such as the Ecological Trading Company (now Ecotimber), forestry academics from university departments, and flora and fauna preservation societies. The possible scope and structure of "an umbrella organisation of forestry certification" slowly emerged, and the ad hoc group commissioned the first draft of what were to become the principles and criteria of good forest management, and are now the cornerstone of the FSC.

The principle of the three chambers (economic, social and environmental) was also established early on, although at the FSC's founding conference the economic chamber had to settle for 25% voting rights only, following strong opposition from some hard line environmental groups who were opposed to any economic voting rights at all. At the founding conference, the first board was elected from the delegates and the board then appointed Tim Synott of the Oxford Forestry Institute as the FSC's first executive director. Their first headquarters were based at Oaxaca in Mexico for a variety of symbolic and practical reasons, Mexico being midway between a developed and developing nation, neither quite north or south, nor tropical or temperate. The fledgling FSC received grants from the Mexican and Austrian governments and initial funding from the Ford and McArthur foundations.

One of the FSC's first tasks was to create and approve the generic criteria and principles against which forest operations would be certified: the template for country specific standards. Applicant certifying bodies (such as SGS, Smartwood and Soil Association in the UK) had to be vetted against new practises (which needed also to be created) as meeting minimum process standards for the issuing of FSC approved certificates. But creating definitions was not enough. Forest managers needed to be tested against these definitions, and would either pass or fail in the manner of an examination. Although the FSC had to set the questions they had also to design the examination process. Certifying bodies were the examiners and the FSC had to train the examiners as well.

This work took around three years and by 1996 the first forests were being certified, with products bearing the newly created FSC logo appearing in the market place shortly afterwards.

Mitre Master

In 1993 the joinery section of the Seddon group of Edgefoldin Bolton, Lancs, produced window sections in a non-traditional way. At the time Timbmet was searching for new ideas and additional products.

The range was designed by David Seddon and Peter Hibberts and ideally suited for the replacement window industry which used non-standard sizes and designs. The chevrons were hydraulically pressed into the joints which simplified the manufacturing process. David Seddon contacted an engineering firm who produced pneumatic and hydraulic machines.

Timbmet eventually agreed with Seddons to purchase the system and in addition to pay a royalty for the chevrons used. We christened it 'Mitre Master'. Peter Hibberts joined Timbmet as manager and Malcolm Lawton was engaged to instal the machinery to the fabricators and train staff in how to operate them. When Peter left the company, his successor David Bowers made a number of technical improvements and designed a new roof system.

Despite several changes in management, and a reduction in sales, it became obvious that those using Mitre Master valued the benefits that the system brought. We decided that to help support those manufacturers and further develop the business, additional resources would be invested to take the business forward.

Paul Hickingbotham joined the business in February 2006, which coincided with a market swing from PVC-U back to factory finished timber windows, mainly due to environmental pressure. Timbmet experienced a significant increase in demand for Mitre Master products, and this was reinforced by the group's desire to supply engineered laminated timber products thus enabling fabricators to manufacture windows from defect free timber. With ongoing product development and updated machinery being introduced, Mitre Master is well positioned for the next generation of hybrid windows.

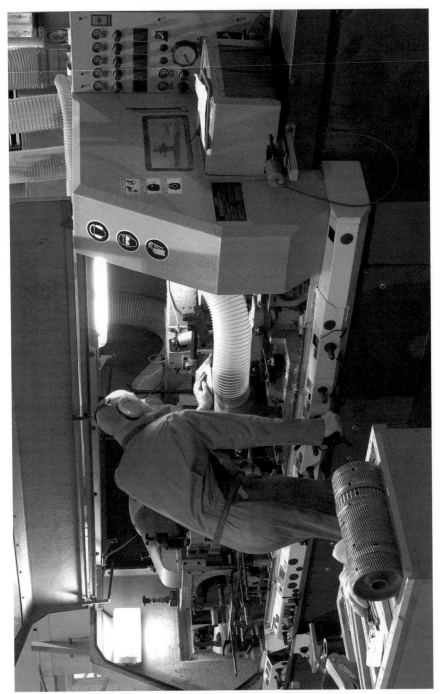

Mill operation in Glasgow 1994

Section of domestic doors assembly in Glasgow, 1993

Stocks in Glasgow

English oak logs air-drying at Oxford

CHAPTER 48

1994-1995
Fifty years at the helm

In March 1994 the Chancellor, in his budget speech, stated that in the previous twelve months the number of unemployed had been reduced by 450,000 and was still falling. He was most satisfied with the economic improvements achieved and announced tax concessions to encourage exports. Interest rates in this period varied between 5 to 6% as opposed to 13 to 14% in 1989. Inflation was reduced to just under 3%, and the general outlook was a good deal better.

As a result we gradually regained our lost business, and in the year ending March 1995, Timbmet's turnover was £60,500,000 (at 2005 value about £63,000,000).

The company did not make any major investments. Apart from maintenance, the only building work undertaken was the last extension to our offices at Cumnor. We continued to replace our fleet of lorries, side-loaders and forklift trucks.

In the tool room at Rochdale's sawmill, we replaced the original OMA setting system by an opti-control system which did the work electronically and saved setting up time on the moulders.

The NCR staff at the Bristol branch helped us with our software requirements. When two of their employees left the company, the management introduced us to Ambridge, an independent small software house in Devon: Frank Conboy and Geoff Clough worked alongside them to improve our systems.

Gradually I began to realise that at the age of seventy three I ought to be handing over the reins to a younger team. I felt it would be ideal to continue the family ownership and invited my son–in–law, Simon Fineman, to join Timbmet. He had graduated in law in 1982 and worked for six years for the inner London probation service. He and my daughter Evelyn married, and moved to Israel. After due consideration, Simon decided to return to England and accept my offer. He joined us in April 1993, initially at Rochdale, and subsequently gaining experience in various departments of the business. Ultimately he became the managing director, and today he bears the title and duties of chief executive officer of the Timbmet Silverman group.

In the spring of 1994 we needed temporary assistance in the accounts department. The agency recommended a mature, capable and well-qualified candidate, John Dobson, who was doing temporary work until he could find a suitable permanent position to satisfy his ambition. A few weeks later Timbmet made him an offer to of the post of finance director and, crucially, guide us in the introduction of computer systems and help to make us all aware of the benefits. John accepted the challenge. He thought also that to work nearer home could have many attractions. Previously, John had held senior positions with the Sears and Ladbroke groups.

When Edward Greenbury, senior partner of Hacker Young, retired in 1990, we invited him to become the first non-executive director of Timbmet. He was always prepared to give advice, and was a real friend in times of crisis as well as a confidant of the Kemp family. He was exceptionally well suited to his new role. Sadly, he died in 1999 at a comparatively young age, and is very much missed.

Adrian Sumner, one of our long-serving employees, having earlier served in various other departments, understudied me for a number of years on the purchasing side of the business. He was appointed purchasing director, and completed the new team charged with the day-to-day management and future policy of the group.

*****

My colleagues and I came to an agreement that I should remain on the board and use my many years of expertise and experience visiting and keeping in touch with older customers, some whom were my personal friends, as well as meeting many of our overseas shippers who were known to have a good deal of respect for me. For some years I still dealt fully with the purchasing of European hardwoods, mainly oak and beech. Due to my intimate knowledge and love of the native species I continued to buy home-grown round logs for a time, assisted by Peter Manion.

I also undertook a few business journeys to Europe, and one to the United States, but at a more leisurely pace than in the past and accompanied by my wife. I visited the Rochdale and Glasgow branches regularly; I received a particularly warm welcome in Scotland, and was taken to meet some of their customers. On one occasion I was taken to three notorious prisons to advise on the use of beech for various products which the inmates were manufacturing. Jim Alexander introduced me to his favourite tipple, Macallan whisky, which I became quite fond of.

I handed over the reins at a time when the company was strong and the envy of our competitors. We had yards in the best possible locations to distribute to manufacturers and inland merchants nationwide, from Anglian Windows down to numerous small craftsmen. We ran a very tight ship, earned good profit margins and had the backing of a loyal workforce. In any inter-firm comparisons published, we scored highly on profit per capital employed and profit per employee.

We had many offers regularly to purchase the family business from companies inside and outside our industry. The boldest and the most straightforward offer came in a letter from a Yorkshireman, Mr Sam Oxford, then chairman of Magnet Southerns (the joint company of Southern Evans Timber Importers and Magnet Joinery.) It read, "Dear Mr Kemp, why do you plough your own narrow furrow? Do come and join us!"

Gradually Timbmet added the import and distribution of clear softwoods, sheet materials and panel products to its traditional hardwood business. We are moulding manufacturers, and in Glasgow also trading in Scandinavian softwoods and manufacturing domestic house door sets.

Have I done the right thing with my business life? I must leave others to judge. I have succeeded where others have failed and given personal service and attention to many hundreds of customers; I have proved the usefulness of hardwoods in this modern electronic age as it has been from "time immemorial."

The timber trade has been underrated for generations and has never received recognition for the time and effort required when a tree is planted, grows to maturity, is felled and becomes a finished product. Young people starting in our industry need to be given good theoretical and practical training in all aspects to ensure the trade is rightly served.

I have not achieved all of this; perhaps no single individual can. My conscience is clear. I have always been a fair and honest trader and Timbmet enjoys an excellent reputation in the timber world both in the UK and abroad.

A wall relief sculpture by John Bye of Oxford in Croatian Bog Oak.
The wood has been radiocarbon dated and dendrochronologically checked
to between 2,500 and 3,000 years B.C.

AFTERWORD

My close family, especially my grandchildren, and friends in the trade have urged me for many years to write my memoirs. It took me a long time to decide to make a start as I find recollections revive too many bitter memories.

Most of my relations perished in the death camps of Auschwitz where virtually all the Slovak Jewry was transported en masse in 1942 and included the majority of our family living in Bratislava, Nitra and Topolcany. The relatives living in the south of Slovakia, which was annexed to Hungary at the time of the Munich agreement in 1938, fared little better. When the German armies had to retreat from Russia and arrived in Hungary in 1944, they forced the Hungarian government to send the Jews to the death camps. This included all my relatives from Surany.

Like most of us in our daily lives I fail to keep a diary and, in spite of being blessed with a good memory, I have to thank many colleagues for the assistance they have given. I cannot possibly mention everyone who has helped me, but I would like to thank, among those in Oxford, Chris Cox, Di Fisher, Natasha Parker-Coughlin, Jim Pitts and Jan Palejowski; in Rochdale, Bob Macdonald and David Johnson, and in Glasgow, Jim Alexander.

I only "took to the mouse" late in life and, as my eyesight is not brilliant and my fingers not so dexterous, I could not have written the story without the assistance of Karen Jackson and Rachel Green.

I am very grateful to my wife Rosie who guided me in English phraseology, and most especially in this connection to Geoff and Kathy Clough who read the entire original text and corrected a number of errors and omissions.

I could never have been as successful in building the company without the help and loyalty of many of our employees, especially those who were with me at the start when working conditions in the yard were much harder than in the more recent period. I hope that this book will be of interest to all past and present employees, and to my business contacts and personal friends in this country and abroad.

Dan Kemp
May 2007

Index of Names

An index of people, businesses, and organizations connected to the author, his father, and Timbmet Ltd.

A

B